States' Fiscal Management and Regional Equity

States' Fiscal Management and Regional Equity

An Overview

edited by

M. Govinda Rao

and

Anwar Shah

OXFORD
UNIVERSITY PRESS

OXFORD
UNIVERSITY PRESS
YMCA Library Building, Jai Singh Road, New Delhi 110 001

Oxford University Press is a department of the University of Oxford. It furthers the University's objective of excellence in research, scholarship, and education by publishing worldwide in

Oxford New York

Auckland Cape Town Dar es Salaam Hong Kong Karachi Kuala Lumpur Madrid Melbourne Mexico City Nairobi New Delhi Shanghai Taipei Toronto

With offices in
Argentina Austria Brazil Chile Czech Republic France Greece Guatemala Hungary Italy Japan Poland Portugal Singapore South Korea Switzerland Thailand Turkey Ukraine Vietnam

Published in India
by Oxford University Press, New Delhi

First published 2009

ISBN 13: 978-0-19-569879-4
ISBN 10: 0-19-569879-7

Typeset in Adobe Garamond Pro 10.5/12.5
by Excellent Laser Typesetters, Pitampura, Delhi 110 034
Printed in India at De-Unique 110 018
Published by Oxford University Press
YMCA Library Building, Jai Singh Road, New Delhi 110 001

Contents

Tables, Figures, and Box

Figures

Box

Preface

This book deals with important aspects of state-level fiscal management in India. The eight chapters in the volume deal with a variety of issues relating to state finances, regional development policies, and the design and implementation of inter-governmental transfers, including the recently enacted National Rural Employment Guarantee Act. It analyses state finances not merely from the perspective of coordinated calibration of macroeconomic stabilization policy between state and central governments but also from the viewpoint of creating an enabling environment for balanced regional development of the country.

The standard of living of people in a country or a region is determined by its resources, policies, and institutions. Endowment of natural resources, investment of capital, and efficiency with which resources and capital are used determine levels of income and growth rates. Efficiency of resource use depends on the enabling environment and, in creating this, standards of social and physical infrastructure play an important role. Given the public good characteristics and high degree of generalized externalities implicit in these services, their provision is mainly a government responsibility. The Constitution of India assigns states the predominant responsibility of providing social services and co-equal responsibility of providing economic services. Therefore, fiscal management at the state level is extremely important not only for efficient provision of public services but also to ensure inclusive regional development of the country.

In all multi-level fiscal systems, the calibration of macroeconomic policies calls for a certain measure of coordination. This calls for systems and processes to control overall deficits and debt to calibrate sustainable fiscal policy. In an open economy environment, accelerating economic growth, creating full employment, stabilizing prices, and encouraging exports call for significant policy coordination between central and state governments. Furthermore, in a globalizing environment, compensating revenue loss from reduction in customs duties calls for coordinated calibration of domestic trade taxes by both central and state governments. Similarly, calibration of policies to achieve stabilization and redistribution, to be successful, will have to be designed and implemented in the spirit of cooperative federalism.

Inclusive development requires that all the regions are provided with a level playing field to harness their potential. A critical component of ensuring a level playing field is to enable all the regions in the country to provide comparable levels of social and physical infrastructure. This calls for appropriate regional policies, implementation of general purpose transfers to offset fiscal disabilities of disadvantaged states, and specific purpose transfers to ensure minimum standards of meritorious services. Indeed, the transition to liberalizing and globalizing reforms provides greater opportunities to states with better market development to access capital, technology, and exports. Ensuring a level playing field is an important precondition and, for this, both regional policies and transfer systems are important. It is important to evaluate the transfer system from this perspective.

Curiously, in India, some states well endowed with natural resources are the lagging ones. Although this emphasizes the role of institutions or, more precisely, the structure of incentives in determining the growth process in the economy, it also underlines the importance of infrastructure investments in reaping the benefits conferred by nature. There is also the issue of compensating these states for the opportunity cost of providing global public goods. These, along with states' own efforts to raise revenues and efficiently deliver public services, form the core of the volume.

The book is an outcome of a seminar on 'Fiscal Management in Lagging States' organized by the National Institute of Public Finance and Policy in collaboration with the World Bank Institute. We are grateful to officials of Bihar, Orissa, Jharkhand, Uttar Pradesh, and West Bengal who made presentations on various aspects of fiscal management in these states and participated in the discussions. We would like to thank the World Bank Institute for providing financial assistance to the seminar.

M. Govinda Rao
Anwar Shah

Abbreviations

AIFI	All-India Financial Institution
CENVAT	Central Value Added Tax
CPA	Central Plan Allocation
CSF	Consolidated Sinking Fund
CSS	Centrally Sponsored Schemes
CST	Central Sales Tax
DSS	Debt Swap Scheme
EGS	Employment Guarantee Scheme
FD	Fiscal Deficit
FRL	Fiscal Responsibility Legislation
GFD	Gross Fiscal Deficit
GRF	Guarantee Redemption Fund
GST	Goods and Services Tax
MIS	Management Information System
NDC	National Development Council
NIPFP	National Institute of Public Finance and Policy
NFB	Net Fiscal Benefit
NREGA	National Rural Employment Guarantee Act
NSDP	Net State Domestic Product
NSSF	National Small Savings Fund
PMGSY	Prime Minister's Gram Sadak Yojana
PSE	Public Sector Enterprises
PURA	Provision of Urban Amenities in Rural Areas
RD	Revenue Deficit
RBI	Reserve Bank of India
RNR	Revenue Neutral Rate
SGRY	Sampoorna Gramina Rozgar Yojana

SGSY	Swarnajayanti Gram Swarozgar Yojana
SDP	State Domestic Product
SSGS	Special State Government Securities
TIN	Tax Information Network
TRR	Total Revenue Receipts
VAT	Value Added Tax
WMA	Ways and Means Advance

States' Fiscal Management and Regional Equity

An Overview

M. Govinda Rao and Anwar Shah

The Constitution of India assigns states a predominant role in the provision of social services and co-equal role with the central government in the provision of economic services. Their responsibility with regard to human development is particularly important and, therefore, the state of their fiscal health determines both the nature and quality of economic growth in the country. As states raise about 40 per cent of the aggregate revenues and incur 58 per cent of the aggregate expenditures, they also determine the inter-sectoral and inter-regional resource allocation and growth pattern within the country.

The market-oriented economic reforms since 1991 have enabled states with better physical infrastructure and more developed market institutions to grow at faster rates than others. Further, with reforms impacting more the manufacturing and service sectors, states with a predominant primary sector have lagged behind. Thus, the benefits of growth have bypassed the 65 per cent of population that continues to live in rural areas, and the problem is particularly severe in the lagging states. Inclusive growth requires creation of an enabling environment in the states lagging in infrastructure and market development.

Creation of an enabling environment requires provision of efficient physical and social infrastructure and raising of adequate resources for financing the infrastructure in a least distortionary manner, besides responsive and proactive governance. In a multi-level fiscal system, an important precondition for balanced development of the regions is to enable the lagging states to provide a level playing field in terms of social and physical infrastructure. For this, it is important to institute an equitable transfer system to offset the fiscal disadvantages of the lagging states so that they are enabled to provide comparable levels of public services at comparable tax rates and minimum standards in respect of services critical for development are ensured. The states, on their part, should institute efficient fiscal management. Thus, inclusive development is inextricably intertwined with fiscal management in states, particularly those that are lagging, and the design and implementation of the transfer system.

Fiscal management in India is characterized by some important features that must be noted. First, the focus of fiscal reforms and much of the discussion on reforms throughout the 1990s was on central finances. There were some isolated discussions on the need for reforming the tax and expenditure system but there was hardly any discussion and much less action on fiscal reform at state level. Second, and related to the first, is that the fiscal reforms focused mainly on macroeconomic stabilization and the measures were directed at compressing fiscal and revenue deficits and not improving efficiency and the tax and expenditure system. This is not surprising, for the reforms in 1991 were initiated in the background of fiscal crisis and even as the deficits were brought down in the initial years of reform, the pay and pension revision combined with decline in central tax revenue, owing mainly to fall in revenue from customs and excise duties reversed the trend to increase deficits to unsustainable levels. Aggregate fiscal deficit hovered around 8–9 per cent from 1997–8 to 2004–5 and the revenue deficit reached the highest level of close to 7 per cent of the GDP in 2001–2. Thus containing deficits and debt was the focus of the Fiscal Responsibility and Budget Management Act (FRBMA) passed by the central government and it was also the principal focus of the fiscal restructuring plan worked out by the Twelfth Finance Commission (TFC).

The third important feature of the fiscal adjustment is that the focus on reducing fiscal deficits at state level had adverse implications for the developmental role of states and more importantly the lagging states. The fiscal incentive scheme recommended by the Eleventh Finance Commission had serious design problems (Rao 2003). The TFC, on the other hand, recommended a 'one size fits all' target, mandating each state to phase out the revenue deficit and to compress fiscal deficit to 3 per cent of the gross state domestic product (GSDP) by 2009–10; it neither recognized the differences in fiscal health between states nor took cognizance of varying developmental needs of different states. In particular, the fiscal restructuring plan caused many of the lagging states to reduce their developmental expenditures and this has widened the differences in states' spending on physical and social infrastructures.

Realizing the developmental potential of the country will depend upon the management of fiscal resources by the centre to create a common market and enable a level playing field for lagging states. Equally important is the latter's own efforts at efficient raising and management of resources. This book provides a review of the challenges of fiscal management by states and national challenge of regional fiscal equity, and provides a scorecard on the performance so far as well as policy options to overcome existing hurdles.

Chapter 1 by Govinda Rao and Pratap Jena analyses recent trends in state finances. The sharp increase in employees' emoluments and decline in intergovernmental transfers combined with stagnancy in states' own revenues during the latter part of the 1990s created severe fiscal problems. Thus, both revenue and fiscal deficits of the states reached the highest levels in 2001–2. While the fiscal stress continued until 2003–4, the subsequent years have seen significant improvement and, by 2007–8, estimates show that revenue deficits have been phased out and fiscal deficit has been contained at 3 per cent of the GDP. The chapter shows that the improvement has come about largely due to higher central transfers, and in some part to states' own revenues. Notably, every state has shown an improvement in fiscal health, more so states with lower than average per capita incomes, which have not only compressed their revenue and fiscal deficits as per the fiscal restructuring plan recommended by the Finance Commission, but also increased their capital expenditures. However, despite this improvement, per capita development expenditures in these states remain much lower than those in more advanced states. This accentuates inequalities, in infrastructure and investment flows, and causes per capita incomes to diverge.

In Chapter 2 Kavita Rao presents an overview of the performance of states in mobilizing tax revenues and identifies options for broadening the tax base, simplifying the tax system, and minimizing distortions. Increase in revenue productivity of the tax system should be achieved while promoting the common market and minimizing relative price distortions. Raising resources in a non-distortionary manner is extremely important, particularly in the lagging states where investment requirements to overcome infrastructure backlog are large and increasing.

The trends in states' tax revenue show that total own tax collections of the states have been growing at an average rate of about 14 per cent per annum over the last two decades. Viewed as a ratio to the GDP, own tax collections registered a decline in the first decade, from 5.48

per cent in 1987–8 to 4.98 per cent in 1998–9, but thereafter steadily increased to reach 5.9 per cent in 2005–6. These figures suggest that while own tax revenue collections failed to keep pace with the growth in GDP till 1998–9, in subsequent years, there has been a sharp recovery in buoyancy.

This performance, however, was not uniform across all states. States can be classified into two categories based on the performance of tax to GSDP—below and above national average. Interestingly only four states have moved from being below the national average as compared to 1997–8—Jammu & Kashmir, Orissa, Madhya Pradesh, and Uttar Pradesh. The average for 1987–8 was 5.44. The states that performed relatively poorly in terms of their tax effort, are also states with relatively lower per capita incomes—West Bengal and Rajasthan being exceptions to this description. This is reinforced by the fact that Orissa, Uttar Pradesh, Madhya Pradesh as well as Jammu & Kashmir belonged to the less than national average category.

The major taxes in the states portfolio are sales tax/value-added tax (VAT), state excise duties, transportation taxes which include motor vehicles tax and passenger and goods tax, electricity duty, professional tax and stamps and registration fees. In addition to the above, in some states land revenue and agricultural income tax (on plantation incomes) too play an important role. State tax collections are dominated by the performance of sales tax collections. At an aggregate level, sales tax collections account for close to 60 per cent of total own tax revenue collections of states. State Excise collections come a poor second with a share of about 14 per cent. Transport taxes and stamps and registration fee tie at the third place with average shares of 8–9 per cent each. Electricity duty accounts for about 4 per cent. All the other taxes put together bring in the balance of 5 per cent.

While sales tax constitutes the most important source for all the states, the role played by other taxes varies across states. There are some states where stamps and registration fee plays a dominant role—Himachal Pradesh, Jammu & Kashmir, Meghalaya, Punjab, Sikkim, and Uttaranchal derive more than 20 per cent of own tax revenue from this source. Orissa and Goa get more than 15 per cent of own tax revenue from transport taxes, while Andhra Pradesh, Arunachal Pradesh, Maharashtra, Uttar Pradesh, and Uttaranchal get over 12 per cent of revenue from state excises.

The sales tax system followed by the states in India till recently was largely a first point tax system, on sales within the state. VAT was introduced in April 2005. A few key observations by Rao on VAT are: (i) it is a tax on the sale of goods to replace the present sales tax; (ii) the input tax credit form of VAT is to be implemented; (iii) tax credit will also be available against central sales tax (CST) paid on inter-state sale; (iv) petrol and diesel are to remain out of the VAT system, while alcohol is to be taxed at a floor rate of 20 per cent; (v) measures to facilitate incorporation of 'declared goods' as well as sugar, textiles, and tobacco into the VAT regime have been initiated; (vi) very small dealers are to remain outside the tax net; and (vii) it is desired that the draft acts too achieve some degree of convergence in terms of definitions, charging sections, and procedures.

The overall performance of VAT suggests that alongside good performance by the VAT states, the revenue performance of the non-VAT states too has been good. This could be attributed either to good economic performance, which translates through buoyancy into higher tax revenues, or partly to improved compliance in the VAT states having spillover effects for the rest of the states. The performance of individual states, however, varied a good deal. Only two states recorded negative or zero increase in revenue in 2005–6—Bihar and Sikkim.

Two major limitations in the coverage of tax systems are identified. First, they do not cover services. As per the constitutional assignment of tax powers, states in India do not have the right to tax services. Second, the programme of phasing out the CST has been initiated to make the VAT system destination based by reducing the rate from 4 per cent to 3 per cent from April 2007, and further to 2 per cent from April 2008.

The unaddressed issues of CST reforms and taxation of services have been identified as areas where reforms are most needed. These reforms are necessary also to make the transition towards the goods and services tax (GST) slated for 2010. While it is commonly recognized that CST reforms are an essential component of the reform of the sales tax regime, there are apprehensions of evasion of tax if the present regime is replaced by a pure system of zero-rating. The difference between zero and 12.5 is considered large enough to induce efforts in favour of evasion, wherein local sales are sought to be passed off as inter-state sales. The chapter discusses various options for the reform of the CST and argues that a conservative revenue safe approach with minimal costs to taxpayers is one of a pre-payment system. This system would ensure that incentives to evade local taxes by passing off local sales as inter-state sales are minimized.

Chapter 3 by D.K. Srivastava examines the aggregate states' debt, its trend and composition, and various components of the TFC's recommendations in order to bring down state debt to sustainable levels, and a host of current issues regarding the management of state debt and progress in implementing fiscal responsibility legislation. This chapter shows that the debt–GDP ratio of the states was at about 22 per cent at the end of 1990–1 and remained at close to this level up to 1996–7. Thereafter, it increased steadily to reach 33 per cent by 2003–4. The sharp deterioration in state finances since the latter half of the 1990s may be attributed to three main factors: the impact of salary revision in the wake of the recommendations of the Fifth Central Pay Commission, which the states also followed, a sharp rise in nominal interest rates towards the end of the 1990s, and low growth rates in the first three years of the new decade. The sharp rise in debt also led to a rise in interest payments.

The components of outstanding liabilities of state governments have also changed. The share of centre's debt to states has fallen sharply after March 2000 mainly due to the debt-swap scheme introduced by the central government. The share of market loans and small savings loans has been progressively increasing since 1990–1.

Srivastava outlines the TFC's recommendations on restructuring government finances, which have important implications for the management of state debt. Issues such as discontinuation of the centre's intermediation, external assistance loans, fiscal targets and responsibility legislation, debt relief schemes (that is debt restructuring, debt write-off), longer term management of state debt, loan council, annual borrowing programme, and effective use of Article 293 (2), Srivastava argues, have significant bearing on states' debt management.

The TFC recommended that, in future, the central government should not act as an intermediary and should allow the states to approach the market directly. If, however, some fiscally weak states are unable to raise funds from the market, the centre could resort to lending, but the interest rates should remain aligned to the marginal cost of borrowing for the centre. The TFC also recommended that external assistance be transferred to states on the same terms and conditions as originally envisaged by the external funding agencies, thereby making Government of India a financial intermediary without any gain or loss. It is suggested that in considering a strategy for fiscal consolidation, two phases can be distinguished: adjustment and stabilization. In the adjustment phase, the debt–GDP ratio should steadily fall. After the debt–GDP ratio has fallen to desirable levels, primary deficit and fiscal deficit should be stabilized. This debt restructuring programme has two components: a consolidation of all state debt to the centre outstanding at the end of 2004–5 at an interest rate of 7.5 per cent to be repaid in twenty years, and a debt relief scheme linked to achievement in reducing revenue deficits. It has also been suggested that states should enact their fiscal responsibility legislations, bringing down the revenue deficit to zero and fiscal deficit to sustainable levels by 2008–9. In order to achieve a sustainable debt structure, it would be important to ensure that the ceiling for annual borrowing prescribed for each state is consistent with the fiscal deficit target for all states taken together in view of the restructuring programme that has been drawn up taking into account macro considerations, and that such a ceiling is consistent with the sustainability requirements of each state.

Current issues of debt management such as the role of the National Small Savings Fund (NSSF), repayment profiles of states, surplus cash balance with states, ways and means advances (WMA), and contingent liabilities have drawn much attention from policy makers. The NSSF was set up in April 1999 as a separate public account that invests in Special State Government Securities (SSGS) from the net small savings collections to facilitate the states in financing their fiscal deficits. This means that all net subscriptions to small savings instruments become a borrowing by the states. The NSSF has thus become a supply-driven source of borrowing for the states.

The Reserve Bank of India (RBI) (2005) observes that the redemption profile is sharply skewed resulting in large bullet repayments during 2012–13 to 2014–15. Repayment of market borrowings would double by 2007–8 (Rs 14,544 crore) from the 2005–6 level (Rs 6274 crore). The repayment schedule of market loans has a bearing on the future volume of gross borrowings by states. The liquidity position of states has been considerably improved since 2005–6. The build-up in surplus cash balances has implications for the revenue balance of states, centre's cash management, and open market operations of the RBI.

In Chapter 4, Chakraborty and Mukhopadhyay present an early assessment of the implementation of the National Rural Employment Guarantee Act (NREGA). This is the most extensive anti-poverty initiative in the form of a legal guarantee of unskilled employment in rural areas. The initiative differed in significant ways from existing centrally sponsored schemes (specific-purpose transfers) and, in particular, made resources available more easily, had less counterpart funding requirements from the sub-national governments, and a substantially higher level of transparency with respect to both physical and financial information. The initial evaluation of the initiative seems to indicate that the implementation has been better than for earlier schemes, but a number of questions remain, especially about the quality of works being constructed (about which little information is available) and the effect of the scheme on the implementation experience of other special-purpose transfers.

Govinda Rao analyses the implications of inter-governmental transfers for balanced regional development in India in an environment of economic reforms and globalization in Chapter 5. When there are significant inequalities in physical and social infrastructure, market-based resource allocation could make poor regions poorer. The chapter argues that although the Indian transfer system has equalizing elements, these are not adequate to offset the fiscal disabilities of poorer states. Thus, some low income states, despite an abundance of natural resources, have not been able to provide basic social and physical infrastructure, and this results in lower physical and human capital and thus growth.

The analysis shows that the GSDP growth rate in the 1990s accelerated by about half a percentage point over that of the previous decade. Much of the acceleration was seen in the middle income states of Andhra Pradesh, Karnataka, Kerala, Tamil Nadu, and West Bengal. In contrast, the growth rate decelerated in Bihar, Orissa, Rajasthan, and Uttar Pradesh. Positive correlation between the level of per capita GSDP in the initial year and growth rates of per capita GSDP has also been found and this indicates a steady increase in inter-state inequalities. Economic liberalization and the opening up of the economy during the 1990s seems to have benefited states with a stronger industrial base and better access to markets, more than states that are predominantly agricultural.

Rao focuses on two regional policies to underscore the incidence of regional distribution—distribution of the central government's own investments and the direction of credit disbursal from commercial banks. It is found that low per capita income states with a population share of 45 per cent accounted for only 29 per cent of the total investments and 41 per cent of the total employment in central government enterprises. In contrast, the above-average-income states with 49 per cent of population accounted for 58 per cent of the investments and 65 per cent of the employment in central public enterprises. Regarding credit disbursement of commercial banks, the relative density of commercial banks in poorer regions is found to be lower than in middle- and high-income states. The chapter also shows that credit–deposit ratios were generally higher in states with relatively greater manufacturing activity. Thus, states such as Tamil Nadu and Maharashtra had much higher credit–deposit ratios than Punjab, Haryana, Uttar Pradesh, and Bihar. The ratios in the last two states were abysmally low and further declined over the last two decades.

The per capita transfer in 1975–6 was estimated at Rs 198 and total transfer constituted 32 per cent of central revenue, 39 per cent of state revenue, and 45 per cent of state expenditure. However, by 2003–4 per capita transfer had increased to Rs 637.4 and total transfer was 35 per cent of central revenue, 36 per cent of state revenue, and 27 per cent of state expenditure. A notable feature of the transfer system in India is the existence of multiple channels. First, the constitutional body—the Finance Commission—recommends devolution of proceeds from central taxes to states and gives them grants for their non-plan spending requirements. Second, the Planning Commission gives assistance for implementing development plans and, finally, various ministries give grants to their counterparts in the states for specified projects.

The trends in the relative shares of the three channels of central transfers show that the share of Finance Commission transfers in the total declined from 65 per cent during the Fourth Plan (1969–74) to a little over 62 per cent during the Eighth Plan. The proportion of formula-based transfers made by the Finance Commission and Planning Commission has declined and that of discretionary transfers has increased in recent years. The share of grants given under the central sector and centrally sponsored schemes increased from 12 per cent during the Fourth Plan to 17 per cent in 1990–1 before declining to about 15 per cent in 2003–4. However, there has been a steady increase in assistance under state plan schemes from 13 per cent in the Fourth Plan period to 20 per cent in the Ninth Plan, climbing to 22 per cent in 2003–4. More importantly, until 1991–2, the assistance under state plan schemes was predominantly formula-based as 80 per cent of the grants were given according to the formula devised by the National Development Council (NDC), but by 2004–5, formula-based state plan assistance was just 48 per cent of the total.

The methodology of transfer of these channels, the chapter points out, has some drawbacks. None of the Finance Commissions assessed the overall resource position and requirements of the centre on any objective basis and also the transfers made by the Finance Commissions were not designed specifically to offset fiscal disadvantages of the states arising from lower revenue-raising capacity and the higher unit cost of public services. It is also argued that the 'gap-filling' methodology has led to both inequity and disincentives for fiscal management in states. The methodology has no incentive for greater tax effort or fiscal austerity as more transfers will be received by states with larger gaps. Moreover, taking the base-year numbers, standardized non-plan expenditures do not take note of the differences in the existing level of services. Therefore, the author argues, the methodology has failed to offset the fiscal disability of poorer states.

An interesting feature of regional development in India is that a number of states well endowed with natural resources are lagging in development. Govinda Rao and Subrata Mandal explore this issue in Chapter 6 and analyse the reasons for the same. With the examples of a few lagging states, such as Bihar, Chhattisgarh, Jharkhand, Madhya Pradesh, Orissa, and Uttar Pradesh, the authors point out that even the natural-resource-abundant regions of a country will fall behind in development if central transfer does not offset the fiscal disadvantages of these regions, and this may exacerbate regional disparity and income inequality.

The six states of Bihar, Chhattisgarh, Jharkhand, Madhya Pradesh, Orissa, and Uttar Pradesh account for 40 per cent of population but less than 20 per cent of GSDP. Interestingly, these six lagging states have an abundance of natural resources. A large proportion of the undivided states of Uttar Pradesh and Bihar forms part of the Indo-Gangetic plain and has fertile alluvial soil and tremendous irrigation potential. The states of Orissa and Madhya Pradesh also have a significant proportion of area covered by forests. The undivided states of Bihar and Madhya Pradesh and the state of Orissa are rich in mineral deposits—almost 78 per cent of the coal deposits (including proved, indicated, and inferred deposits) in the country being concentrated in the six states. The states of Bihar, Madhya Pradesh, and Orissa also have significant deposits of iron ore, copper, and bauxite. In fact, almost 25 per cent of the iron ore comes from Madhya Pradesh and almost 42 per cent of the copper ore is produced in Orissa and another 18 per cent in Bihar. Similarly, almost 42 per cent of the estimated deposits of bauxite are in Orissa, Bihar accounts for another 18 per cent, and Madhya Pradesh for 10 per cent. These states also have an overwhelming proportion of the estimated deposits of other major minerals such as lead, zinc, and manganese.

It is also shown in the chapter that the tax–GSDP ratios for these lagging states are comparable to other regions. Despite this, per capita development expenditures as well as total expenditures in the lagging states are less than the respective averages of non-special category states. The shortfall is particularly significant in Bihar and Uttar Pradesh where the per capita expenditures are lower than the average by 47 per cent and 42 per cent respectively. In other words, per capita development expenditure in Bihar is just about 53 per cent of the average. With a shortfall of such magnitude, the standards of services in these states are significantly lower and naturally they have lagged behind in both social and physical infrastructure.

The intergovernmental transfer systems are designed to offset the fiscal disabilities of states to ensure equity across regions. Therefore, given the fact that these six states are lagging behind other regions despite abundance of natural resources, the question is whether the transfer system has offset their fiscal disabilities. The six lagging states that account for over 40 per cent of population accounted for only 26 per cent of the capital stock of central government enterprises which shows that the central government's own investment pattern, despite the rhetoric on balanced regional development in successive plans, did not really address the issue. Although the employment share of these states is commensurate with population share, indirect employment generation by these enterprises is quite low for two important reasons. First, most public enterprises in the lagging regions, such as steel and heavy electricals, are capital intensive, and the highly skilled labour requirement has to be met from among migrants as the native population of these states lacks the skills. Second, although these industries have a high degree of backward linkages as they depend on the resources of the states, they have very few forward linkages. Third, whatever forward linkages could have resulted from these investments were, to a large extent, nullified by the 'freight-equalization scheme' which subsidized transportation costs of items such as coal and steel used by manufacturers in other places, thereby denying locational advantage for the ancillary units.

Another explicit method of impacting regional resource allocation is through intergovernmental transfers. But the problem is, with multiple agencies making transfers from the centre, each working independently of the others, achieving economic objectives of the transfer system has been rendered difficult. The authors also question the methodology adopted by the Finance Commissions: although it helps achieve some degree of equalization, it is not targeted to offset fiscal disabilities from lower revenue capacity or higher unit cost of providing public services. The high weight given to the backwardness factor in the tax-devolution formula results in some measure of equalization, but this is more an outcome of random policy choice than a targeted attempt to offset fiscal disabilities. The problem of poor targeting is, the authors argue, equally true of plan grants as of transfers given under the central sector and centrally sponsored schemes. Plan grants are distributed according to the NDC formula (called the Gadgil formula) and this formula is again based on general economic indicators and, not surprisingly, poorly targeted. Grants for central schemes are basically for specific purposes and are given according to a separate formula for each scheme.

Chapter 7 by Somik V. Lall addresses regional disparities in infrastructure and urban service delivery in India. The author first asks why two major states are performing worse than other states in providing basic services. Second, do public services improve with the size of transfers from higher levels of government, or do own source revenues have considerable role to play in improving service provision? With a model of supply and demand of public services, local service delivery responds to expansion in local revenue bases but is not sensitive to increases in general-purpose transfers from higher levels of government. From a policy perspective this raises an important concern on stimulating own source revenues in areas with limited administrative capacity and weak revenue bases.

Service delivery, such as water supply, sanitation, roads, transportation, and waste management, though inadequate across the country, is particularly so in India's lagging states such as Bihar, Uttar Pradesh, and Orissa. It is found that local bodies in lagging states spend less on local infrastructure services relative to normative levels, defined by the Zakaria Committee, than in other states. Statistics from 151 Indian cities in 1992–3 and 1997–8 show that, on average, expenditure on sewerage and drainage was just 12.2 per cent of the required normative expenditure level. It was 7.3 per cent for water supply, 56.7 per cent for roads, and only 13 per cent for street lights. The (weighted) mean of overall local infrastructure expenditures (relative to normative levels) in lagging states is 13.3 per cent of the required normative level, which is considerably lower than in other states (78 per cent).

However, the shortfall in public service provision can be attributed to the low revenue base of local governments. Therefore, the author compares normative infrastructure level and municipal revenue base which is a good proxy for local infrastructure resource gap. Own revenue receipts are found to finance only half the required expenditure level. The average ratio of total revenue incomes including various transfers from higher levels of governments was 90.8 per cent. When the resource gap between municipal corporations and municipalities is compared, municipal corporations are in more favourable positions. The own revenue receipts of municipal corporations were enough to meet the required local core infrastructure expenditure level, but those of municipalities were less than half the required level (102.9 per cent vs 49.0 per cent). In sum, only 13 per cent of cities in the sample could afford to meet local core infrastructure needs from their own revenue sources, and 30 per cent of cities from their total revenue receipts.

The author estimates a simultaneous model of supply and demand for local infrastructure provision. The estimates show that both local own source tax revenues and transfers from higher levels of government have a positive effect on infrastructure supply; the effect of source revenue is higher than that of transfers. The price elasticity of local infrastructure supply has the expected positive sign, but is not statistically significant. This may imply that local governments provide infrastructure services on a non-market-pricing basis, emphasizing the role of governments as public good providers. Local infrastructure provision costs have a negative effect on supply, as expected. Interestingly, it is found that municipal tax receipts (per capita, real) have a statistically significant and positive effect on local infrastructure supply, but the effect of transfers from higher levels of governments is not significant. Therefore, one can argue that raising municipal taxes is a more effective way of financing and increasing local infrastructure service supply.

Raja Shankar and Anwar Shah, in Chapter 8, examine the impact of regional development policies on regional inequality. Reduction in regional disparities is a major concern for governments in most countries. Large regional inequalities represent serious threats to the unity of a country and, in extreme cases, lead to calls for separation both by the richest and the poorest regions. While the poorest may consider such inequalities as manifestation of regional injustice, the richest may view a union with the poorest as holding them back in their drive to prosperity. The centrifugal effect of regional disparities is often exacerbated by the fact that regions in most countries also differ ethnically, culturally, linguistically, or religiously. These differences are a barrier to the flow of labour from the poorer to the richer regions. As regional disparities cannot be reduced through the large-scale movement of people from the poorer to the richer regions, each region has to develop on its own. Even if mass migration were possible, it may not be desirable because it may lead to congestion in the richer regions. Further, there is ample evidence that the migration of labour to the richer regions does not automatically lead to wage increases in the poorer regions. It is often the better educated and more skilled who migrate, leaving the poorer region even worse off.

Therefore, it is not surprising that reduction in regional disparities has been a major policy objective of most governments, especially in developing countries, where these disparities are two to six times more than in the developed countries. In this chapter, the authors discuss different regional development policies that have been pursued in developing countries to address regional disparities. Using India as a case, they show that most of these policies have not been effective in reducing regional inequality. They show that the failure of these policies is due to their strong centralized and paternalistic bias, and the incentives inherent in the design of such policies incline sub-national governments to abdicate their responsibility for development and become dependent on central aid. They also show that contrary to conventional wisdom that calls for a central role in reducing regional inequality, a strong sub-national government is pivotal to the catch-up process by poorer regions.

The authors summarize theory and evidence on regional convergence/divergence and theoretically discuss the relationship between regional development policies and regional inequality. While increasing regional disparities might be affected by factors other than government policies, they focus on the latter in this chapter. They present regional inequality trends in India, and review and evaluate regional development policies to reduce such disparities.

The main conclusion drawn in this chapter is that regional inequality between Indian states has increased since 1980. Explicit government transfers have not been successful in reducing regional inequality. Rather, they may be contributing to increased inequality by creating dependency in poorer states. Implicit transfers such as subsidized lending have gone disproportionately to richer states. This could primarily be due to better opportunities for investment in these areas. In this sense, implicit transfers (including inter-state tax exportation) shift resources to more productive states, while explicit transfers transfer some income to poorer states which use these transfers to buy goods and services produced in the richer states (Rao and Singh 2005). Therefore, government policies have not reduced regional disparity as they have not been aimed at helping or forcing poorer states to catch up in productivity terms. The results presented in this chapter show a negative association between per capita SDP and explicit transfers (that are not productivity related) and a positive association between per capita SDP and implicit transfers (that are productivity related). The authors acknowledge that much more work needs to be done to achieve a better understanding of the underlying reasons for differential growth of various states. In this context, they advocate further research on the effect of central government spending on regional inequality and how the composition of state spending is affected by central incentives. Further, such research should also look at how state spending itself affects regional inequality.

The eight chapters in the volume deal with important policy issues relating to fiscal management of the states and design and implementation of intergovernmental transfers. Indeed, there are many other related policy and institutional issues of importance that need to be analysed in detail, but we had to be necessarily selective in focusing on fiscal issues. Hopefully the chapters included here will provide useful guidance to policy makers.

References

Rao, M. Govinda (2003). 'Incentivising Fiscal Transfers in the Indian Federation', *Publins*, 33(4): 43–62.

Rao, M. Govinda and Nirvikar Singh (2005). *Political Economy of Federalism in India*, Oxford University Press, New Delhi.

Reserve Bank of India (2005). 'State Finances: A Study of Budgets of 2005–06', *RBI Bulletin*, December.

I

Fiscal Challenges of States in India

1

Recent Trends in State Finances

M. Govinda Rao and P.R. Jena

There has been considerable concern about high and growing inter-state disparities in development in India. The per capita income in the most prosperous state (excluding the small state of Goa) in 2005–6 was eight times that of the poorest state and the difference has been steadily increasing over the years. This magnitude of inter-state differences in per capita incomes is not seen in any of the developed countries and indeed among very few even of the developing countries. High inter-state inequalities are seen in India not only in per capita incomes but also in human development indicators. Low-income states are home to an overwhelming proportion of poor people. Both education and health standards in low-income states are much lower than in high-income states.

Differences in per capita incomes among the states can be caused by differences in resource endowment, investments, policies, and institutions. Mere richness of resources—both physical and human—may not lead to development unless there are incentives for growth and an enabling environment (Rao and Mandal 2008). The enabling environment determines the volume of investment and is contributed by accommodating policies including level and quality of infrastructure and structure of incentives as provided by the institutional environment including the quality of governance.

A critical component of an enabling environment is provision of quality infrastructure—both physical and human. States in India have a predominant role in providing human capital and co-equal role with the central government in providing physical infrastructure. In developing countries, absence of the private sector in infrastructure provision and a nascent stage of development of the framework for private participation makes investment in infrastructure a predominantly government responsibility. Thus creation of an enabling environment for development critically depends on the state governments making the required investments in physical infrastructure and human development on the one hand and spending efficiently on the other.

Provision of efficient standards of physical and social infrastructure calls for efficient fiscal management in the states and a properly designed intergovernmental transfer system to offset vertical and horizontal fiscal imbalances. In other words, the states should efficiently raise revenues from the handles assigned to them and should ensure allocative and technical efficiency in spending so that the expenditures incurred translate into public outputs and outcomes. At the same time, it is important to design the transfer system to offset vertical fiscal imbalance to ensure that states are provided with adequate resources to finance the functions assigned to them satisfactorily. Similarly, offsetting horizontal imbalance is necessary to place all the states on a level playing field. This chapter analyses the recent trends in states' finances and highlights salient features of their fiscal management.

Recent Trends in State Finances

During the decade of the 1990s, there was very little reform in state finances and, barring a few exceptions, much less discussion on the need to undertake it. Of course, there have been discussions on the need to reform the sales tax system in the country both in the report of the Tax Reform Committee (Government of India 1991) and in a report prepared by the National Institute of Public Finance and Policy (NIPFP 1994). Towards the end of the decade, sharp deterioration in state finances reflected in increases in revenue and fiscal deficits and steady accumulation of debt created a destabilizing impact on state finances calling for urgency in reforms. However, attempts to contain deficits in the latter part of the 1990s and early part of the present decade have resulted in expenditures on social and physical infrastructure being compressed. The impact of these policy responses has been particularly harsh on the poorer states that are already lagging in infrastructure standards.

An important point to be noted, however, is that the focus of fiscal trends has been on burgeoning deficits. Thus much of the analysis of states' fiscal management has been from the viewpoint of macroeconomic stabilization which is largely a central function and not from the viewpoint of government's role in resource allocation which is largely the function of states. Thus concerns have been expressed about sharply increasing revenue and fiscal deficits. Fiscal deficits in the states increased from 2.7 per cent in 1996–7 to 4.7 per cent in 1999–2000 and revenue deficits from 0.85 per cent to 2.4 per cent in the same period. Thus, not only did the volume of fiscal deficit increase sharply, but also the quality of deficits deteriorated as the ratio of revenue deficit to fiscal deficit increased from 26 per cent to 59 per cent during this period. States' indebtedness relative to gross domestic product (GDP) increased from 21 per cent in 1995–6 to 30 per cent in 2001–2. Expenditures on social and economic services as a ratio of GDP remained at about 9.5 per cent, but with a sharp increase in the unit cost of providing these services following the pay revision, the real allocation to these sectors declined.

There are four important reasons for the declining fiscal health of the states during the latter part of the 1990s. The first was declining central transfers following a fall in central tax revenues. Gross central tax revenues relative to GDP declined from 10.2 per cent in 1991–2 to 8.2 per cent in 2001–2. During this period, even though revenue from income taxes increased by 1 percentage point thanks to the reduction in marginal tax rates, the ratio from indirect taxes declined due to falling revenue from import duty (2 percentage points) and central excise duty (2 percentage point). Thus transfers to the states declined by 1 percentage point. The second and probably most important factor was the pay and pension revision of employees. The spillover effect of the implementation of the Fifth Pay Commission recommendations at central level was to sharply increase the burden of wages, salaries, and pensions to state government employees. It is estimated that the burden of pay and pension revision was not less than 2 percentage points to GDP. In fact, due to the pay revision, virtually every state got into a revenue deficit situation. Third, increasing government deficits and steady accumulation of debt had adverse impact on interest rates which caused significant increases in states' borrowing costs. Many states tried to manage the hardening fiscal situation by taking increasing recourse to more expensive small savings loans by providing various types of incentives to depositors. Thus there was sharp increase in borrowing costs due to both larger volume of borrowings and higher interest rates. Finally, the emergence of coalition politics at the centre and in the states and a declining time horizon of political parties as well as politicians has made it difficult to cut down subsidies and transfers. As a result, attempts to contain fiscal deficits invariably translated into phasing out productive expenditures on creation and maintenance of infrastructure.

Indeed, crisis is the mother of reforms. The sharp increase in revenue and fiscal deficits not only vitiated the macroeconomic environment, but also compressed expenditures on infrastructure and essential public services. Although the reform conditionalities initiated by the recommendations of Eleventh Finance Commissions were ill designed (Rao 2003), state finances started showing steady improvements since 2001–2 and by 2006–7, the states were well on course to achieve the deficit reduction targets set by the Twelfth Finance Commission (TFC).

More recent trends show significant improvement in state finances. There was a 3 percentage point improvement in revenue deficit from 2.6 per cent of gross state domestic product (GSDP) in 2001–2 to a marginal surplus in 2007–8. The improvement resulted in reducing the fiscal deficit relative to GSDP from 4.2 per cent to 2.4 per cent during the period, which meant that capital expenditures increased by about 1.2 percentage points. Thus fiscal adjustment by states has led to overreaching the fiscal deficit targets.

It would, however, be inappropriate to attribute the improvement to the fiscal restructuring plan of the TFC. Of course, the fiscal restructuring plan required states to pass fiscal responsibility legislation to phase out revenue deficits and reduce fiscal deficits to 3 per cent of GSDP by 2009–10. The progress in the reduction in revenue deficits was also linked to the writing off of debt to the central government. While this has provided the direction in which the adjustment should take place, the mechanism to achieve this recommended by the Commission was too general and there is nothing to show that the sources of improvement can be attributed to these recommendations.

The analysis of the various sources of improvement summarized in Table 1.1 shows interesting features. During the period from 2001–2 to 2007–8, revenue deficit relative to GDP was reduced by 3 percentage points. Of this, 2.5 percentage points were due to increase in revenues and 0.5 point to expenditure compression. Within revenues, an almost 1.4 percentage points rise was due to increase in transfers equally distributed between tax devolution and grants. Much of this increase is attributable to the high buoyancy of central direct taxes. The gross tax revenue of the central government increased at 26 per cent during this period and this was partly due to the high growth of manufacturing and service sectors during the period and more importantly, strengthening of the information system through establishing the Tax Information Network (TIN).

TABLE 1.1
Improvement in State Finances since 2001–2

	Fiscal trends (per cent of GDP)		Improvement in 2007–8 over 2001–2 (percentage points)
	2001–2	2007–8 (BE)	
Fiscal deficit	4.2	2.4	1.8
Revenue deficit	2.6	–0.4	3.0
Revenue receipts	9.8	12.3	2.5
Own tax revenue	5.6	6.7	1.1
Tax devolution	2.3	3.0	0.7
Grants	1.9	2.6	0.7
Revenue expenditure of which:	13.8	13.2	0.6
Interest payment	2.7	2.3	0.4

Note: BE—budget estimates.
Source: NIPFP Database.

Own tax revenues of state governments increased by over 1 percentage point during the period and a close examination shows that much of the increase is attributable to the reform of the sales tax system with the cascading-type sales tax being replaced by the value-added tax (VAT) in April 2005. Of course, rationalization of stamp duties and boom in the real estate market also contributed in terms of significant increases in stamp duties.

On the expenditure side, the adjustment was only 0.6 percentage point and this is almost entirely attributable to reduction in interest payments mainly due to lower interest rates on states' borrowings. Besides lowering of interest rates due to the debt swap scheme adopted in 2004–5, lower volume of borrowings from the National Small Savings Fund (NSSF) and, to some extent, write off of debt repayment as per the recommendation of the TFC have contributed to the improvement. Thus much of the improvement in state finances has come about due to higher transfers from the central government and the introduction of VAT in the states. It is also important to note that the improvement is likely to sustain in the medium term as revenues from central direct taxes are likely to show high buoyancy with progressive strengthening of the information system and reforms to introduce the goods and services tax (GST).

Interestingly, almost all states have shown significant improvement in their fiscal health (Table 1.2). Both revenue and fiscal deficits have been reduced in every state except Kerala among general category states.

TABLE 1.2
Fiscal Consolidation since 2001–2

	Fiscal deficit			Revenue deficit			Capital outlay*		
	2001–2	2007–8 (BE)	Improvement (2–3)	2001–2	2007–8 (BE)	Improvement (5–6)	2001–2	2007–8 (BE)	Improvement (9–8)
1	2	3	4	5	6	7	8	9	10
I. General Category States									
High-income states									
Andhra Pradesh	4.28	2.90	1.38	1.83	0.01	1.82	2.44	2.88	0.44
Goa	5.82	4.47	1.35	3.22	0.05	3.17	2.60	4.42	1.82
Gujarat	5.27	2.15	3.12	5.45	–0.59	6.04	–0.18	2.74	2.91
Haryana	4.32	1.28	3.04	1.66	–0.89	2.56	2.65	2.17	–0.48
Karnataka	5.39	2.95	2.44	3.01	–0.68	3.70	2.37	3.63	1.26
Kerala	4.22	5.02	–0.80	3.37	3.55	–0.19	0.86	1.47	0.61
Maharashtra	4.02	2.01	2.00	3.02	–0.09	3.11	1.00	2.11	1.11
Punjab	6.22	4.79	1.43	4.74	1.48	3.26	1.48	3.31	1.84
Tamil Nadu	3.18	2.86	0.32	1.84	0.04	1.80	1.34	2.82	1.48
West Bengal	7.51	3.90	3.62	5.64	2.43	3.20	1.88	1.46	–0.41
Average	**4.85**	**2.88**	**1.97**	**3.38**	**0.40**	**2.97**	**1.47**	**2.48**	**1.01**
Low-income states									
Bihar	4.47	2.96	1.51	2.28	–3.27	5.55	2.19	6.23	4.04
Chhattisgarh	3.60	2.31	1.29	1.88	–2.66	4.54	1.73	4.97	3.25
Jharkhand	3.89	5.79	–1.89	0.87	0.66	0.21	3.02	5.13	2.11

Table 1.2 (*contd...*)

Table 1.2 (contd...)

1	2	3	4	5	6	7	8	9	10
Madhya Pradesh	4.20	3.40	0.79	3.64	–1.47	5.11	0.56	4.87	4.31
Orissa	8.45	0.85	7.61	6.04	–0.86	6.90	2.42	1.71	–0.71
Rajasthan	5.21	3.74	1.46	3.25	–1.84	5.10	1.95	5.59	3.63
Uttar Pradesh	6.28	3.45	2.83	4.14	–0.14	4.28	2.13	3.59	1.46
Average	**5.25**	**3.28**	**1.98**	**3.37**	**–1.42**	**4.80**	**1.88**	**4.70**	**2.82**
Average–I	**4.97**	**3.00**	**1.97**	**3.38**	**–0.14**	**3.52**	**1.60**	**3.14**	**1.54**
				II. Special Category States					
Arunachal Pradesh	11.70	3.78	7.92	–2.62	–4.38	1.76	14.32	8.16	–6.16
Assam	3.79	2.93	0.86	2.30	–1.27	3.58	1.48	4.20	2.72
Himachal Pradesh	8.81	4.32	4.50	5.02	0.80	4.22	3.80	3.52	–0.28
Jammu & Kashmir	8.17	6.44	1.73	1.85	–8.81	10.67	6.32	15.25	8.94
Manipur	10.22	1.46	8.76	4.84	–5.56	10.40	5.38	7.02	1.64
Meghalaya	4.79	1.08	3.71	0.73	–6.66	7.38	4.06	7.73	3.67
Mizoram	21.70	3.84	17.86	13.38	–5.50	18.88	8.32	9.34	1.02
Nagaland	8.09	3.61	4.48	2.46	–9.29	11.75	5.63	12.89	7.27
Sikkim	5.88	10.76	–4.88	–12.58	–16.69	4.11	18.47	27.46	8.99
Tripura	8.45	6.11	2.34	–0.86	–5.80	4.95	9.30	11.91	2.61
Uttarakhand	3.83	4.54	–0.71	2.06	–2.94	5.00	1.77	7.48	5.71
Average	**6.38**	**4.11**	**2.27**	**2.40**	**–3.50**	**5.90**	**3.99**	**7.61**	**3.62**
Average–All States	**5.06**	**3.06**	**2.00**	**3.32**	**-0.34**	**3.65**	**1.74**	**3.40**	**1.66**

Notes: Negative sign for revenue deficit (cols 5 & 6) indicates surplus GSDP figures are projected using trend growth rate on last two available years.
* Capital outlay includes net lending.
Source: Finance accounts and budget documents of state governments.

Another interesting point is that, non-special category states performed better, on the whole, than special category states. Among non-special category states, low-income states performed better than high-income states. Between 2001–2 and 2007–8, while low-income states improved their average revenue deficit–GSDP ratio by 4.8 points, the improvement was only by about 3 points in the case of high-income states.

The improvement in revenue deficit was partly used to compress fiscal deficit and partly to increase capital outlay. Both high-income and low-income states brought down fiscal deficits by 2 percentage points, but while the high-income states increased their capital outlay by about 1 percentage point, the increase in the case of low-income states was 2.8 percentage points. Among the states, the greatest improvement in revenue deficit was in Orissa (6.9 points) and it was more than 5 percentage points for Bihar, Uttar Pradesh, and Madhya Pradesh. Similarly, among the general category states, fiscal deficit reduction was highest in Orissa. Thus capital expenditure relative to the GSDP increased by over 4 percentage points in Bihar and Madhya Pradesh and over 3 percentage points in Chhattisgarh and Uttar Pradesh. In contrast, Orissa reduced capital spending by 0.7 percentage point.

Table 1.3 presents the sources of improvement in revenue deficit in each of the states. It can be seen that the improvement was overwhelmingly due to increase in revenues and, more particularly, higher central transfers. There was hardly any compression of revenue expenditures even as the ratio of interest payments to the GSDP in 2007–8 was lower than in 2001–2 by 0.4 percentage point. Since 2005–6, some of the states have been able to avail of the benefits of the debt rescheduling and write-off recommended by the TFC.

The pattern of fiscal adjustment since 2001–2, however, shows significant variation among the states. In general, higher central transfer to states by way of tax devolution and grants helped to significantly reduce revenue deficits in every state. However, high-income states improved their revenue efforts as well. In these states, of the 3 percentage points improvement in revenue deficit, higher tax effort contributed 1.5 points or almost 50 per cent mainly due to the introduction of VAT. However, own non-tax revenues declined by 0.23 point. Tax devolution and grants together increased by 1.07 points during the period. These states compressed their revenue expenditures by 0.6 point of which, almost 0.3 point was due to lower interest payments. The increase in own tax effort was more than 3 percentage points in Andhra Pradesh, more than 2.5 points in Punjab and Tamil Nadu and more than

Table 1.3

Sources of Improvement in Revenue Deficit from 2001–2 to 2007–8

(per cent of GSDP)

States	Reduction in revenue deficit	Increase in				Change (+/-) in interest payments	
		Own taxes	Own non-taxes	Share in central taxes	Grants	Revenue expenditure	Interest payments
I. General Category States							
High-income states							
Andhra Pradesh	1.82	3.20	0.45	0.50	0.41	2.73	–0.02
Goa	3.17	–0.60	1.96	0.43	0.42	–0.96	–0.61
Gujarat	6.04	–0.01	–1.65	0.32	0.20	–7.18	–0.63
Haryana	2.56	1.69	0.28	0.34	0.28	0.03	–0.61
Karnataka	3.70	2.19	–0.19	0.24	0.88	–0.58	–0.44
Kerala	–0.19	1.68	0.07	0.49	0.58	3.00	0.02
Maharashtra	3.11	0.43	–0.63	0.38	1.10	–1.83	–0.18
Punjab	3.26	2.71	0.09	0.73	2.06	2.32	–0.48
Tamil Nadu	1.80	2.63	0.05	0.85	0.22	1.96	–0.32
West Bengal	3.20	0.68	–0.05	0.69	–0.16	–2.05	–0.16
Average	**2.97**	**1.50**	**–0.23**	**0.48**	**0.59**	**–0.63**	**–0.30**
Low-income states							
Bihar	5.55	0.65	–0.12	3.41	4.78	3.16	–0.88
Chhattisgarh	4.54	2.31	0.19	1.01	1.91	0.88	–0.65
Jharkhand	0.21	0.07	–0.36	1.63	0.86	1.99	0.71
Madhya Pradesh	5.11	3.17	–0.07	2.16	2.28	2.43	0.51

Table 1.3 (contd...)

Table 1.3 (contd...)

States	Reduction in revenue deficit	Increase in				Change (+/-) in interest payments	
		Own taxes	Own non-taxes	Share in central taxes	Grants	Revenue expenditure	Interest payments
Orissa	6.90	0.39	–0.17	–0.23	1.05	–5.86	–2.70
Rajasthan	4.28	2.18	0.55	2.04	0.50	0.98	–0.26
Uttar Pradesh	5.10	2.91	1.11	2.89	1.84	3.65	–1.00
Average	**4.80**	**2.01**	**0.42**	**2.16**	**1.86**	**1.65**	**–0.67**
I. Gen. Cat. States	**3.52**	**1.68**	**–0.04**	**0.93**	**0.96**	**0.02**	**–0.43**
II. Special Category States							
Arunachal Pradesh	1.76	0.69	1.42	6.79	2.89	10.02	0.47
Assam	3.58	1.66	1.01	1.53	4.29	4.92	–0.14
Himachal Pradesh	4.22	0.88	1.46	0.18	–0.85	–2.55	–0.42
Jammu & Kashmir	10.67	2.22	0.32	1.73	2.11	–4.28	–1.85
Manipur	10.40	0.22	1.16	2.84	–1.55	–7.74	–1.70
Meghalaya	7.38	1.39	0.31	3.34	12.95	10.61	0.16
Mizoram	18.88	1.32	1.01	9.26	9.21	1.93	–0.28
Nagaland	11.75	0.65	0.44	4.51	9.52	3.38	–0.07
Sikkim	4.11	2.63	1.11	0.47	–2.88	–2.78	–1.29
Tripura	4.95	1.15	–0.82	1.14	2.44	–1.04	–0.44
Uttarakhand	5.00	2.47	1.74	2.93	4.62	6.76	0.41
Average	**5.90**	**1.67**	**0.94**	**1.95**	**3.11**	**1.78**	**–0.44**
All States	**3.65**	**1.69**	**0.02**	**0.99**	**1.04**	**0.09**	**–0.43**

Note: GSDP figures are projected using average growth rates of last two available years.
Source: Finance accounts and budget documents of state governments.

2 points in Karnataka. Except Goa and Gujarat every state improved its tax effort. In the case of Kerala too, the tax–GSDP ratio increased by 1.7 points and central transfers increased by over 1 percentage point, but as revenue expenditures increased by over 3 points, the revenue deficit actually increased by 0.2 point.

The low-income states, on the other hand, reduced their revenue deficit–GSDP ratio by 4.8 percentage points. This was achieved even as non-interest revenue expenditures on social and economic services increased by 2.3 points. Due to lower interest payments, however, total revenue expenditure increased by 1.7 points. Thus larger transfers from the centre increased the revenues of these states by 4 points and better revenue effort from own sources increased the revenues by another 2.4 points. However, easing of resource constraints enabled these states to make additional allocation to social and economic services in both revenue and capital accounts.

Significant improvement in fiscal health since 2001–2 was also seen in the Special Category states. The revenue deficit relative to the GSDP was compressed by 5.9 percentage points mainly on the strength of higher central transfers. The ratio of tax devolution and grants to the GSDP from the central government increased by over 5 percentage points since 2001–2 and the increase in own revenues was about 2.5 points. At the same time, revenue expenditures too increased by 1.8 points. Although revenue deficits were reduced by 5.9 points, an only 2–3 point compression of fiscal deficit since 2001–2 was achieved as a significant portion of revenue deficit reduction (3.6 points) was used to augment capital expenditures.

Despite the improvements, there are significant risks and the fiscal situation is likely to show a substantial deterioration. Most of the states will follow the centre in revising the pay scales and the burden of this will be more on the states than the centre. The states' own revenues are likely to decelerate due to slowdown in the economy, particularly from the VAT, motor vehicles tax, and stamps and registration. Given the deceleration in central tax collections due to slowdown in the economy and reduction in the Central Value Added Tax (CENVAT) rate and various concessions given in excise duties, the tax devolution to the states is likely to decelerate. The impact of these will be particularly adverse for the poorer states, as at the margin, it is the capital expenditures that will be displaced.

The analysis of the indicators of fiscal health in different states summarized in Table 1.4 shows that going purely by deficit indicators, the performance of low-income states was as good if not better than that of high-income states. In fact, in 2006–7 (Revised Estimates [RE]), average revenue and fiscal deficits in the latter were higher than in the former. While low-income states, on average, had a revenue surplus of 0.65 per cent of the GSDP, high-income states had a deficit of 0.77 per cent. Similarly, average fiscal deficit of low-income states (3.9 per cent) was only marginally higher than that of the high-income states (3.3 per cent). Revenue and fiscal deficits in individual states do not show a clear pattern with their per capita income levels. The correlation coefficient of revenue deficit with per capita income in the general category states was 0.15 indicating that the deficits were higher in high-income states, though the coefficient was not significant. Similarly, the correlation coefficient of fiscal deficits with per capita income was not significant (–0.09). It can also be seen that among the low-income states every state except Bihar and Jharkhand had revenue surpluses whereas among the high-income states all the states except Karnataka and Gujarat had deficits.

However, per capita development expenditures (on social and economic services) in low-income states were significantly lower than in the high-income states (Table 1.4). As is evident from Figure 1.1, there exists a positive relationship between per capita development spending and per capita GSDP in general category states. The average per capita development expenditure in the low-income states at Rs 2706 was lower than the all-states average (Rs 3802) by 29 per cent and general category states average (Rs 3606) by 25 per cent. In contrast, high-income states at Rs 4445 could spend 23 per cent more on developmental heads than the average of general category states. Even leaving aside Goa, which is an outlier, the highest spending on development heads was in Haryana at Rs 5718 and this was higher than the average for general category states by 59 per cent. At the same time, Bihar, the poorest state could incur only Rs 2105 expenditure per capita on developmental heads which was 42 per cent lower than the average for general category states and 36.8 per cent of the expenditure incurred by Haryana.

Analysis shows that the tax–GSDP ratio in low-income states on average is less than in high-income states (Figure 1.2). However, it would be misleading to argue from this that the tax effort in low-income states is low because the relationship between per capita income and tax revenue is non-linear, for taxable capacity increases faster than per capita incomes. At lower levels of per capita incomes, non-market transactions are higher and these cannot be taxed. Nevertheless, it is

TABLE 1.4

Important Fiscal Performance Indicators in States, 2006–7

	Average per capita GSDP (Rs) 2006–7	Revenue deficit (per cent of GSDP) 2006–7 (RE)	Fisal deficit (per cent of GSDP) 2006–7 (RE)	Per cent of revenue to fiscal deficit 2006–7 (RE)	Per capita dev. spending (Rs) 2006–7 (RE)	Tax–GSDP ratio (per cent) 2006–7 (RE)
I. General Category States						
High-income states						
Andhra Pradesh	32,533	0.02	2.99	0.68	4977	9.56
Goa	95,663	0.24	4.93	4.93	15,460	8.26
Gujarat	44,332	–0.73	2.51	–29.24	4558	7.52
Haryana	48,214	0.57	0.57	100.80	5718	9.27
Karnataka	36,038	–1.39	2.63	–52.71	5174	11.71
Kerala	39,742	4.46	6.28	71.01	4244	9.04
Maharashtra	46,308	0.65	3.19	20.44	4587	8.24
Punjab	43,436	1.92	4.87	39.35	4886	8.54
Tamil Nadu	37,635	0.10	2.69	3.73	4698	11.37
West Bengal	30,739	3.19	4.49	71.14	2419	4.75
Average	**39,040**	**0.77**	**3.29**	**23.37**	**4445**	**8.71**
Low-income states						
Bihar	10,286	0.80	7.32	10.91	2105	4.80
Chhattisgarh	26,125	–2.83	2.41	–117.57	4440	8.99
Jharkhand	23,591	1.56	7.54	20.73	3992	4.48
Madhya Pradesh	18,984	–1.38	3.56	–38.90	2872	7.98
Orissa	25,998	–0.74	0.91	–81.17	2650	5.66

Table 1.4 (*contd...*)

Table 1.4 (contd...)

	Average per capita GSDP (Rs) 2006–7	Revenue deficit (per cent of GSDP) 2006–7 (RE)	Fisal deficit (per cent of GSDP) 2006–7 (RE)	Per cent of revenue to fiscal deficit 2006–7 (RE)	Per capita dev. spending (Rs) 2006–7 (RE)	Tax–GSDP ratio (per cent) 2006–7 (RE)
Rajasthan	22,211	–0.07	3.58	–1.93	3201	8.09
Uttar Pradesh	16,308	–1.11	3.67	–30.29	2369	8.07
Average	**17,947**	**–0.65**	**3.93**	**–16.52**	**2706**	**7.22**
General Category States	**28,867**	**0.34**	**3.48**	**9.88**	**3606**	**8.27**
			II. Special Category States			
Arunachal Pradesh	27,748	–12.63	7.76	–162.83	16,942	2.10
Assam	21,948	0.99	5.75	17.27	4580	5.62
Himachal Pradesh	43,535	0.19	3.92	4.87	7542	5.36
Jammu & Kashmir	26,334	–6.61	5.05	–130.74	8067	6.57
Manipur	27,992	–12.06	3.54	–340.68	9822	1.72
Meghalaya	28,343	–4.82	1.22	–395.59	7400	3.81
Mizoram	27,820	–6.34	10.36	–61.17	16,250	2.27
Nagaland	27,740	–6.66	6.42	–103.77	9209	1.95
Sikkim	34,821	–22.00	9.87	–222.82	22,765	7.53
Tripura	29,500	–5.46	4.70	–116.31	6600	3.52
Uttarakhand	30,956	–1.24	6.52	–19.07	6427	8.16
Average	**27,189**	**–2.51**	**5.35**	**–46.94**	**6730**	**5.59**
Average of All States	**28,762**	**0.18**	**3.59**	**4.89**	**3802**	**8.11**

Note: The GSDP figures are projected for the last two years.
Source: Budget documents of state governments and state finances, RBI.

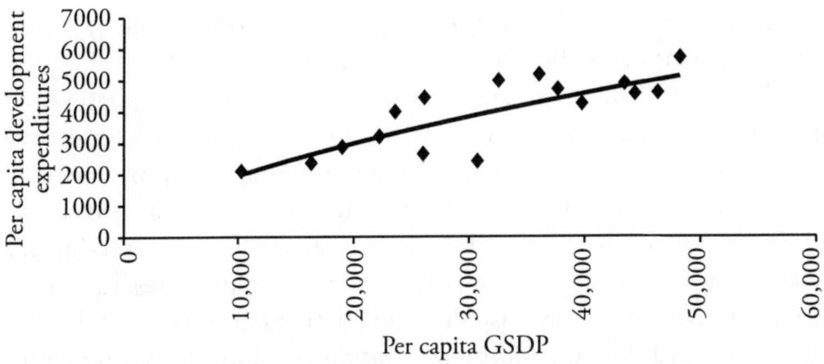

FIGURE 1.1: Relationship between Per Capita Development Spending and Per Capita GSDP in General Category States

Source: NIPFP Database.

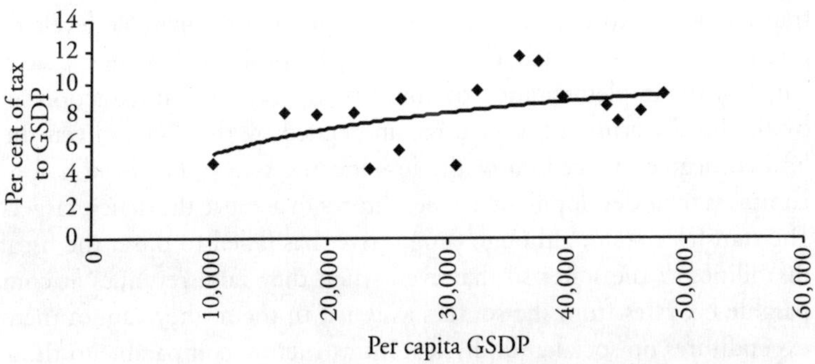

FIGURE 1.2: Relationship between Tax–GSDP Ratio and Per Capita GSDP

Source: NIPFP Database.

seen that some of the low-income states have higher tax ratios than some of the high-income states and, curiously, the lowest tax ratio was in West Bengal, which is a high-income state.

Analysis shows that there is indeed a negative relationship between per capita central transfers and per capita GSDP, though the correlation coefficient is not significant. In other words, even when we adjust the per capita expenditures of the states for lower tax–GSDP ratios by taking into account states' own revenues at an all-state average level, in states where it is lower the estimated per capita expenditures are positively correlated with per capita GSDP. This implies that central transfers have failed to offset the fiscal disabilities of poorer states due to their low tax base. The problem of low resource base and poor revenue effort is reinforced by large and growing expenditures on committed items such as wages, salaries and pensions, and debt servicing. Fiscal stress in low-income states has displaced spending on developmental items, thereby jeopardizing their future growth prospects.

The focus of the fiscal restructuring plan has been on phasing out revenue deficits and reducing fiscal deficits of the state to 3 per cent of GSDP. Recent trends show that though significant improvements in central transfers and, to some extent, own revenues have helped restore the fiscal balance, per capita development expenditures in low-income states are significantly lower than in high-income states. This tends to accentuate inter-state disparities in infrastructure levels and living standards. Inability to achieve a level playing field for states through the transfer system could pose a severe strain on Indian federalism.

The reasons for high and increasing inter-state disparities in per capita expenditures have to be found in the inability of the intergovernmental transfer system to enable these states to provide comparable levels of public services at comparable tax rates. The problem has been exacerbated by the implementation of uniform targets of deficit reduction set by the fiscal restructuring plan recommended by the TFC. Given the limited degree of freedom of the low-income states, they have had to compress their developmental expenditures to achieve the deficit targets. The transfer system, although progressive, has failed to offset the fiscal disabilities of the states so that even when they raise revenues at comparable tax rates from the sources assigned to them, they cannot incur expenditures on social and physical infrastructure comparable to those by high-income states. The next stage of the fiscal restructuring plan should not merely have the objective of macroeconomic stabilization but should also take account of the developmental requirements of the low-income states.

References

Government of India (1991). *Report of the Tax Reform Committee*, Chairman: R.J. Chelliah. New Delhi: Ministry of Finance, Government of India.

NIPFP (1994). *Reform of Domestic Trade Taxes in India: Issues and Options*. New Delhi: National Institute of Public Finance and Policy.

Rao, M. Govinda (2003). 'Incentivising Fiscal Transfers in Indian Federation', *Publius: The Journal of Federalism*, 33(4): 43–62.

Rao, M. Govinda and Subrata Mandal (2008). 'Resource Endowment, Fiscal Flows and Regional Equity in Indian Federalism', in M. Govinda Rao and Anwar Shah (eds), *Fiscal Management Challenges of Indian States and Regional Equity in India*, pp. 207–30. New Delhi: Oxford University Press.

2

Reforming the State Tax System in a Globalizing Environment

R. Kavita Rao

Apart from the fiscal stress that states are already going through, there are immediate pressures building up to focus more effort on raising tax revenues. The next pay commission has recently been constituted. The recommendations of the last pay commission had seriously upset the fiscal balance of states. Demands for infrastructure are growing by the day. Even the major initiatives being taken by the central government on Providing Urban Amenities in Rural Areas (PURA) and urban renewal programmes require a degree of counterpart funding from states, in situations where the fiscal flexibility of the states is rather limited. The spurt of special economic zones is likely to take its toll on central tax revenues, and thereby on transfers that states receive from the centre.

This chapter presents an overview of the performance of states in terms of mobilization of tax revenues and attempts to identify options for strengthening the tax base. The next section discusses trends in state taxes; this is followed by five more sections each dealing with one particular tax, namely, value-added tax (VAT), state excise, stamp duties and registration fees, on income/earning, and taxes on transportation. Each of these sections seeks to identify the weak links in the existing system and outline options for reform, some of which can be implemented by the states themselves while others may require the initiative of the union government.

Trends in State Taxes

States' own tax revenues have grown at an average rate of about 14 per cent per annum over the last two decades. There is evidence of a trend decline in total own tax collections—the mid 1980s began with growth rates of 16 per cent per annum but settled down to more modest levels of around 14 per cent in more recent times, though since 2001–2, there has been a reversal of the trend. Viewed as a ratio to gross domestic product (GDP), own tax collections registered a decline in the first decade, from 5.48 per cent in 1987–8 to 4.98 per cent in 1998–9, but thereafter steadily increased to reach 5.9 per cent in 2005–6 (Figure 2.1). Thus, while own tax revenue collections failed to keep pace with the growth of GDP till 1998–9, there has been a recovery in subsequent years. Since the late 1990s, thanks to the initiatives taken to improve tax collections, there has been greater tax buoyancy. In sales tax, after a prolonged period of tax competition among states both in terms of rates of tax and incentives for investment, an agreement was reached to adhere to floor rates and phase out sales-tax-based industrial incentives. Reforms in stamp duties and registration fees were initiated—a reduction in the rates of tax and computerization of land records were two such measures. Some states explored options for stemming the decline in performance of state excise collections as well.

This performance, however, was not uniform across all states. States can be classified into two categories based on the performance of ratio of tax to gross state domestic product (GSDP). (Table 2.1 provides a listing of the states above and below national average.) Interestingly only four states have moved up from being below the national average when

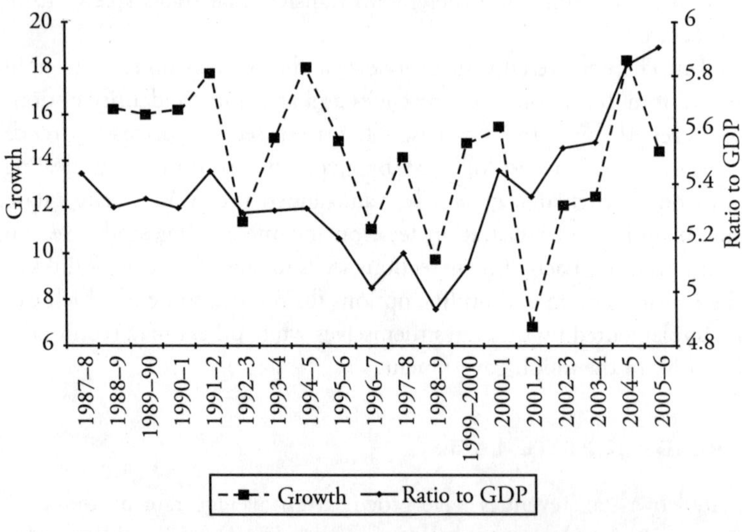

FIGURE 2.1: Trends in Own Tax Revenue
Source: Finance accounts of state governments/NIPFP Database.

compared to 1987–8—Jammu & Kashmir, Orissa, Madhya Pradesh, and Uttar Pradesh. The average for 1987–8 was 5.44.

TABLE 2.1
Comparison of Performance of States, 2003–4

Ratio above 6 per cent		Ratio less than 6 per cent	
State	Ratio	State	Ratio
Orissa	6.07	Nagaland	1.44
Jammu & Kashmir	6.10	Mizoram	1.54
Uttar Pradesh	6.32	Arunachal Pradesh	1.80
Chhattisgarh	6.71	Manipur	1.86
Gujarat	6.74	Tripura	3.09
Rajasthan	6.90	Meghalaya	3.69
Madhya Pradesh	6.92	West Bengal	4.70
Uttaranchal	7.06	Jharkhand	4.99
Goa	7.35	Assam	5.14
Andhra Pradesh	7.48	Himachal Pradesh	5.45
Punjab	7.57	Bihar	5.53
Maharashtra	7.67	Sikkim	5.86
Haryana	8.58		
Kerala	9.04		
Tamil Nadu	9.47		
Karnataka	9.66		

Source: Finance accounts of state governments/NIPFP Database.

Table 2.1 brings to light an interesting pattern—the states performing relatively poorly in terms of own tax revenue are also states with relatively lower per capita incomes—West Bengal and Rajasthan being exceptions to this description in each category. This is reinforced by the fact that Orissa, Uttar Pradesh, Madhya Pradesh, as well as Jammu & Kashmir too belonged to the less than national average category till 1987–8.

The major taxes in the states portfolio are sales tax/VAT, state excise duties, transportation taxes including motor vehicles tax and passenger and goods tax, electricity duty, professional tax, and stamps and registration fees. In addition to these, in some states land revenue and agricultural income tax play an important role. State tax collections are dominated by sales tax collections. At aggregate level, sales tax collections account for close to 60 per cent of total own tax revenue of the states. State excise collections come a poor second with a share of about 14 per cent. Transportation taxes and stamps and registration fee tie at the third place with average shares of 8–9 per cent each. Electricity duty accounts for about 4 per cent. All the other taxes put together bring in the balance of 5 per cent (Table 2.2).

TABLE 2.2

State-wise Composition of Own Tax Revenue

(per cent)

	Electricity duty	Profession tax	State excise	Stamps and registration	Sales tax	Transport taxes	Other taxes
Andhra Pradesh	0.85	1.11	12.87	8.54	67.92	7.59	1.12
Arunachal Pradesh	0.02	0.00	35.51	0.92	56.38	4.40	2.77
Assam	2.28	3.49	5.31	2.67	77.34	5.55	3.36
Bihar	0.61	0.00	10.30	13.13	60.93	12.72	2.32
Chhattisgarh	9.57	0.82	7.68	14.20	51.86	14.84	1.04
Goa	0.00	0.00	6.46	4.17	66.22	18.90	4.25
Gujarat	14.12	1.03	7.43	0.36	64.12	9.42	3.52
Haryana	0.83	0.00	9.77	13.62	63.99	11.36	0.43
Himachal Pradesh	7.03	0.00	6.02	23.96	43.32	11.67	8.00
Jammu & Kashmir	3.65	0.00	2.90	20.16	59.52	12.90	0.86
Jharkhand	1.52	0.00	3.63	6.12	78.96	8.75	1.02
Karnataka	0.23	1.76	11.16	17.79	55.17	11.25	2.63
Kerala	0.11	0.00	8.65	8.33	74.76	6.81	1.35
Madhya Pradesh	9.10	1.93	10.15	15.34	50.33	12.31	0.85
Maharashtra	5.47	3.51	13.45	7.25	61.48	5.24	3.60
Manipur	6.09	14.15	2.71	3.75	67.24	4.98	1.08
Meghalaya	0.01	0.49	2.19	30.18	60.74	4.87	1.50
Mizoram	0.00	11.03	3.68	0.26	71.73	11.03	2.27
Nagaland	0.01	16.96	0.94	2.64	67.78	10.73	0.96

Table 2.2 (contd...)

Table 2.2 (contd...)

	Electricity duty	Profession tax	State excise	Stamps and registration	Sales tax	Transport taxes	Other taxes
Orissa	6.27	1.41	4.74	7.34	59.17	17.31	3.75
Punjab	3.62	0.00	13.91	21.41	54.95	5.82	0.29
Rajasthan	5.26	0.02	9.72	15.16	57.01	11.42	1.40
Sikkim	0.00	0.00	1.62	37.20	54.84	3.69	2.64
Tamil Nadu	1.26	0.00	8.29	13.17	67.14	9.19	0.96
Tripura	0.01	7.80	5.04	14.16	67.39	3.62	1.97
Uttar Pradesh	2.26	0.00	17.09	17.12	56.64	5.46	1.43
Uttaranchal	2.60	0.00	14.39	20.22	54.94	6.85	1.01
West Bengal	2.72	2.39	10.14	6.77	57.60	5.32	15.06

Note: The data for Tripura relate to 2003–4.
Source: Computed from the finance accounts for various states, 2004–5.

While sales tax constitutes the most important source for all the states, the role played by other taxes varies across states. There are some states where stamps and registration fee plays a dominant role—Himachal Pradesh, Jammu & Kashmir, Meghalaya, Punjab, Sikkim, and Uttaranchal derive more than 20 per cent of own tax revenue from this source. Orissa and Goa get more than 15 per cent of own tax revenue from transportation taxes, while Andhra Pradesh, Arunachal Pradesh, Maharashtra, Uttar Pradesh, and Uttaranchal get over 12 per cent of their revenue from state excises. Table 2.2 captures the variations across states, in terms of composition of own tax revenue.

The importance of sales tax in the states' portfolio of taxes is also reflected in the close correlation between the ratios of own tax revenue to the GDP and sales tax to the GDP, for all the states put together—an exceptionally high correlation of 0.91. States with low volatility in own tax revenue as a percentage of the GSDP are Gujarat, Himachal Pradesh, Maharashtra, Meghalaya, Karnataka, Kerala, Punjab, and Tamil Nadu.[1]

Reforming the Sales Tax System

The sales tax system followed till recently by states in India, was largely a first point tax system, on sales within the state. Inter-state sales are governed by the Central Sales Tax Act, which assigns the right to tax to the exporting state and places a 4 per cent ceiling on the tax.[2] A logical consequence of this structure is input taxation and resultant cascading and tax exportation. Since each state had a separate jurisdiction, there was basis for intense tax competition among the states, in the choice of tax rates as well as in the provision of tax-based industrial incentives. With industrial incentives being offered by all the states, these failed to influence location of industry in any major way. There is no evidence of increase in dispersion of industry. In this context, the relatively more industrial states stood to lose more revenue. Some anecdotal evidence suggests that considerable revenue was forgone by way of industrial incentives—in Maharashtra, the figures were 22 per cent of sales tax revenue for 1999–2000.

In November 1999, a consensus was arrived at to address some of these problems. It proposed the following:

1. Adherence to agreed floors on rates of tax on a pre-specified list of about 200 commodities.

2. Withdrawal of tax-based industrial incentives for new projects from January 2000.
3. Replacement of existing sales tax by VAT with a common design.

The first two items in the consensus were made effective by January 2000. This did contribute to stabilizing of the revenues of states, as was to be expected. An exercise to examine the buoyancy subsequent to the introduction of the first two measures indicates an improvement from a level of 1 prior to 1999–2000 to 1.29.

The improvements, however, have not been uniform across all states. Some have benefited more than others. In terms of significant improvement in the growth of sales tax revenue, very few states can be identified as beneficiaries—Assam, Jammu & Kashmir, and Tripura. However, when viewed as a ratio of the GSDP, the trends appear to have altered for a number of states. In regression of the tax to GSDP ratio on time, there is a perceptible change in trend in all the following states: Assam, Haryana, Himachal Pradesh, Jammu & Kashmir, Maharashtra, Mizoram, Orissa, Punjab, Rajasthan, Sikkim, Tamil Nadu, and Tripura, indicating that the impact was quite widespread.

The third measure was introduced only in April 2005. A consensus design of VAT was hammered out by the Empowered Committee of State Finance Ministers, constituted to coordinate and monitor transition to the new tax regime. Since the proposed regime sought only to replace the existing tax with a more rational version, the new tax is effectively a VAT limited in coverage only to taxation of goods within the state. The principle features of this tax can be summarized as follows:

1. VAT is proposed as a tax on the sale of goods to replace the present sales tax, along with all related taxes such as turnover tax, additional tax, and surcharges. Entry taxes levied in order to protect the sales tax revenue from diversion of trade would have to be integrated into the VAT. However, entry taxes levied as a replacement for octroi would continue to remain as separate taxes.
2. An input tax credit form of VAT is to be implemented. It provides for credit of any input/purchase taxes paid in the state against taxes collected on sales. The input tax credit on capital goods is to be spread over a maximum of three years. A negative list of goods excluded from the domain of input tax credit is to be prescribed by each individual state.
3. Tax credit will also be available against central sales tax (CST) paid on inter-state sales. In the case of exports, full credit/refund

is available. In the case of consignment and branch transfer, the state would retain tax of up to 4 per cent on the inputs and the rest would be available as credit.[3] There is provision for carry forward of excess tax credits. There is no instant refund provision in the event of credit exceeding the tax due in any period. In the first two years, there is no provision for refund of excess credit in the case of local sales/inter-state sales. The refund becomes due at the end of a financial year, except in the case of exporters, who can get refund in three months.

4. Following up on the work done for the floor rates regime, 550 major commodities have been classified into three broad categories—those to be exempt from tax, those to be taxed at 4 per cent, and those to be taxed at 12.5 per cent.[4] These rates are to remain uniform across all states. Petrol and diesel are to remain out of the VAT system, while alcohol is to be taxed at a floor rate of 20 per cent. For gold and bullion a special VAT rate of 1 per cent has been agreed upon.
5. Measures to facilitate incorporation of 'declared goods' as well as sugar, textiles, and tobacco into the VAT regime, have been initiated. The latter, however, are not yet formally being taxed within the state VATs.
6. Very small dealers are to remain outside the tax net. A ceiling of Rs 500,000 has been proposed for the exemption threshold. Further, a simplified scheme for dealers below a certain threshold is allowed—they can pay a turnover tax on their entire turnover as an alternative to adopting the entire system of VAT. The ceiling for this category was specified at Rs 5 million.
7. It is desired that the draft acts too achieve some degree of convergence in terms of definitions, charging sections, and procedures. The Empowered Committee specified a list of twenty-two points for convergence.

In the first year of the transition to the new regime, twenty-two out of the twenty-nine states and two union territories with legislature implemented the new tax. Of the remaining, eight implemented it in the second year and Uttar Pradesh changed over in 2008. The revenue performance of states in the new regime has been better than anticipated. The union government had budgeted for Rs 50,000 million to compensate the states for any loss of revenue. It may be mentioned that the basis for compensation was worked out by comparing actual revenue collections with a potential collection figure where the latter was arrived at by applying the average growth rate of the best three out of the five-year period 1999–2004.

Table 2.3 captures the performance of states in the first year after introduction of VAT. The overall performance suggests that alongside good performance by VAT states, the revenue performance of non-VAT states too has been good. This could be attributed either to good economic performance which translates through buoyancy into higher tax revenue or partly to improved compliance in the VAT states having spillover effects for the rest of the states. The performance of individual states, however, is quite varied. Only two states recorded negative or zero increase in revenue in 2005–6—Bihar and Sikkim. The relatively more industrialized states exhibit lower growth rates, possibly owing to the change in regime and the resultant elimination of input taxes. The extent of compensation paid exceeds the budgeted amount but examined in terms of magnitude—8.8 per cent of the total revenue collected in 2005–6, or spread—only eight of the twenty-five states and union territories that implemented VAT required compensation—the transition should be considered remarkably smooth. For the states that did not need compensation, annual growth averaged 26 per cent. The good revenue performance of VAT has continued.

While this is heartening, it is useful to focus on some of the weaknesses in the design. Some of the salient points are as follows:[5]

1. Problems with the proposed rate structure
   - A large number of goods including industrial inputs have been placed in the 4 per cent category. This was ostensibly done to minimize demands for refund. However, with a large difference between the two rate categories, there are perverse incentives to misclassify goods, as well as demands for increasing the number of goods to be placed in the lower rate category. It is both desirable and more efficient to confine the lower rate to very few commodities of essential consumption and place all the rest in the higher rate category.
   - There are no mechanisms to ensure that the present consensus design based on uniform tax rates can be sustained beyond the initial years, where the compensation package could provide the necessary binding force. While it is in the interest of every single state to adhere to the consensus—since initiating

TABLE 2.3
Revenue Performance during 2005–6

(vis-à-vis past performance)

Sl no.	State/UT	Tax revenue (Rs crore)			
		2004–5	2005–6	Per cent change	Compensation received
A.	VAT states/UTs:				
1.	Andhra Pradesh	11,022.58	12,569.91	14.0	404.06
2.	Arunachal Pradesh	28.25	34.50	22.1	
3.	Assam	1529.92	1823.02	19.2	
4.	Bihar	2393.25	2387.49	–0.2	272.98
5.	Dadra & Nagar Haveli	81.83	121.76	48.8	
6.	Daman & Diu	61.69	116.85	89.4	
7.	Delhi	4201.38	5686.02	35.3	
8.	Goa	502.90	669.83	33.2	
9.	Haryana	3731.12	4400.85	17.9	
10.	Himachal Pradesh	504.92	646.10	28.0	
11.	Jammu & Kashmir	609.05	740.19	21.5	
12.	Karnataka	7545.56	8078.93	7.1	1272.2
13.	Kerala	6648.07	6937.24	4.3	692.7
14.	Maharashtra	16,815.80	18,669.55	11.0	2374.6
15.	Manipur	42.76	51.35	20.1	
16.	Meghalaya	101.38	145.43	43.5	
17.	Mizoram	27.98	41.16	47.1	
18.	Nagaland	52.41	82.08	56.6	
19.	Orissa	2080.73	2541.09	22.1	
20.	Punjab	3366.16	4281.28	27.2	
21.	Sikkim	48.07	48.33	0.5	5.9
22.	Tripura	159.46	196.61	23.3	5.1
23.	West Bengal	5086.40	5406.35	6.3	278.8
24.	Uttaranchal	698.18	916.35	31.2	
25.	Chandigarh	303.03	401.60	32.5	
	Sub-total (A)	**67,642.88**	**76,993.87**	**13.8**	**5306.4**
B.	Non-VAT states/UTs:				
1.	Chhattisgarh	1296.15	1641.58	26.7	
2.	Gujarat	6763.04	8691.74	28.5	
3.	Jharkhand	1322.57	1565.34	18.4	
4.	Madhya Pradesh	3336.97	3902.17	16.9	
5.	Pondicherry	246.49	303.82	23.3	
6.	Rajasthan	4500.77	5245.00	16.5	
7.	Tamil Nadu	11,461.86	13,657.79	19.2	
8.	Uttar Pradesh	8535.10	11,012.67	29.0	
	Sub-total (B)	**37,462.95**	**46,020.11**	**22.8**	
C.	**Grand total (A+B)**	**105,105.83**	**123,013.98**	**17.0**	

Note: The figures in the last column would be higher by Rs 1456.14, which is the amount of claims still being processed. These would accrue to Kerala (Rs 313.7 crore) and Maharashtra (Rs 1142.4 crore).

Source: Sales Tax Desk, Ministry of Finance, Government of India.

a divergence would trigger off some more rate wars—this logic by itself may not be adequate to ensure that states do not default on some of the agreed rates. Some divergence is in evidence even today.

2. Limitations in coverage
   - The tax does not cover services: As per the constitutional assignment of tax powers, states in India do not have the right to tax services. Introducing a goods tax does not eliminate cascading from the system. Since services are closely interlinked with goods—transportation services and electricity are prime examples—a base that does not include these activities retains a large measure of cascading. Under the present constitutional dispensation, the right to tax services rests solely with the union government. While there is discussion about some sharing of these tax powers, the sharing arrangement is yet to be finalized.
   - Reform of CST is not yet clear: The initial discussions mentioned a phased withdrawal of the CST alongside the introduction of VAT. The phase-out has been initiated, in 2007–8, by a reduction in the CST ceiling to 3 per cent, from 1 April 2007. A reduction in the CST to zero presents large incentives to mask local sales as inter-state sales. There is, therefore, need to establish an effective and reliable system of inter-state transactions, to prevent revenue leakages. However, there is not much happening on this front. While the National Tax Information Exchange System (TINXYX) was proposed as a database to address these concerns, in setting up the database, the existing system of documentation was taken as given. Further, no consensus was arrived at on the form and frequency of data collection and updation. These glitches need to be ironed out before elimination of the CST can be contemplated.[6]

The process of reform in commodity taxes has since been pushed one step further. The Finance Minister of India, in his budget speech for the union budget of 2006–7 proposed that India would move to a national level goods and services tax (GST) by 2010. The contours of this new regime are just beginning to emerge, after extensive discussions between the various levels of government involved in the transition. The salient features emerging are as follows:

1. The proposed regime would be a dual VAT, covering both goods and services—a central GST and a state GST.
2. There will be more than one rate category for taxation of goods but only one rate for services, with set-offs provided within each of these tax regimes.
3. An attempt will be made to merge most of the existing levies on goods and services into this new tax.

As is evident, the proposed regime shift can take care of both the concerns with regard to the present regime. The proposed extension of the state GST to cover services would allow for a more comprehensive and rational tax at state level. However, before such a tax can be put into place, it is essential to define an acceptable system of taxation for services involving more than one state. Turning to the second issue, the establishment of a comprehensive dual VAT will also address the concerns for the reform of the CST. A pure zero-rating system can work, provided the administration of both these taxes is closely coordinated, if not integrated. However, if the final design retains two distinct administrations that do not work together, there will continue to be need for an effective system of monitoring inter-state transactions. In what follows, as attempt is made to outline the options available for assigning the right to tax in case of services spanning multiple states and for establishing a reliable system for capturing information on inter-state transactions.

Options for Reform

Table 2.4 provides a comparison of the options for reform of the CST. As is apparent from the Table, while none of the options emerges as a clear winner, a conservative revenue safe approach with minimal costs to the taxpayers is one of a pre-payment system. This system would ensure that the incentives to evade local taxes by passing off local sales as inter-state sales are minimized. The system can be designed so as to reduce the costs to the taxpayer as well—the tax payment cycle and the refund claims can be processed along with the tax returns. Transaction-wise details need to be captured both for the buyer and the seller and any mismatch could work as a trigger for action by the department.

Turning to the taxation of services which span more than one state, it is essential to work out a suitable mechanism for taxation of such services, before states can implement a regime involving comprehensive

Table 2.4
Reform of CST: Comparison of Alternatives

	Pure zero rating	Pre-payment system	Pair-wise clearing	Clearing house
Comparison with local sales	High benefits from evasion	High benefits from evasion	No benefits	No benefits
Comparison with local purchases	Inter-state purchase cheaper	No difference	No difference	No difference
Dependence on other states for revenue	None	None	On all inter-state transactions	On all inter-state transactions
Dependence on transaction-wise information	Complete	Complete	Complete	Alternative redistribution mechanism may be devised
Compliance costs	Report individual transactions independent of return (for both buyer and seller)	Report individual transactions independent of return (for both buyer and seller)	Not required	Not required
Possible mechanism for fraud	Exporter can set up a fake dealer in the importing state and	Provisions have to allow for the importer to reallocate the pre-paid	Exporting state and exporting dealer have no incentive to document	Same as in the pair-wise clearing case.

Table 2.4 (*contd...*)

Table 2.4 (*contd...*)

	Pure zero rating	Pre-payment system	Pair-wise clearing	Clearing house
	record the receipt of transactions. The importer can then disappear. If the department is not vigilant, then this can be a source of major revenue loss. If the department is vigilant, these transactions cannot be sustained over long periods.	tax, in the event of the goods being lost/damaged in transit or the value of the goods being lower than when the tax was paid. If this provision is made, there are issues of valuation and verification of the receipt of goods to authenticate the transactions, without which there can emerge scope for tax evasion.	inter-state sales. Exporting dealer can record the transaction as a local sale to an unregistered person, when a transaction involves inter-state sales. This reduces the transaction costs for the seller and the buyer can pass off these goods without paying tax in the importing state. The exporting state can afford to ignore such transactions since there is a revenue gain from ignoring them. In other words, this system may require a strong set of check-posts too, to monitor inflow of goods.	

Source: Rao (2005).

taxation of services. Taking the solution for treatment of inter-state sales discussed in the previous paragraph, it is possible to work out a destination-based treatment of services with inter-state character. The following principle may be applied:

The place of origin would define the location or jurisdiction for taxation, with the qualification that for services having an inter-state dimension, if the supplier is registered in both the jurisdictions, the transaction can be taxed as per destination state for a registered dealer of the destination state.[7]

In the case of localized services, the supply as well as consumption of service would converge into the same jurisdiction. Non-localized services, services that have an inter-state dimension, would be services that can be delivered over a space of two states. Passenger and goods transport as well as telecommunication services are important examples of the latter. Hence the place of origin of the services would be different from the destination place. The principle suggests that the transaction can be taxed as per the destination for a dealer registered in the destination jurisdiction, provided the service provider is registered in both the jurisdictions. An alternative could be for purchasers who are registered dealers to undertake the payment of the tax on services received and provide a document of tax paid to the service provider, in place of the tax due. An example of the application of the proposed approach is as follows:

Goods Transport

Case I: Supplier of the service is registered in State A while purchaser is registered in State B.

1. If goods owned by purchaser are to be transported from State A to State B, the tax would have to be paid in State A. This would be similar to a case where a non-registered person or a final consumer requires transport of goods from one state to another.
2. If goods are purchased from a registered dealer in State A and the seller of the goods contracts the transport of goods also, the supply of service would be to a registered dealer within the state and would be taxed in State A. The value of transport services too would become part of the price of goods when sold and in the process of zero rating this inter-state sale, the cost of transport too gets zero rated. The buyer in State B can acquire the goods with no taxes attached.

Case II: Supplier is registered in both jurisdictions. The transaction can be billed in the destination state provided the buyer is a registered dealer there. The transaction would be zero rated in the state of origin and taxed in the state of destination.

Passenger Transport

Cases I and II would work in the same manner as in the goods transport example. In addition, it is possible to imagine passengers undertaking a journey from a place in State A, to another in State B, and further on to a third destination in State C before finally returning to place of origin in State A. According to the principle, each leg of this journey would be taxed in a different state.[8] Given the qualifier spelt out in the principle, if the same journey were undertaken by the employees of a business enterprise registered in State A, and if the service provider were registered in all three states, it would be possible to zero rate the transactions in States B and C and bill and tax them from State A, provided the journey begins and ends in State A. This would facilitate the mechanism for tax credit for the concerned enterprise.

All this discussion on reforms for state VAT is applicable to the existing framework of taxation and seeks to address the problems therein. In the budget of 2006–7, the Union Finance Minister announced the intention to make a transition to a comprehensive GST by the year 2010. While there is still no firm design of the regime that is being proposed, it is worthwhile to note that the reforms discussed in the preceding pages would have to be an integral part of any such design.

State Excise

State excise revenue is generated from the levy of duties on the production and import of alcohol in a state and through a number of licence fees for wholesale and retailing permits, for registering brands, and so on. All the levies tend to be specific duties, with an effort at progressivity through variation in the duty depending on specific features such as the alcohol content. As discussed in the section on trends, state excise duties contribute a sizeable 14 per cent to the total own tax revenue of states. With some states committed to prohibition, the averages for states that do collect these revenues should be higher.

State excise has not been a very buoyant source of revenue. This is reflected in a consistent decline in the ratio of tax collections to GDP, from close to 0.85 per cent in the early 1990s to less than 0.68

per cent in 2004–5. It is, however, noteworthy that the last few years have been witness to relative stability in this ratio at around 0.70 per cent. The performance of individual states is quite volatile. While some states exhibit marginally rising trends, most others witness a lot of fluctuations. Tripura, Tamil Nadu, Orissa, Assam, and Arunachal Pradesh are the only states that exhibit an increasing trend.

This revenue category faces two kinds of problems: problems relating to policy and those relating to administration. On the administrative side, this tax is dogged by rampant evasion—the interim report of the Revenue Reforms Commission of Government of Karnataka quantified the extent of evasion at three times the revenue collected. On the policy front, persistence with specific duties hampers the buoyancy of the tax. Specific duties respond to changes in only quantities and not prices. With evidence of widespread evasion, the duty fails to reflect changes in quantities as well. The attraction of specific duties lies in the fact that collections are not sensitive to the revealed prices of the goods, unlike an ad valorem duty. However, specific duties require frequent revision to ensure inflation adjustment.

The solutions explored by states to address these problems are broadly of two kinds: some states have chosen to regulate the market through the introduction of state-owned monopolies for wholesale (Karnataka and Andhra Pradesh) and/or retail trade (Delhi and Tamil Nadu), especially in Indian made foreign liquor (IMFL). This measure reduces scope for evasion through suppression of the volume of transactions, and addresses the price issue as well. For achieving adequate control on the trade, operations at wholesale level are adequate; extending the coverage to retail activities as well might not be necessary. On the other hand, some other states have sought to address the problem by regulating the prices of the products as shown in Box 2.1 on Maharashtra's excise duty reforms, and thereby translating the specific duties effectively into ad valorem duties. Maharashtra is one such example.

The performance of the states that experimented with these measures does register improvement. The Maharashtra experience however translates into a one-shot increase in revenue, with not much impact on the long-term buoyancies, given that the basic character of the tax remains specific. West Bengal attempted another variant of the same approach by allowing for an abatement on the retail price in determining the production costs, which constitute the basis for levy of excise duty.

Given the willingness of states to undertake ad valorem taxation of most other commodities, it is useful to explore the possibility of

Box 2.1
Maharashtra Excise Duty Reforms

In order to address problems of valuation of the product and buoyancy of the tax at the same time, the government introduced the notion of maximum retail price which was linked to production costs. The products were classified into two categories—for products with production costs less than Rs 72 per proof litre, the ratio was pegged at four times, that is, the retail price could be up to four times the production cost. For other products the ratio was eight times. Since manufacturers/suppliers of each brand of product had to get the brand 'recognized', the information on production costs and the proposed MRP was a part of this process.

Excise duty applicable was specified as an ad valorem rate. With the declaration of the production costs, the administration of the tax became relatively straightforward and the revenue increased by 54 per cent in the first year.

In subsequent years, however, the downward trend in the tax to GSDP ratio resumed, as reflected in the graph. This, it is argued, resulted from the fact that the prices continue to need monitoring and the threshold for upgrading from a ceiling of 400 per cent value addition to 800 per cent value addition did not take place on a regular basis. In other words, the system does not capture the full gains from transformation to an ad valorem mode.

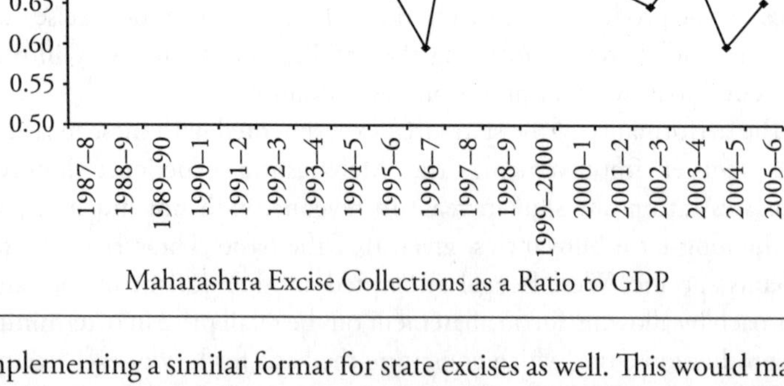

Maharashtra Excise Collections as a Ratio to GDP

implementing a similar format for state excises as well. This would make feasible greater coordination with the VAT administrations which are currently making efforts to improve their systems of tax administration, with a proposed move towards selective audit systems. These systems have to devise mechanisms for identifying revenue under risk, they will develop systems of analysis drawing on multiple sources of information, all of which would be useful to improve the administration of the excise collections as well. Extending the efforts of state VAT departments in monitoring the quantum of goods transacted by examining input–output ratios and supplies of raw materials could contribute towards improved administration/compliance of the tax.

Stamp Duties and Registration Fees

The Constitution of India segregates stamp duties and registration fees into two categories: those that are to be imposed by the union government (entry 91 of List I in Seventh Schedule) and those that are to be imposed by the state governments (entry 63 of the List II of the Seventh Schedule). For the former, the union government sets the rates, while the states collect and retain the receipts therefrom. This ensures that the rates are uniform across states. For the latter, the states have their own acts and the instruments covered can vary from state to state.

While stamp duty is a tax on the value of instruments used in various business transactions, registration fees are payments made for a specific service provided by the government—that of recording contracts and deeds.[9] Stamp duties are generally imposed on the following broad categories of instruments

- Instruments relating to the transfer of property
- Instruments connected with loans and advances
- Instruments relating to capital market transactions
- Instruments used in daily business and commercial transactions
- Instruments executed for record-keeping purposes under other Acts

National Institute of Public Finance and Policy (NIPFP) (1995) documents the predominance in terms of contribution to revenue of the first category. This report also documents the high rates of basic stamp duties imposed by states, which are often topped up by additional charges—the latter varying with the size of the underlying transactions.

The main problems with this source of revenue are often related to the high rates. It is argued that high rates encouraged evasion and avoidance, which is made worse by the presence of additional charges relating to the size of the transaction. There emerges an incentive to undervalue. To address the former problems, states are working towards a reduction in rates. To give a few examples, at present Rajasthan taxes transactions in property at 2 per cent of the market value of the property, while in Maharashtra these transactions are taxable at 5 per cent. Most states expect to reach the 5 per cent mark before the end of the Tenth Plan period, as part of their commitment towards the Jawaharlal National Urban Renewal Mission. On the valuation front, states have set up mechanisms for establishing benchmarks for acceptable values. This information is publicly available through government websites as well. In some states, these numbers are arrived at by working through a Central Valuation Committee involving both government officials and other stakeholders such as builders, so as to provide credibility and acceptability to the benchmarks. These benchmarks are treated as the floor value below which no property can be registered.

There are a number of alternative routes for masking such transactions so as to avoid payment of stamp duty on the transfer of property (see Sen 1999). To address such issues of avoidance and to expand the tax base, states are attempting to bring a larger number of instruments into the tax net.[10] One of the major routes of avoidance relates to transactions in property through the formation of a cooperative society. The land is acquired through a cooperative society which then constructs flats for its members and allocates the same. West Bengal has brought these transactions into the tax net, by making the transfer of flats from cooperative to individual members subject to stamp duty. Assam has sought to address this problem by proposing a separate Assam Apartments (Construction and Transfer of Ownership) Bill, 2006, which pre-empts the masking of sale of apartments as works contracts undertaken on behalf of a cooperative society. In Karnataka such a regulation has been in operation since 2001.

Another route involves the masking of sale as a long-term lease. Some states treat documents governing lease transactions also as documents requiring registration. Assam has sought to capture lease transactions where the term of the lease is over thirty years. The Maharashtra Rent Control Act makes it mandatory to register all lease documents from 2003 onwards. Valuation of the terms of the lease too has been pegged to the benchmark market value of the property.

Stamp duties and registration fees are viewed only as a source of revenue by the government. The only benefit these confer on the payer is to maintain a record of the details of transactions undertaken, which, in the event of a dispute, provides a basis for arbitration. For transactions involving inter-temporal events, this would involve some gains, however in the case of property transactions, since the documents only capture a transaction that has already elapsed, the gains are limited. For instance, the payment of a registration fee does not entitle the payee to a guaranteed legal title over property. To increase the effectiveness and attraction of complying, it would be useful to integrate these taxes with some value-added services. Given the booming property market, it is important for the security of especially small property owners/purchasers that the legal status of the property be confirmable. Since change in ownership of property and mortgage of property are transactions requiring registration in most states, this information should be available to the general public for, say, a fee. For this to be useable information, registration of the change in the ownership of a particular property should ideally update the property records as well and should be able to generate the updated status of the identity of the property.

Prior to computerization, this would be a difficult goal to aim for, since it requires coordination among a number of agencies and hence their records. A number of states in India are computerizing their land records, supported through a centrally sponsored scheme. With the generation of these land records, it is easy to visualize a relation between the updation/mutation of land records and the registration process. With information on ownership easily accessible even to the general public, the registration department can be assigned the additional responsibility of verifying the ownership details of the property concerned. Further, if a photo-identity card can be made mandatory, the registration process can lead straight on to mutation with its due procedure. Karnataka requires photographs to be affixed in the case of transactions involving registration of property. The E-governance initiative of the Government of Karnataka on this front—BHOOMI—does allow for initiating mutation through designated kiosks with the time required for mutation being reduced from around 200 to thirty-five days.

Such initiatives will be useful for the government departments as well, since the tax base for both land revenue and property tax would be better monitored. Apart from the functioning of the levy and its administration, an important aspect of reforms relates to the potential for fraudulent stamp paper circulating in the market. The scam unearthed in 2001 suggests that the dimensions of the problem are humongous. This is sustained by the prevailing system of printed stationery for stamp paper. Maharashtra and Karnataka—the two states most affected by this scam—have changed their systems. Karnataka has done away with stamp paper and replaced it with a system wherein registration of plain paper documents can be undertaken with duty paid at the sub-registrar's office. Some other states too are experimenting with this system. In some states banks have been authorized to accept the duty as well. Eliminating the need for pre-printed and pre-notarized stamp paper would be a first step in this direction.

Taxation of Income

While the constitution assigns the union government the power to tax non-agricultural income, the power to levy a tax on trade and profession as well as a tax on agricultural income is assigned to the states. The former is not a tax on income earned, however, states vary the rate payable in accordance with the income earned, thereby mimicking a tax on income. For all the states put together, these sources of revenue do not yield much—less than 2 per cent of total revenue and less than 0.2 per cent of the GDP. Further, these are not considered buoyant sources of revenue—as a ratio of the GDP, the collections from these taxes have been declining till 1998–9; thereafter there has been a reversal, with a few states introducing a profession tax, but given the inherent inflexibility in this levy, the correction is not expected to be sustained over time. There is some inter-state variation in performance, but the overall trends remain consistent. While some options for reform of these levies individually are indicated in the discussion that follows, an alternative approach, examining a more comprehensive change, too is proposed.

Profession Tax

Article 276 of the constitution assigns the states the power to collect a tax on professions, trades, callings, and employments, within a ceiling of Rs 2500 per capita per annum. The rationale for imposing a ceiling on the per capita tax was to prevent the introduction of parallel tax on non-agricultural income since the list of activities covered by the provisions of this tax corresponds quite closely with non-agriculture. However, most states follow a graduated levy, where the amount of tax due changes with level of income. In this sense, the similarities with an income tax do remain.

Any reform within the structure of this tax would imply two things: first, not all states collect this tax, and of those that have the provision, in some the revenue collected is assigned to urban local bodies. It would be worthwhile for all states to collect the tax, whether it be used by the state government or assigned to the local bodies.[11] Second, the ceiling for this levy was last fixed in 1988. Simply in terms of purchasing power, the present price equivalent of this level would be around Rs 10,000. This explains the clamour by the states for revision in the ceiling. This becomes important given that the graduated structures were determined at the time the ceiling was revised and most taxpayers have reached the ceiling, suggesting thereby that increase in tax collections is only to the extent of net new entrants into the taxable activities.

Land Revenue and Tax on Agricultural Income

The right to tax agricultural income rests with the states but very few actually collect any revenue on this count. Land revenue too has receded in importance for most states. Some states have assigned the revenue from this levy to rural local bodies. In the process, there is no tax that is recovered from a major part of economic activity in a state. As of today only five states receive some revenue from agricultural income tax—Assam, Karnataka, Kerala, Tamil Nadu, and West Bengal. In each of these states, the collections have been declining in nominal terms. In Assam, the revenue has declined from Rs 104 crore in 1991–2 to Rs 5 crore in 2004–5. In Karnataka, it has declined from a peak of Rs 50 crore in 1995–6 to Rs 2 crore in 2004–5. A similar trend is observed in the other states as well. In nominal terms, the trends in land revenue collections have been positive for most states, however, the levels are very low. The only state that gets a noticeable sum from land revenue is West Bengal—it accounts for almost 50 per cent of all India collections and over 5.5 per cent of own tax revenue of the state.

Since agriculture is perceived to be a low-income domain, with a large number of people dependent on it for livelihood, there is reluctance to bring this part of income within the ambit of taxation, whether by states or through some tax rental arrangement by the centre. Kerala and Assam are two states that do levy tax on incomes from plantation crops, mainly tea. The time, however, is ripe to revisit this issue for the following reasons:

1. As is becoming increasingly apparent, the character of agriculture is undergoing a change—new activities with a predominance of commercial interests are emerging in the scenario. Two examples are contract farming with integrated processing and marketing

arrangements, and plant breeders involved in the generation of new varieties of crops. In addition to plantation crops, these are activities that do not conform to the traditional notion of agriculture as a low-income source of livelihood for a large number of people, and hence can be brought into the tax net.

2. There are studies which suggest that a considerable degree of evasion in income tax is induced by the existence of an exemption for incomes from agriculture. The Kelkar Committee Report on Reform of Direct Taxes places this figure at Rs 1000 crore for 2001–2. A part of this therefore amounts to revenue loss for states, given the present revenue-sharing formula.

Within the current constitutional assignment of tax powers, two options for reform exist:

1. States take on the task of introducing a tax on agricultural income. Since assessment of the income may pose problems, the tax could either be limited to certain kinds of activities like plantations and other commercial forms of agricultural operations, where large players dominate or a presumptive tax could be levied as has often been suggested (Rajaraman 2004). The former would have to be administered by state governments, maybe in coordination with the union income tax department, while the latter could potentially even be delegated to rural local bodies so as to strengthen their revenue base. Implementation could be made mandatory and a conservative estimate of the potential revenue could be incorporated into the state finance commission's calculus, in determining the transfers from states to local bodies. The presumptive tax could serve as a close approximation of the land revenue levy as well.
2. The states could enter into a tax rental arrangement with the union government, wherein the latter collects tax on all income instead of only non-agricultural income and the states are returned the tax collected on agricultural income, on origin basis. This option has been proposed a number of times (see Government of India 2002; Bagchi et al. 2005). The advantage of this approach would be, as indicated earlier that not only do the states get tax on agricultural income, they also get a share of the evaded tax on non-agricultural income. It may be mentioned here that with the present exemption threshold of Rs 100,000, poor farmers would remain outside the tax net.

A Comprehensive Alternative

It has often been argued that states in India are unwilling or unable to undertake consistent reform in indirect taxes, since their tax base does not include some taxes on incomes. For instance, efforts at reform of the CST face a demand for compensation, since a change in the economic environment and any resultant expansion in economic activity is not perceived as tangible gains in terms of revenue collections. Reforms, therefore, are expected to result in lower tax collections, in spite of evidence to the contrary from the introduction of VAT. However, if some form of income tax did exist in the tax base of the states, an expansion in the level of economic activity would yield direct tangible benefits.

As discussed earlier in the section, the base for these taxes is some part of income. Instead of attempting to reform each of these taxes individually, so as to restore them a degree of buoyancy, it would be worth exploring an alternative scheme whereby the union government taxes all incomes and collects, on behalf of states, a piggyback levy on all incomes, to be distributed among the states on origin basis. This approach would reduce the extent of evasion in income tax and thereby increase the shareable pool of taxes. Further, it provides states access to a buoyant source of revenue, which depends on the scale of economic activities in the state.

In terms of administration of such a levy, it may be pointed out that the present income tax system, especially for corporate incomes, works on a registered office basis, irrespective of where the incomes are actually generated. This might have to change if the origin basis for distribution of the piggyback tax is to be implemented. Further, since both profession tax and agricultural income tax are collected by a department within the state government, which also collects a number of other taxes, elimination of these levies may require some restructuring, without making any department redundant. Since most state VAT administrators claim inadequacy in number of employees, redeployment might be mutually beneficial.

Taxes on Transportation

Transport taxes include motor vehicles tax and passenger and goods tax. While their importance as a source of revenue for the government has declined over time, given the proliferation of vehicles and the need to monitor the same, it is important to focus on these taxes as well. The motor vehicles tax is a tax on the ownership of a motor vehicle and is usually described as a levy towards the use of roads in the jurisdiction. The tax started off as an annual levy but got transformed into a one-time levy imposed at the time of sale of the vehicle, so as to reduce compliance and administrative costs. It is often argued that this is inefficient for two reasons:

1. The revenue of the government gets related to additions in the fleet of vehicles in the states and not to the use of vehicles and hence is subject to all the fluctuations in asset formation. High interest rates may adversely affect the purchases. Poor overall economic performance may hinder growth of demand and all these factors would contribute to fluctuations in the revenues of the government.
2. Given the increase in pollution in urban areas and the extent of congestion in traffic, and the inefficiency of older vehicles, it is useful to focus on the green tax version of motor vehicles tax (Sarma 2005). Higher taxes can be used to phase out older vehicles only if the tax is reverted to its earlier version of being an annual levy.

It may be pointed out that annual payment of tax is not necessary for addressing either of these concern—any periodicity of less than a lifetime could serve the purpose. A periodicity of five years, say, would ensure that the vehicle returns for payment of tax, and if the rate of tax increases with age, there would be incentive to replace an old vehicle. Such an option would keep compliance and administrative costs too within manageable limits.

Another problem with the current version of the tax, as pointed out in World Bank (2005) is that its rate structure is lopsided: private transport vehicles are taxed at low rates while public transport vehicles are taxed at excessively high rates. As reflected in Table 2.5, while all vehicles cover their respective costs vis-à-vis maintenance of roads, only buses yield enough to cover the capital cost as well. This suggests that some rationalization of rates is called for. Such a rationalization should either result in enhanced revenue buoyancy (if demand is insensitive to prices) or to a containment of the congestion on roads, with a fillip for public transportation. Either of these outcomes would be desirable.

The passenger and goods tax is a tax on the use of a motor vehicle for commercial purposes, that is, for transport of goods and passengers.

TABLE 2.5
Revenue from Sales Tax and Transport Tax
per Vehicle vs Road Costs, 2000–1

Category	Two-wheelers	Cars	Jeep/taxi	Bus	LCV	HCV	MAV
Revenue (normalized to two-wheeler revenue = 1)	1.0	9.4	10.1	322.3	12.2	32.6	59.0
Ratio of revenue to road capital and maintenance cost	0.4	1.1	0.5	19.4	0.8	0.4	0.4
Ratio of revenue to road maintenance cost	1.8	4.9	2.0	82.5	3.3	1.5	1.9

Note: MAV: multi axle vehicles; HCV: heavy commercial vehicles and LCV: light commercial vehicles.
Source: World Bank (2005).

While this levy too started off as directly related to the actual transactions of transportation, the difficulty in administering the same resulted in a change to a compounded scheme where the tax was related to the capacity of the vehicle rather than the actual transactions undertaken. Given that this is a tax on services, it is desirable that this levy be ultimately merged with the value-added tax at state level. At least in the case of transportation of goods, it would become a part of the trail of invoices and thereby reduce the incentive to under-report the extent of transactions undertaken.

NOTES

1. Volatility is measured through the coefficient of variation of the ratio, with low volatility referring to states where the coefficient of variation is less than 0.10. For the newly formed states, including the parent states of Bihar, Madhya Pradesh, and Uttar Pradesh, data exist for only a brief four years and hence do not provide adequate basis for assessing volatility.
2. Four states—Punjab, Haryana, Delhi, and Himachal Pradesh—are exceptions to this rule. These states followed the last point tax principle. However, given rampant evasion in taxes, some goods were taxed at the first sale, while keeping input taxation out of the system. These states, therefore, did not suffer from cascading within the state. Transactions of inter-state character, however, did suffer taxes, like in all other states.
3. The CST Act excludes consignment transfers/branch transfers from the purview of the tax. This, it is argued, creates perverse incentives for companies to establish branches in all states with a reasonable market size and thereby avoid tax. To prevent complete loss of revenue on this account, the tax credit in these instances is limited.

4. The initial discussions on the rate structure proposed a three-rate VAT, following up on the scheme of floor rates that were implemented in 1999. Further, the highest rate category was to be associated with a revenue neutral rate (RNR), which would vary from state to state and would ensure that each individual state received the same revenue as in the pre-VAT regime. Problems in identifying the RNR and, further, difficulties envisaged in implementing the identified RNR—many states found the computed rates too high—on the one hand and the central government's assurances of compensation on the other, led the discussion towards uniform rates of tax across all states in the country.
5. A detailed analysis can be found in Rao (2005).
6. However, if the CST regime is not phased out in a systematic manner, it can have some perverse consequences: some realignment of economic activity is likely. Since tax credit in VAT is limited to purchases made within the state, most producers would like to procure their inputs locally. This raises the question of choice of location for establishment of industry—most activities are likely to go close to the final consumer, that is, to states with high demand or economically advanced states.
7. For suppliers registered in all jurisdictions, the registered dealer purchasers could supply the service provider with a C-form at the beginning of the transaction period. The supplier can use the VAT ID or create fresh internal ID in the event of frequent transactions with these dealers. All transactions by these dealers can then be billed and taxed at the jurisdiction of registration of the concerned purchasing dealer. Detailed information of these transactions can be provided to the relevant tax departments as well for improved surveillance and associated improvements in tax compliance.
8. This is different from suggesting that the revenue from a journey passing through multiple states should be allocated to all the states involved in proportion to the distance covered in that state. The latter approach would apply if the tax concerned is visualized as a tax on the use of infrastructure in the state. VAT, however, does not follow this principle. It is meant to be a tax on consumption of services and goods and the consumption of this service can only be identified either with the originating jurisdiction or the destination.
9. Judicial stamp duties are fees collected from litigants in courts and are in the nature of fees as well. Non-judicial stamp duties are being discussed here.
10. Mortgage documents are now covered in Karnataka, while Maharashtra has brought into its net the following agreements: advertisement on mass media; rights of telecasting, broadcasting, or exhibition of an event or film; specific performance by a person or group of persons; creation of any obligation, right, or interest having monetary value; assignment of copyright under the Copyright Act, 1975; project under Built, Operate, and Transfer System (BOT) with or without toll or fee collection rights; and works contracts.

11. Arunachal Pradesh, Bihar, Goa, Haryana, Jammu & Kashmir, Jharkhand, Kerala, Punjab, Sikkim, and Uttarakhand do not collect profession tax. Sikkim collects an income tax from its residents and hence presumably refrains from collecting profession tax.

References

Alm, James, P. Annez, and A. Modi (2004). 'Stamp Duties in Indian States: A Case for Reform', World Bank Policy Research Working Paper 3413, Sept.

Bagchi, A., R. Kavita Rao, and Bulbul Sen (2005). 'Raising the Tax Ratio by Reining the "Tax Breaks": An Agenda for Action', Tax Research Unit Working Paper Number 2, NIPFP, New Delhi.

Government of India (2002). *Report on the Reform of Direct Taxes*, (known as the Kelkar Committee Report on Direct Taxes). New Delhi: Ministry of Finance.

NIPFP (2000). *Study of Maharashtra's Finances*. New Delhi: NIPFP.

———— (1995). *Economic Reforms and the Stamp Act*. New Delhi: NIPFP.

Rajaraman (2004). 'Taxing Agriculture in a Developing Country: A Possible Approach', in J. Alm, J. Martinez-Vazquez, and S. Wallace (eds), *Taxing the Hard: Lessons from Theory and Practice*. Amsterdam: Elsevier.

Rao, R. Kavita (2005). 'Reforming the State Tax System: Transition to VAT', paper commissioned for Policy Research Networking for Policy Reform, 2004.

Sarma, J.V.M. (2005). *An Overview of the State Tax System in India (Other than Sales Taxation)*, report written for the Asian Development Bank, http://adb.org/Documents/Reports/Consultants/TAR-IND-4066/GovtBudget/sarma.pdf.

Sen, Tapas K. (1999). *Reform of Stamp Duty Administration in Orissa*. New Delhi: NIPFP.

World Bank (2005). *State Fiscal Reforms in India: Progress and Prospects*. India: Macmillan.

3

Debt Management in States

Emerging Issues

D.K. Srivastava

The indebtedness of Indian states grew sharply after 1997–8. According to Reserve Bank of India (RBI 2005), states' liabilities relative to the gross domestic product (GDP) were 21 per cent in end March 1997. These rose to 33.5 per cent by end March 2005, an increase of 12.5 percentage points in a period of seven years. An increase of this order in such a short period of time is unprecedented in the evolution of state debt since the early 1950s. To arrest this trend, several institutional changes have been brought about in the management of state debt. The overall environment for state borrowing has been considerably changed after the recommendations of the Twelfth Finance Commission (TFC). The TFC recommendations have changed many of the ground conditions as well as the ground rules for state debt. This chapter looks at the emerging issues and prospects in regard to the growth of state debt in the light of these changed conditions.

Under the TFC recommendations, the centre's intermediation in state debt is being discontinued. States have been asked to raise subscription to their loans directly from the market through the RBI. States have also been given a major one-time debt relief by consolidating and rescheduling their outstanding debt to the central government provided they enact fiscal responsibility legislation (FRL) with given conditionalities. The relief given by the TFC was preceded by three years of a debt-swap scheme initiated by the central government. In an Appendix to their Report and in the concluding chapter, the TFC has also suggested that state debt should be overseen by an independent authority like a loan council with representation from the Ministry of Finance, Planning Commission, and states. Some of the emerging issues in the context of state debt relate to (i) whether the TFC recommendations and other institutional changes have successfully arrested the growth of debt; (ii) what the progress is in regard to states enacting the FRL; (iii) how successful states have been in raising loans from the market; (iv) what the special position of the National Small Savings Fund (NSSF) is in state debt and (v) what the medium term prospects regarding achieving debt sustainability and related fiscal corrections are.

The outline of the chapter is as follows. The following section analyses the growth of state debt since the early 1990s by decomposing this growth as due to cumulated primary deficit and the impact of growth–interest rate differential. It also examines the comparative profile of interest payment relative to revenue receipts for individual states and changes in composition of state debt. The next section highlights the recommendations of the TFC in regard to state debt. It is followed by a section looking at the important emerging issues in managing state debt including changes introduced by the RBI in regard to loans by the states, particularly modification in the facility for ways and means advances (WMA). The fifth section examines the initiatives by state governments themselves in regard to the FRL and other initiatives and success achieved so far. The next section looks at progress in market borrowing and the case of special category states. Concluding observations follow.

Growth of State Debt in India since the 1990s

Aggregate State Debt–GDP Ratio

The debt–GDP ratio of the states was around 22 per cent at the end of 1990–1 and remained close to this level up to 1996–7. It started increasing in 1997–8 following deterioration in state finances. By 2003–4 it had risen to a level more than 33 per cent of GDP. The deterioration of state finances from the latter half of the 1990s was caused by three main factors: the impact of salary revision in the wake of the recommendations of the Fifth Central Pay Commission, which the states also followed, a sharp rise in the nominal interest rates towards the end of the 1990s, and low growth rates in the first three years of the new decade.

In order to examine the reasons for the growth of state debt during 1991–2 to 2003–4, I look at the relative roles played by (i) change in cumulated primary deficit and (ii) the impact of the excess of growth over interest rates. Following Rangarajan and Srivastava (2003), the debt accumulation for the state governments can be decomposed into the relative contributions of cumulated primary deficit and the relative contribution of weighted growth–interest rate differential.

The increment in the debt–GDP ratio between any two periods 0 and T ($b_T - b_0 = z_t$) can be written as

$$b_T - b_0 = \sum_{t=1}^{T} p_t - \sum_{t=1}^{T} b_{t-1}[(g_t - i_t)/(1+g_t)] \quad \ldots (1)$$

In the case of state debt, since Σp_t has been much larger than Σz_t and the role of the growth–interest rate differential has been to absorb the impact of the cumulated primary deficits from getting translated into accretion to the debt–GDP ratio, it is, therefore, useful to write equation (1) as

$$\sum_{t=1}^{T} p_t = \sum_{t=1}^{T} z_t + \sum_{t=1}^{T} b_{t-1}[(g_t - i_t)/(1+g_t)] \quad \ldots (2)$$

The first term on the right-hand side shows the extent to which cumulated primary deficit was translated into an increase in the debt–GDP ratio while the second term shows the extent to which it was absorbed due to the excess of growth rate over interest rate.

Table 3.1 shows the profile of cumulated growth in the aggregate debt of states relative to the GDP. The increase in debt in successive years remained negative from 1991–2 to 1996–7. It is after this that the increase in debt–GDP ratio was sharp and large. This was due to continued rise in primary deficit and the reversal of the sign of excess of growth over interest rate. For the period as a whole, from 1991–2 to 2003–4, cumulated primary deficit would have caused an increment of 17.51 percentage points in state debt relative to GDP. Of this, 6.62 percentage points were neutralized by an excess of growth over interest rate, leading to an overall increment in the debt–GDP ratio of 10.89 percentage points during 1991–2 to 2003–4.

The sub-period 1997–8 to 2003–4 is of particular importance. During this period, incremental cumulated primary deficit accounted for a growth in debt–GDP ratio of 12.46 percentage points. All of it was due to cumulated primary deficit. The growth–interest rate differential, instead of neutralizing any part of the pressure marginally added to the growth of state debt–GDP ratio. The reversal of role of this factor is clearly depicted in Figure 3.1, bringing out the difference between the first sub-period upto 1996–7 and the second sub-period from 1996–7 to 2003–4. The TFC had argued that the slump in growth in the early years of the decade was partly due to a fall in the saving rate, which was

TABLE 3.1
Growth of State Debt in India since the Early 1990s

(per cent)

	Debt–GDP ratio (end March)	Cumulated changes in			Cumulative absorption by weighted growth–interest rate differential
		Debt–GDP ratio	Primary deficit–GDP ratio	Growth–interest rate differential	
1991–2	22.50	–0.023	1.214	6.305	1.237
1992–3	22.49	–0.037	2.298	5.595	2.335
1993–4	21.87	–0.655	2.743	5.424	3.398
1994–5	21.43	–1.097	3.700	7.540	4.797
1995–6	21.11	–1.413	4.698	7.197	6.112
1996–7	20.95	–1.571	5.452	4.971	7.023
1997–8	22.09	–0.434	6.735	0.777	7.169
1998–9	22.82	0.299	8.179	3.681	7.880
1999–2000	26.07	3.549	11.405	–0.119	7.856
2000–1	28.37	5.842	13.129	–2.355	7.287
2001–2	30.17	7.645	14.459	–1.812	6.814
2002–3	32.38	9.857	16.003	–2.401	6.146
2003–4	33.42	10.890	17.512	1.650	6.623
Memo Debt–GDP ratio (1990–1)		22.53			(percentage points)

		Change in debt–GDP ratio	Contribution of cumulated primary deficit		Absorption by weighted growth–interest rate differential
1990–1 to 1996–7	–1.571	5.452			7.023
1996–7 to 2003–4	12.46	12.060			–0.400

Source (Basic Data): RBI (2005).

the result of high fiscal deficit and high interest payments while the revenues had remained stagnant, giving rise to a large revenue deficit.

Changes in Interest Payments Relative to Revenue Receipts: Inter-state Profile

The sharp rise in debt also led to a rise in interest payments. For some states, there was an inordinate increase in the level of interest payments

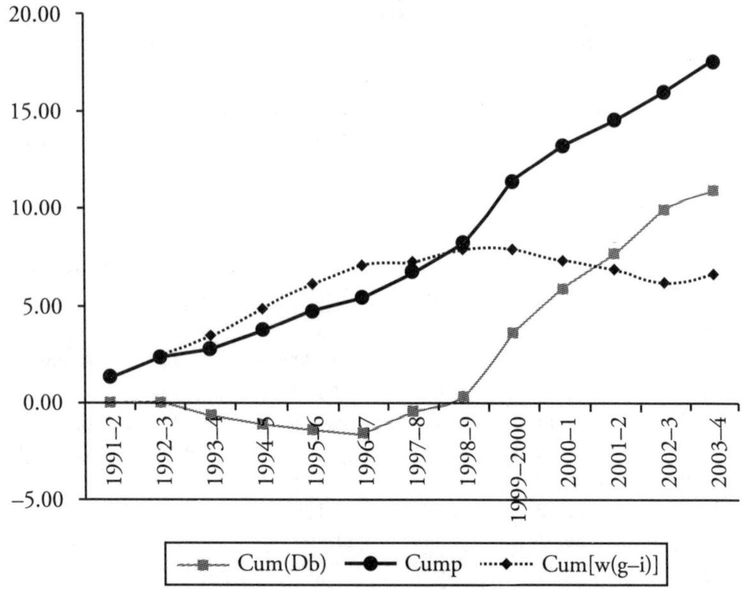

Figure 3.1: Factors Contributing to Debt–GDP Ratio

relative to revenue receipts. Table 3.2 gives the interest payments to revenue receipts position for two three-year averages—1993–4 to 1995–6 and 2000–1 to 2002–3—for individual states as well as general and special category state groups. It is shown that for the general states, the average interest payment–revenue receipts (IP–RR) ratio increased from 16.7 per cent to 25.5 per cent, comparing the 1993–6 average to the 2000–3 average. For the special category states, the corresponding increase was from 13.5 per cent to 17.0 per cent. The all-state average increased from 16.4 per cent during 1993–6 to 24.6 per cent in 2000–3.

In the case of general states, considering the 2000–3 average, the states that show a higher than average IP–RR ratio, listed in order of the magnitude of excess over the group average are West Bengal, Punjab, Orissa, Rajasthan, Uttar Pradesh, Kerala, and Bihar. For the special category states, compared to group average, the states with above-average IP–RR ratios are Himachal Pradesh, Uttaranchal, Manipur, and Assam. By 2002, it had become clear that state finances had come under severe pressure and some relief was needed even before the recommendations of the TFC were at hand.

Table 3.2
Trends in Interest Payments Relative to Revenue Receipts: State-wise and Group-wise

	Average (1993–4 to 1995–6)	% of group average	Average 2000–1 to 2002–3	% of group average	% increase (average 2000–3 over 1993–6
Andhra Pradesh	14.07	84.33	22.37	87.76	58.99
Bihar*	21.78	130.52	26.27	103.05	20.62
Chhattisgarh		0.00	15.84	62.13	
Goa	14.26	85.50	19.62	76.96	37.52
Gujarat	15.18	90.99	24.60	96.51	62.05
Haryana	15.46	92.69	23.29	91.38	50.62
Jharkhand		0.00	20.69	81.18	
Karnataka	12.08	72.42	18.07	70.91	49.59
Kerala	17.66	105.86	27.39	107.46	55.09
Madhya Pradesh*	13.34	79.98	19.04	74.68	42.67
Maharashtra	11.93	71.52	20.76	81.45	74.01
Orissa	22.39	134.20	35.85	140.64	60.11
Punjab	32.27	193.43	38.77	152.12	20.15
Rajasthan	17.48	104.79	30.57	119.93	74.86
Tamil Nadu	11.98	71.84	18.64	73.13	55.53
Uttar Pradesh*	21.88	131.13	28.99	113.73	32.51
West Bengal	20.35	121.97	44.35	173.99	117.95
Total-Non-Spl.Cat.	**16.68**	**100.00**	**25.49**	**100.00**	**52.78**
Special Category States					
Assam	16.39	121.70	17.16	100.77	4.67
Arunachal Pradesh	5.04	37.43	11.34	66.57	124.82
Himachal Pradesh	15.93	118.26	28.76	168.90	80.55
Jammu & Kashmir	16.57	122.99	14.75	86.60	–10.99
Manipur	8.78	65.16	17.48	102.64	99.14
Meghalaya	7.52	55.83	11.10	65.17	47.57
Mizoram	5.40	40.07	14.11	82.84	161.37
Nagaland	10.72	79.55	15.08	88.55	40.71
Sikkim	9.90	73.46	11.67	68.52	17.90
Tripura	10.09	74.91	14.27	83.83	41.47
Uttaranchal			17.87	104.95	
Total Sp. Cat. States	13.47	100.00	17.03	100.00	26.41
All States	**16.36**		**24.58**		**50.28**

Note: * Refers to undivided states.
Source: GoI (2004).

Changing Composition of State Debt

Table 3.3 shows that the share of centre's debt to states has fallen sharply after March 2000. The share of market loans and the small savings loans has been progressively increasing since 1990–1. A part of the reason for the fall in states' debt to centre in the early part of this decade was the debt-swap scheme introduced by the central government.

TABLE 3.3
Components of Outstanding Liabilities of State Governments

(per cent to total)

Components of outstanding liabilities	End March 1991	End March 2000	End March 2004	End March 2005
1. Internal debt	15.0	22.9	46.4	50.4
of which:				
(i) Market loans	12.2	14.9	19.5	20.5
(ii) Small savings (NSSF)	–	5.2	18.2	21.3
(iii) Loans from banks & financial institutions	2.0	3.4	6.6	6.8
2. Loans and advances from the centre	57.4	46.6	29.1	26.3
3. Public account liabilities	26.9	30.1	24.5	23.3
of which:				
(i) State small savings & provident funds	13.2	15.9	13.3	12.9
(ii) Reserve funds	3.7	3.9	4.2	4.3
(iii) Deposits and advances	10.0	10.3	7.0	6.1
4. Contingency fund	0.8	0.3	0.0	0.0

Source: RBI (2005).

Debt-Swap Scheme: Precursor to TFC's Scheme of Debt Relief

Nominal interest rates started falling after reaching a peak in late 1990s. This would have benefited the states in the normal course but the adjustment would have taken a long time because the states were locked in with high-cost debt owed to the centre with long-term maturities. In order to tackle the problem of high level of interest payments and expedite the process of adjustment, the central government proposed a debt-swap scheme in September 2002 to give relief to the states on the 'high-cost debt' owed by the states to the central government. High-cost debt was defined as the debt which carried an interest rate of 13 per cent or above. Only state plan loans and small savings loans given up to 31 March 1999 qualified for debt swap. By 31 March 2002, such high-cost debt amounted to Rs 1,14,325 crore. Two borrowing sources were identified for swapping the 'high-cost' central government loans, namely additional open market borrowings and state governments' investment in small savings securities. In 2002 additional market borrowings could be raised at around 7 per cent. As the states had over Rs 65,000 crore of small savings debt, which carried an interest rate in excess of 14.5 per cent, this swap was expected to give state governments clear interest savings of over 6 to 8 percentage points in respect of small savings loan swapped with additional market borrowings. The states' investments in NSSF securities carried an interest obligation of 9.5 per cent. Here also, the expected saving was from a fall in the interest rate of 3.5 to 5.5 percentage points. The scheme envisaged that during the year 2002–3, 20 per cent of net small savings loans payable to states from September 2002 would be used to pre-pay the past debt. Further, 30 per cent of net small savings in the year 2003–4 and 40 per cent in the year 2004–5 were envisaged for additional debt swap. While the debt-swap scheme provided some relief, more structural changes were needed to curb the growth of state debt in India. The TFC recommendations aimed to bring about these structural reforms. It might be noted that in spite of the debt-swap scheme, states carried relatively high interest on a large part of their debt as shown by Table 3.4.

State Debt and TFC Recommendations

The TFC suggested a comprehensive scheme of restructuring government finances in India. A significant part of this scheme had important implications for the management of state debt. The TFC emphasized the need to bring state (and central) debt down to sustainable levels so that growth can be supported and adverse incentives are removed, particularly those attached to plan assistance.

Discontinuation of Centre's Intermediation

The TFC recommended that the central government should phase out its intermediation in borrowing by the states. Where necessary, this should be managed through a public account. However, there is a need

TABLE 3.4
Interest Rate Profile of Outstanding State Government Securities
(end March 2005)

Sl no.	Range of interest rate (per cent)	Outstanding amount (rupees crore)	Percentage to total
1.	5.00–5.99	34,612	16.22
2.	6.00–6.99	58,563	27.44
3.	7.00–7.99	27,872	13.06
4.	8.00–8.99	8004	3.75
5.	9.00–9.99	5412	2.54
6.	10.00–10.99	14,563	6.82
7.	11.00–11.99	17,062	7.99
8.	12.00–12.99	25,362	11.88
9.	13.00–13.99	15,720	7.37
10.	14.00	6274	2.94
	Total	2,13,443	100

Source: RBI (2005).

to determine borrowing limits for each state taking into account borrowing from all sources including small savings and states' public accounts and reserve funds. The prescribed borrowing limit on states' aggregate fiscal deficit in the TFC restructuring plan is 3 per cent of the GDP. At the same time, it was suggested that the total all-state revenue deficit should be brought down to zero by 2008–9. The TFC observed that central lending to states, which is done at much higher rates of interest than the marginal cost of borrowing for the centre, results in a reverse subsidy from states to centre. In most federal countries, the federal government's loan intermediation role has been discontinued over the years, subjecting the states to market discipline. Such a dispensation allows the constituent units to borrow on terms that reflect their credit risk. While fiscally prudent states manage to borrow at rates lower than those offered by the federal government, the fiscally imprudent states would find their access to loan finance curtailed. The TFC recommended that, in future, the central government should not act as intermediary and should allow states to approach the market directly. If, however, some fiscally weak states are unable to raise funds from the market, the centre could resort to lending, but the interest rates should remain aligned to the marginal cost of borrowing for the centre.

With particular reference to Central Plan Assistance (CPA) from the Planning Commission, the TFC highlighted that the rate of interest charged is, at times, higher by 300 to 400 basis points than the cost of funds for the centre. Furthermore, such an arrangement is pushing states into higher indebtedness on account of structurally mandated borrowings as part of plan assistance. In this context, the TFC has recommended doing away with plan loans and extending entire plan assistance in the form of grants only, giving states the freedom to complement this by borrowing according to their capacities.

External Assistance Loans: Recasting Terms of On-lending

The terms and conditions for external assistance to states vary according to projects and lending agencies. There are grants, soft loans, and non-concessional loans provided by external agencies, depending upon the nature, the financial viability, and the revenue-earning potential of a project. All external assistance was hitherto passed on as 70 per cent loan and 30 per cent grant (10 per cent and 90 per cent respectively in case of special category states). Interest rates applied were those applicable to state plan block loans. While external assistance from some sources and for some projects is highly concessional, in other cases it is on commercial terms. In the process of pooling and fixing a uniform interest rate in rupee terms, an element of cross-subsidization occurs at two levels: between centre and all states, and among the states. The TFC suggested that this is not desirable. In the case of cross-subsidization between centre and states, the gain/loss to one side vis-à-vis another depends on the rate of depreciation of the Indian rupee against major foreign currencies. Cross-subsidization also takes place among states, when states having a relatively larger share of grants and soft loans for long-gestation, low return projects relating to social welfare and poverty alleviation in their assistance portfolio are required to pay a higher rate of interest to sustain the relatively larger share of high-cost loans for often commercial projects used by other states. The TFC recommended that external assistance be transferred to states on the same terms and conditions as originally envisaged by the external funding agencies, thereby making the Government of India a financial intermediary without any gain or loss. States would get the same maturity, moratorium, and amortization schedule, as the Government of India receives from the external lender.

Fiscal Targets and Responsibility Legislation

The TFC observed that targets for revenue and fiscal deficits are essential ingredients of a restructuring programme. It suggested the following conditions to be considered for stabilizing debt and fiscal deficit relative to GDP, where the nominal growth rate (g) and the nominal effective interest rate (i) are given:

1. Stabilized debt–GDP ratio will be at a level b^* where $b^* = p(1 + g)/(g - i)$.
2. Corresponding fiscal deficit to GDP ratio is f^* where $f^* = p.g/(g - i)$

Indicating the ratio of revenue receipts to GDP indicated by (r), these conditions can also be written equivalently, in terms of the ratio of interest payments to revenue receipts $(ip)^*$ instead of primary deficit, as follows:

1. Debt–GDP ratio: b^* where $b^* = (ip)^* r (1 + g)/i$
2. Fiscal deficit to GDP ratio: f^* where $f^* = (ip)^* r.g/i$

Considering a nominal growth of 12 per cent as benchmark, the TFC suggested that the debt–GDP ratio for states as a whole should be stabilized at 28 per cent and combined with aggregate state-level fiscal deficit of 3 per cent of GDP. This will be consistent with bringing down the ratio of interest payments to revenue receipts to 15 per cent for the states.

The TFC suggested that in considering a strategy for fiscal consolidation, two phases can be distinguished: adjustment and stabilization. In the adjustment phase, the debt–GDP ratio should steadily fall. After the debt–GDP ratio has fallen to desirable levels, primary deficit and fiscal deficit should be stabilized. While these adjustments were bound to take time, in order to provide immediate relief, the TFC suggested a debt-relief scheme linked to strengthening fiscal reforms.

Debt-relief Schemes of the TFC

Debt Restructuring

The debt restructuring programme for the states suggested by the TFC has two components: a consolidation of all state debt to the centre outstanding at the end of 2004–5 at an interest rate of 7.5 per cent to be repaid in twenty years, and a debt-relief scheme linked to achievement in reducing revenue deficits. As a precondition for availing the benefit of the scheme, states are required to enact an FRL that provides for eliminating revenue deficit in the respective states no later than 2008–9 curbing fiscal debt relative to the gross state domestic product (GSDP) at 3 per cent, incorporates annual targets for reduction of fiscal and revenue deficits, and presents to the respective legislatures a consolidated growth and fiscal strategy statement along with their budgets.

Debt Write-off

In addition, the TFC devised a scheme of debt write-off based on fiscal performance. Under the scheme, repayments due on central loans from 2005–6 to 2009–10 after consolidation and rescheduling are eligible for write-off. The quantum of write-off of repayment is linked to the absolute amount by which the revenue deficit is reduced in each successive year during the award period. The details of the scheme are given in Annexure 3.1.

Longer-term Management of State Debt: Loan Council

In the plan for restructuring state finances, an overall fiscal deficit target for the states of 3 per cent of the GDP is to be achieved by 2008–9. It has been suggested that the states should enact their FRLs bringing down the revenue deficit to zero and fiscal deficit to sustainable levels by 2008–9. While these reforms are to be undertaken at the initiative of state governments, the TFC emphasized the need for imposing a hard budget constraint and suggested that the overall borrowing programme of a state should be within a prescribed limit, determined annually, taking into account borrowing from all sources.

The TFC suggests that an autonomous body like a loan council should ensure that the borrowing programme of a state is consistent with its sustainability requirements, which should be determined on the basis of relevant state-specific parameters, and, taken together, consistent with the requirements of macroeconomic stability. It suggested that the following steps should be considered for operationalizing the scheme:

1. Determining the fiscal deficit to GSDP ratio relevant for the 'average' state as all-state average
2. Adjusting the all-state fiscal deficit as a percentage of the all-state GSDP by applying an adjustment factor equal to [GDP/(sum of GSDPs)]
3. Determining the relevant interest rate, growth rate, and revenue–GSDP ratio for individual states and corresponding averages for all states, which may be applied to the current year

4. Applying the formula relating to the fiscal deficit of an individual state to that of all states to determine the permissible borrowing requirement for a given state and year

Annual Borrowing Programme

The TFC suggested that for annual borrowing purposes it was important to ensure that the ceiling prescribed for each state is (i) consistent with the fiscal deficit target for all states taken together in view of the restructuring programme that has been drawn up taking into account macro considerations, (ii) that such ceilings are consistent with the sustainability requirements of each state. This could be derived using the target level of interest payments relative to revenue receipts for all states and converting this to individual targets for specific states, with the help of relevant parameters, namely, state-specific growth rate, interest rate and revenue–GSDP ratio, using the relationship[1]

$$(ip)^{*} = f^{*}.i/r.g$$

Considering a fiscal deficit level of 3 per cent to GDP (f^{*}=.03), interest rate at 7 per cent, and revenue receipts to GDP ratio of about 13 per cent, achievable by 2009–10, the target level of interest payments to revenue receipts ratio for all states considered together was estimated at 13.5 per cent. While this may take a longer time to achieve, the TFC suggested a higher target as achievable by 2009–10. As given in the TFC Report (para 3.13 of Chapter 4), which describes the fiscal profile of combined, central, and state finances in accordance with the suggested restructuring plan, states should in the aggregate achieve a level of interest payments to revenue receipts ratio of 15 per cent by 2009–10. Assuming that each state may achieve the same target in regard to IP–RR, $[IP_1/RR_1 = IP_2/RR_2 = \ldots\ldots\ldots = IP_n/RR_n = IP_a/RR]$, it would be implied[2] that states with higher than average interest rates and lower than average revenue–GDP ratio, will need to have lower than average debt–GSDP ratios. If an individual state is denoted by the subscript 'j', and the all-state average, by subscript 'a', we have

$$(i_j/r_j).b_j^{*}/(1 + g_j) = (i_a/r_a).b_a^{*}/(1 + g_a) \text{ (if } IP_j/RR_j = IP_a/RR_a)$$

Rearranging terms, we have

$$b_j^{*} = b_a^{*}[(i_a/i_j)(r_j/r_a)]\,[(1 + g_j)/(1 + g_a)]$$

Similarly, for stabilized levels of fiscal deficit, we can write

$$f_j^* = f_a^* (i_a/i_j)(r_j/r_a)/(g_j/g_a)$$

Thus, in the context of stabilizing the all-state debt-GSDP ratio, the fiscal deficit–GSDP ratio and the debt–GSDP ratio of a state should be lower than the average,

(i) the higher its interest rate,
(ii) the lower its revenue–GDSP ratio, and
(iii) the lower its growth rate,
compared to the respective corresponding averages.

Effective Use of Article 293(2)

The central government has powers to control state borrowing under Article 293(2) of the Constitution and state legislatures also have the power to do so under Article 293(1). Once the FRL is enacted, state legislatures are expected to exercise greater control to ensure that the annual borrowing programme of a state remains within the contours prescribed by the legislation. As long the centre is lending to states through its public account like the NSSF, it will be in a position to approve the borrowing programme of the states. This power should be effectively utilized by the centre and deliberations in the loan council can give a pre-warning about states deviating from sustainability levels.

Managing State Debt: Current Issues

Role of the NSSF

The NSSF was set up in April 1999 as a separate public account. Prior to this, small savings were managed directly by the central government. The NSSF invests in special state government securities (SSGS) from the net small savings collections so as to facilitate states in financing their fiscal deficits. These securities have a twenty-five-year maturity with a five-year moratorium on repayments. The interest rate on SSGSs has been gradually reduced from 13.5 per cent in 1999–2000 to 9.5 per cent since 2003–4. The entire net collections accredited to the NSSF are being invested in SSGSs since 2002–3. This means that all net subscriptions to small savings instruments become a borrowing by the states. The NSSF has thus become a supply-driven source of borrowing for states. It is a very special source of borrowing. For the investor in small savings instrument, it is almost risk free because there is a guarantee of redemption by the central government. The central government determines the interest rates for the savings rates as well as the rate at which states borrow from the NSSF.

The states have used a portion of their borrowing from the NSSF to prepay their high-cost liabilities to the centre under the debt-swap scheme operated between 2002–3 and 2004–5 as discussed earlier. With the discontinuation of the debt-swap scheme in 2005–6, states have access to the entire net small savings collections as against only 60 per cent in 2004–5. According to the RBI (RBI 2005) buoyant small savings collections have led to a sharp increase in the annual investment made by the NSSF in state government securities from Rs 25,753 crore during 1999–2000 to Rs 83,746 crore in 2004–5 excluding the share of Union Territories. As of end March 2005, the outstanding amount of SSGSs was Rs 2,86,357 crore. Maharashtra had the highest outstanding investment made by the NSSF at Rs 47,010 crore, followed by West Bengal (Rs 42,017 crore) and Gujarat (Rs 30,163 crore). Out of the total debt outstanding with the NSSF as at the end of March 2005, Rs 1,39,515 crore was raised at interest rates higher than the present prevailing rate on SSGSs, that is 9.5 per cent.

Some additional debt swap or adjustment is needed to bring down the average rate on NSSF holding of states to close to market rates. Several options may be considered, as discussed in RBI (2005).

1. Allow the existing high-cost debt with interest rates over 9.5 per cent to be swapped with fresh receipts from the NSSF in a phased manner.
2. Allow the states to enter the market to raise the required resources for the debt swap. However, since the demand for state development loans (SDLs) is not strong, only fiscally prudent states would be in a position to raise market borrowings at relatively cheaper rate of interest. Market borrowings would, however, have shorter tenures and better repayments.
3. Increase the tenure of the small savings schemes towards medium to long term as against rescheduling the entire outstanding loans and shortening the maturity of loans to six years.
4. Revert to the 80:20 formula which will limit NSSF investment in SSGSs to 80 per cent of the net collections with the balance to be invested in central government securities.

There is also need to realign the administered interest rates of small savings to market rates. The Advisory Committee on Administered Interest Rates and the Rationalization of Savings Instruments (headed by Dr Rakesh Mohan) has recommended rate reductions in small savings ranging from 0.75 per cent to 2.16 per cent from the prevailing rates. State governments may also reduce the commissions and other incentives offered to small savings agencies to maximize subscription of small savings instruments.

The securities issued to the NSSF constitute over two-thirds of the fiscal deficit of the states. As noted earlier, this is an exogenous source of fiscal deficit for states as neither the quantum nor the cost of these borrowings is within their control. The RBI has observed that given the higher cost of small savings than of market borrowings at present, at least in respect of those states that receive oversubscription in tap issues and a finer spread at auctions, there is need to introduce greater flexibility in managing the NSSF.

There is a clear trade-off that states might consider. On one hand, are securities issued to the NSSF that provide a secure, steady, and regular source of borrowing with a longer redemption profile and, on the other, market borrowings that carry a lower maturity profile of about ten years and large bullet repayments, even though the interest rate is lower. It is time that states are given greater flexibility to exercise a choice across borrowing instruments. Based on the relative advantage for respective states, they may choose a suitable mix of NSSF and market borrowings. The more creditworthy states may prefer market borrowings to take advantage of lower interest rates. Others may prefer a larger share of small savings due to their relative certainty and stability. If a state does not require excess receipts from the NSSF, the centre may either use the excess amount to finance its own fiscal deficit or empower the NSSF to lend to other states that do not have resources to match their approved overall borrowing limits.

Repayment Profile

A major emerging issue relates to the repayment profile of the states. The RBI observes that the redemption profile is sharply skewed resulting in large bullet repayments during 2012–13 to 2014–15 (RBI 2005). The repayment schedule of market loans has a bearing on the future volume of gross borrowings. Repayment of market borrowings is more than double in 2008–9 (Rs 17,278 crore) from the level of 2005–6

(Rs 6274 crore). Further, repayments would rise threefold by 2010–11 (Rs 18,641 crore) and nearly six times by 2014–15 (Rs 36,245 crore). Table 3.5 gives details of the repayment profile of the states. More than 62 per cent of repayment is due in the next five–ten years. Since borrowing is done from the market in gross terms, that is repayment and current borrowing requirement, there is need to plan ahead, if sudden pressure on interest rates is to be avoided.

Table 3.5
Maturity Profile of State Government Securities
(Outstanding as on 31 March 2005)

(percentage)

States/Period (Years)	0–5	5–10	>10
Andhra Pradesh	30.01	64.59	5.40
Arunachal Pradesh	14.17	57.20	28.63
Assam	29.21	60.54	10.26
Bihar	26.83	59.46	13.71
Chhattisgarh	26.59	55.99	17.43
Goa	25.57	60.78	13.64
Gujarat	20.69	66.99	12.32
Himachal Pradesh	15.36	72.65	11.99
Haryana	24.01	64.39	11.61
Jammu & Kashmir	19.21	68.65	12.13
Jharkhand	28.71	63.50	7.79
Karnataka	23.96	66.86	9.18
Kerala	29.89	62.27	7.84
Maharashtra	19.11	60.30	20.58
Madhya Pradesh	27.43	66.36	6.21
Manipur	25.37	54.38	20.25
Meghalaya	31.29	50.18	18.53
Mizoram	22.86	56.17	20.97
Nagaland	30.48	58.63	10.88
Orissa	31.88	57.07	11.05
Punjab	23.73	64.91	11.36
Rajasthan	28.77	63.00	8.23
Sikkim	46.63	32.21	21.16
Tamil Nadu	24.23	68.69	7.08
Tripura	25.09	47.17	27.74
Uttaranchal	13.63	68.85	17.52
Uttar Pradesh	33.43	57.11	9.46
West Bengal	19.26	63.65	17.09
All States	**25.90**	**62.78**	**11.32**

Source: RBI (2005).

Surplus Cash Balances with States

The liquidity position of states has considerably improved since 2005–6. This surplus cash position of state governments can be attributed to the various factors. One reason is the increase in central transfers in the form of grants and share in central taxes as recommended by the TFC and implemented by the central government which has lowered the financing gaps of the states. Second, the enactment of FRLs and adherence to the fiscal restructuring plan of the TFC has enabled some state governments to avail of debt relief in terms of debt write-off and rescheduling of loans from the centre. The RBI observes that if states were able to pursue the roadmap chalked out by the Report of the TFC, their fiscal situation would further improve (RBI 2006). Further, there has been buoyancy in small savings collection over the last few years. At aggregate level, the liquidity position of states is expected to remain in surplus. The build-up in the surplus cash balances has implications for (i) the revenue balance of states, (ii) centre's cash management, and (iii) open market operations of the RBI. The interest cost of borrowings against small savings at 9.5 per cent and of market borrowings at around 7.4 per cent is significantly higher than the return earned by states in investments of their surplus cash balances in 14-Day Intermediate Treasury Bills at 5.0 per cent. This implies a reverse transfer of resources from states to the centre and a lower rate of return to states, which has an adverse impact on their revenue balances.

Whenever states have surplus cash balances, they tend to lock in the funds by investing in a consolidated sinking fund (CSF) and guarantee redemption fund (GRF) to meet future redemptions/devolvements. Investments in CSFs and GRFs are deployed in Government of India dated securities held by the RBI. States, nevertheless, would earn a negative spread on account of their higher cost of market borrowings vis-à-vis the centre that would impact their revenue balances. Some states have sought the RBI's permission to utilize the interest income accrued and invested in CSFs to redeem part repayment of market borrowings for the year 2005–6, with a view to improving upon their fiscal indicators for the current year.

WMA: Modified Scheme

The RBI offers states facilities for WMA under two schemes: normal WMA and special WMA as also facilities for overdrafts (OD). While these are facilities for short-term borrowing, when they are under fiscal pressure states can keep recycling the advances and these facilities become a source of financing fiscal deficit. These also have monetary implications. The WMA scheme has been periodically revised. Up to the late 1990s, the normal and special WMA limits of state governments were fixed in terms of specified multiples of their minimum balances with the RBI. A major change in the WMA scheme was effected in March 1999 in accordance with the recommendations of the Informal Advisory Committee (the Vithal Committee), in that the computation of normal WMA limits of state governments was explicitly linked as a multiple of their budgetary turnover (as proxied by the average level of revenue receipts *plus* capital expenditure during the previous three years). The multiplying ratios to be applied to the base were 2.25 per cent in the case of general states and 2.75 per cent in the case of special category states. The Group of Finance Secretaries (2001) did not change the base but increased the multiplying ratios to 2.40 per cent and 2.90 per cent, respectively. Later, the Ramachandran Committee (2003) changed the base to revenue receipts on the grounds of, inter-alia, transparency, simplicity, and inter-state differences in the computation of capital expenditure. The exclusion of capital expenditure from the base was compensated by adopting higher multiplying ratios. The multiplying ratios were accordingly increased to 3.19 per cent and 3.84 per cent, for non-special category and special category states, respectively. After the recommendations of the TFC, the RBI set up a new Advisory Committee headed by Mr Bezbaruah to examine the question afresh. Based on the recommendations of the Bezbaruah committee a new scheme (2005) was designed with the following features:

Normal WMA

1. Base may be defined as total (revenue *plus* capital) expenditure excluding repayments and adjusted for one-time ad hoc expenditures like lottery expenditures. The base may be so defined in the case of a state government which has a revenue surplus, while for a state having a revenue deficit, the base should exclude the revenue deficit.
2. The base needs to incorporate only actual data, even if these are dated one more year than the revised estimates.
3. Multiplying ratios: The Committee recommended that multiplying ratios may be taken as 3.1 per cent for non-special category states

and 4.1 per cent for special category states, and applied to their respective base. The base should be taken as the average of the latest three years for which actual data are available.

4. The normal WMA limits may be reviewed every year. The Committee anticipated that with the reduction in revenue deficit over time, the limits as computed for 2006–7 may prove to be quite adequate, in which case annual revision of the limits may not be necessary.

Special WMA

Since March 1999, special WMA limits of the state governments are linked exclusively to their holdings of Government of India securities, adjusted for margin. These securities are revalued every quarter by the Central Accounts Section (CAS) of the RBI, Nagpur, and the holdings of such securities by state governments can fluctuate on a daily basis (reflecting addition to holdings and redemption or sale of securities held). The Bezbaruah Committee did not suggest any change in the special WMA scheme. In line with extant scheme, state governments would be required to avail of special WMA before normal WMA. However, keeping in view the evolving fiscal scenario, the Committee highlighted one important and emergent issue from the point of view of monetary management. It recognized that persistent increases in WMA limits have potentially adverse implications for monetary stability even though net RBI credit to state governments has *so far* usually constituted a small component of reserve money. This is because linking special WMA limits exclusively to holdings of Government of India securities, adjusted for margin, renders these limits potentially unbounded. Apart from being potentially unrestrained, these limits bear little relation to the size of budgetary transactions and are, therefore, inequitably distributed across states. Since special WMA is required to be availed of before normal WMA with improvement in the liquidity position of state governments over the medium term, their cash surpluses are likely to increase which would enable them to invest in eligible Government of India securities, and thereby permit them to avail of commensurately larger and unpredictable amount of special WMA. Early traces of such a trend are already evident from the rapid increase in aggregate special WMA entitlements of state governments from Rs 2862 crore as in end March 2005 to Rs 5207 crore as in end June 2005 and further to Rs 7630 crore as on 19 September 2005, that is an increase of over 166 per cent within a span of less than six months, with most of the increase concentrated only in respect of three states, namely, Bihar, Karnataka, and Haryana. At the same time, under the present Overdraft Regulation Scheme, states can resort to an unlimited amount of OD for a period of five days, on the first such occasion. Thus, over the medium term, the total (normal plus special) WMA limit and overdraft of state governments, under the existing modalities, could potentially be disproportionately large, if not unlimited. In this context, the Committee suggested that issue of rationalizing the limits for special and normal WMA within a single integrated limit may be examined in future from the standpoint of monetary stability.

Interest Rate on WMA

At present, the interest rate charged on a WMA up to ninety days is at the bank rate, while a WMA beyond ninety days is charged at 1 per cent above the bank rate. The interest on special WMA is, at present, 1 per cent below the bank rate. With the current bank rate at 6 per cent, most state governments have favoured a reduction in interest rate on WMA. However, the interest on WMA should be linked to a more market-related rate rather than the bank rate. The Committee also suggested that there is merit in linking the interest rate on WMA to one that is more reflective of short-term market conditions since the bank rate is a signal for a medium-term monetary policy stance. They suggested that the repo rate be used for this purpose. The repo is an instrument for liquidity injection to meet day-to-day mismatches in the cash flows of commercial banks and, in this context, the repo rate signals a short-term policy rate. The Committee recommended that the interest rate on WMA up to ninety days should be at the repo rate, while WMA beyond ninety days should be charged at 1 percentage point above the repo rate. The Committee also recommended that special WMA may be charged at 1 per cent below the repo rate.

ODs by States

The existing stipulations regarding ODs are based on the recommendations of the Ramachandran Committee. Accordingly, a state can remain in OD up to fourteen consecutive days. Furthermore, if a state's OD exceeds 100 per cent of the WMA limit continuously for five days for the second time, then payments are stopped. Payments are also stopped if a state remains in OD for more than thirty-six days in a quarter. No changes were suggested except there should be an early warning system and states should be warned whenever they avail of WMA in excess of 75 per cent of their normal WMA limit.

Contingent Liabilities

Apart from the borrowings routed through the budget, state governments have resorted to off-budget borrowings. They have taken recourse to borrowings through public sector enterprises (PSEs) under their control, enabling them to float bonds against state government guarantees. Other special purpose vehicles mainly for infrastructure financing have also come into the picture. Although contingent liabilities do not form a part of the debt of states, in the event of default by the borrowing entities, the states will be required to meet the debt service obligations. At the same time, non-adherence to the payment obligations committed by states in respect of guarantees already provided by them would have adverse implications on sovereign credibility. In addition, this may cause difficulties for states to raise resources from the market in future.

The amount of outstanding contingent liabilities (guarantees), based on the information which is available for select seventeen state governments (RBI 2005), has moved up sharply from Rs 40,158 crore as of end March 1992 to Rs 1,84,294 crore as of end March 2003. As per available information in respect of sixteen states, the amount of guarantees has gone up to Rs 1,96,914 crore by end March 2006. While five states have set up guarantee redemption funds, nine state governments have fixed statutory/administrative ceilings on state government guarantees. It would be useful if rest of the states also implemented such institutional measures. In this connection, it is noteworthy that the FRLs enacted by state governments already contain provisions relating to a cap on the debt–GSDP ratios as also on guarantees. Thus progressive enactment of FRLs by the remaining state governments would augment discipline with regard to guarantees.

Progress in Implementing FRL

Even prior to the TFC recommendations, many states had initiated fiscal reforms in the framework of an FRL. Some of them amended the targets and/or target dates to be consistent with those recommended by the TFC. The RBI had set up, on the basis of the deliberations at the RBI's bi-annual conference with state finance secretaries, a group with representatives from several state governments and the Government of India to draft a model FRL. This was meant to facilitate adoption of a rule-based fiscal correction programme at state level. The report of the group was submitted in January 2005. The highlights of the draft legislation are given in Annexure 3.2.

According to available information sixteen states have already enacted their FRLs. Most other states are ready with their FRLs. The main objective of these legislations is to achieve revenue account balance by 2008–9 and remain in balance or revenue surplus thereafter. A summary of the main features of state FRLs is given in Annexure 3.3.

Experience with Market Borrowing in the New Environment

The recommendations of the TFC on doing away with the loan portion of the central plan assistance and discontinuation of central intermediation have significant implications for the future market borrowings of state governments. Assuming all other sources of financing fiscal deficit remain unchanged, the shortfall due to elimination of central plan loans is expected to be compensated by an increase in market borrowings. In resorting to market borrowings, state governments would be exposed to market discipline. It is important to note that the quantum of market borrowings by state governments in the future has to be consistent with the fiscal deficit envisaged in their FRLs and would also critically depend upon the other sources of borrowing in the Consolidated Fund and Public Account.

The immediate concern of the various stakeholders associated with the market borrowings of states is regarding their ability to raise additional resources directly from the market over and above their normal open market borrowings for the current year. Such concerns emanate from the experience of open market borrowings during 2003–4 and 2004–5, when the open market borrowing programme of state governments had received lukewarm response from investors, reflecting in part their excess holdings of government securities for the purpose of maintenance of statutory liquidity ratio (SLR) with the banking system, the increasing availability of alternative avenues for lending as economic activity gathered momentum, and apprehensions regarding the fiscal and economic performance of state governments.

To address various issues related to future market borrowings of the states, the Government of India has constituted a Technical Group (Chairperson: Smt. Shyamala Gopinath, Deputy Governor, RBI). The Group is constituted of representatives from the Government of India, the Reserve Bank, and select state governments.

According to the RBI Monthly Bulletin (August 2006), the market borrowing programme in the states seems to be doing satisfactorily (RBI 2006). The provisional net allocation under the market borrowing programme for state governments was about Rs 17,077 crore during 2006–7. Taking into account the additional allocation of Rs 35 crore and repayments of Rs 6551 crore, the gross allocation amounts to Rs 23,663 crore. During 2006–7, up to 18 July 2006, the states had already raised market loans amounting to Rs 7343 crore (31.0 per cent of gross allocation) through auctions with a cut-off rate in the range 7.65–8.66 per cent. The weighted average interest rate of market loans was in the range of 7.67 per cent during 2005–6 (up to 18 July 2005) and 8.08 per cent during 2006–7 (up to 18 July 2006).

In the context of sharp growth in state debt relative to the GDP in the late 1990s and the early part of this decade, the TFC suggested a comprehensive restructuring of the institutional arrangements for managing state debt. The TFC complemented this by a substantial package of debt relief to the states linked to their enacting FRLs with specified targets and progressive reduction in revenue deficit. The TFC has suggested a three-tier mechanism of keeping state debt within sustainable levels with a view to keeping interest payments limited as a percentage of revenue receipts leaving enough scope for primary expenditures.

The first tier of the strategy is self-control by states through their FRLs. The second tier is to let the market exercise a control through appropriate signals. The third tier is to have a control through an apex body or central intervention so that under no circumstances does state-level debt go beyond prudent limits consistent with achieving adequate growth. According to available information, fiscal correction in states is well on target. As per the RBI, states' aggregate revenue deficit in 2006–7 is estimated at 0.5 per cent of GDP and fiscal deficit at 2.7 per cent of GDP (RBI 2006). While these are budget estimates and there may be some slippage, the adjustments are well on course for achieving balance on revenue account by 2008–9. As revenue deficit falls, a progressively larger share of fiscal deficit would be available for capital expenditure for the states, which can be focused on state-level infrastructure.

Some of the important emerging issues relate to management of the NSSF along with raising of state loans in the market. The present NSSF scheme is too rigid and states are forced to lift subscriptions to the NSSF from their states even if market loans are available to them at lower rates. Greater flexibility in managing the NSSF would involve asking the states to lift part of their quota themselves and allow the remaining part to become available for other states that are not so successful in the market. Any balance should be taken up by the central government.

Annexure 3.1

TFC's Scheme of Debt Relief linked to Reduction in Revenue Deficit

1. Fiscal performance is to be measured with reference to the revenue deficit/revenue surplus, as worked out in absolute numbers by taking an average of three years, viz., 2001–2 (Actuals), 2002–3 (Actuals), and 2003–4 (RE). This average will be taken as the base year figure for 2003–4.
2. For states which were in revenue surplus, as per the base year figure (calculated as the manner indicated above), and continue to remain so in the subsequent years till the end of the award period, the installment of repayment due on the central loans (after consolidation and reschedulement) may be written-off in each of the years from 2005–6 onwards so long as the revenue surplus of the states does not go below the base year level in absolute terms. In the year the revenue surplus is less than that in the base year figure, no write-off is permitted.
3. For the states which were in revenue deficit as per the base year figure, the revenue deficit is expected to be eliminated by 2008–9, fiscal performance is measured by the absolute amount by which the revenue deficit is reduced in each year compared to the deficit in the previous year starting from the base year figure. For the purpose of determining the scale at which the relief will be provided, the ratio of the repayment due by a state during the period 2005–10 (of central loans after consolidation and re-schedulement) to the base year revenue deficit figure has been worked out. This determines the amount of write-off of repayment that will be allowed to each state for the reduction of each rupee of revenue deficit. TFC has indicated the ratios that are applicable to the states for determining the quantum of write-off.
4. The actual reduction in the revenue deficit in each year over the immediately preceding one would determine the amount of write-off for the state in the repayment due in the immediately succeeding year. This is calculated by multiplying the above mentioned ratio by the amount of reduction of the revenue deficit. The total amount of write-off in a year is to be restricted

to the repayments due on the consolidated loans in that year. Further, the write-off will only be admissible if the state reduces the revenue deficit to a level lower than the base year figure.

5. A reduction of revenue deficit is inherent from 2005–6 onwards as a result of the debt relief due to the lowering of the interest rate. The TFC suggested that reduction in revenue deficit which is at least equal to the interest rate relief shall be treated as an eligibility requirement. Each state is required to achieve, in each year of the award period, a reduction in the revenue deficit, which, compared to the base year figure, is cumulatively higher than the cumulative reduction attributable to the interest relief recommended by us.
6. If the reduction in revenue deficit in a year is more than the minimum required for the write-off of the entire repayment due in that year, the excess will be carried forward fully to the next year, provided the revenue deficit continued to follow a downward trend in the next year and is lower than the base year figure. On the other hand, if there is an increase in the revenue deficit in the next year, but the revenue deficit is still lower than the base year figure, the entitlement to write-off shall be determined on the basis of improvement from the minimum revenue deficit figure of the previous year that would have given full relief in the previous year.
7. If the performance of a state deteriorates in a year, with the revenue deficit registering a higher level over the previous year for which relief in repayment has been availed of, any improvement in the succeeding year will be measured, not with reference to that year, but the performance level in the previous year up to which relief has been availed of. If the revenue deficit reduction in that previous year was more than the minimum reduction required to qualify for 100 per cent write-off of repayment, the revenue deficit in that year may be redetermined notionally keeping in view the minimum revenue deficit reduction that would have qualified the state for 100 per cent relief in repayment.
8. The benefit of write-off is made available only if the fiscal deficit of the state is contained to the level of 2004–5. If, in any year, the fiscal deficit exceeds this level, the benefit of write-off, even if eligible otherwise, is to be given.

Annexure 3.2

Reserve Bank's Initiatives: Model Fiscal Responsibilities Legislation

The Group on Model Fiscal Responsibility Legislation at State Level suggested that the FRL Bill of a state government would contain the following, apart from titles, definitions and explanations:

1. *Fiscal Management Objectives*

(i) Taking appropriate measures to eliminate revenue deficit and thereafter build up revenue surplus and contain fiscal deficit at a sustainable level.
(ii) Pursue policies to raise non-tax revenue with due regard to cost recovery and equity.
(iii) Lay down norms for prioritisation of capital expenditure and pursue expenditure policies that would provide impetus for economic growth, poverty reduction and improvement in human welfare.

2. *Fiscal Management Principles*

Transparency, Stability and Predictability, Responsibility and Integrity, Fairness, and Efficiency

3. *Fiscal Policy Statements to be laid before the Legislature*

(i) The Macroeconomic Framework Statement: This Statement shall contain an overview of the State's Economy, an analysis of growth and sectoral composition of GSDP, an assessment related to state government finances and future prospects.
(ii) The Medium Term Fiscal Policy Statement shall contain the three year rolling targets of RD to Total Revenue Receipts (TRR), GFD as a percentage of GSDP and total outstanding liabilities as percentage of GSDP. The statement shall include the various assumptions behind the fiscal indicators and an assessment of sustainability relating to: (i) the balance between revenue receipts and revenue expenditure; (ii) the use of capital receipts including borrowings for generating productive assets; (iii) the estimated yearly pension liabilities worked out on actuarial basis for the next ten years.
(iii) Fiscal Policy Strategy Statement:

The Fiscal Policy Strategy Statement shall contain, inter alia, the following:

(i) Fiscal policies of the state government for the ensuing year relating to taxation, expenditure, borrowings and other liabilities, lending, investments, contingent liabilities, user charges on public goods/utilities and description of other activities such as guarantees and activities of state-level public sector undertakings (PSUs).
(ii) Strategic priorities of the state government in the fiscal area for the ensuing year.
(iii) The key fiscal measures and the rationale for any major deviation in fiscal measures pertaining to taxation, subsidy, expenditure, borrowings and user charges.
(iv) Evaluation of current policies of the state government vis-à-vis the fiscal management principles.

The Fiscal Policy Strategy Statement would have nine disclosure statements regarding select indicators of fiscal situation, components of state government liability and interest cost of borrowings, consolidated sinking fund, guarantees given by the state government, outstanding risk-weighted guarantees, guarantee redemption, assets, revenue demands raised but not realised, and outstanding miscellaneous liabilities.

Fiscal Targets

The state government may prescribe such targets as may be deemed necessary for giving effect to fiscal management objectives. These may include the followings:

(i) Reduction and elimination of revenue deficit. (ii) Reduction of GFD/GSDP ratio (iii) Reduction of outstanding liabilities/GSDP ratio (iii) Limiting the incremental risk weighted guarantees as ratio to TRR and/or GSDP.

The RD and GFD targets will have exclusion clauses on grounds of unforeseen demands on the finances of the state government arising out of internal disturbance or natural calamity or such other exceptional grounds as the state government may specify.

In addition, the Model Bill specifies about measures for fiscal transparency, measures to enforce compliance, power to make rules, which shall be laid before the House or Houses of the legislature. The state government may set up an appropriate agency independent of the government to carry out the periodic review for the compliance of the provisions of the Act in the manner as may be prescribed under the rules framed under the Act.

Appendix 3.3

Progress in State-level Fiscal Responsibility Legislation

S. No.	States	Year of enactment	Fiscal deficit target	Revenue deficit target	Cap on guarantees	Target liabilities
1.	Andhra Pradesh	October 2005	3% of GSDP by 2010	Nil by March 2009	Annual incremental guarantees to be limited to 90% of RR	Not to exceed 35% of GSDP by March 2010
2.	Assam	May 2005	3% by March 2010	Nil by March 2010	50% of state's own RR or 5% of GSDP whichever is lower	45% of GSDP of the previous year by March 2010
3.	Chhattisgarh	September 2005	3% by March 2009	Nil by March 2009		–
4.	Gujarat	March 2005	3% by March 2009	Nil by March 2008	Gujarat State Guarantees Act	30% by March 2008
5.	Haryana	July 2005	3% by March 2010	Nil by March 2009	–	28% by March 2010
6.	Himachal Pradesh	April 2005		Reduce RD/RR ratio by at least 2% points until revenue surplus is achieved	Reduce risk weighted guarantees to 80% of RR of the preceding year	

Annexure 3.3 (cond...)

Annexure 3.3 (cond...)

S. No.	States	Year of enactment	Fiscal deficit target	Revenue deficit target	Cap on guarantees	Target liabilities
7.	Karnataka	April 2003	3% by March 2006	Nil by March 2006	Karnataka Government Guarantees Act, 1999	25% by March 2015
8.	Kerala	March 2003 as amended in May 2005	3.5% by 2005–6 and 2% by 2006–7	2% by 2005–6 and nil by 2006–7		
9.	Madhya Pradesh	August 2005	3% by March 2009	Nil by March 2009	Not to exceed 80% of RR in preceding year	40% by 2015
10.	Maharashtra	April 2005	Rule on interest payment to RR	Nil by March 2009		
11.	Orissa	May 2005	3% by March 2009	Nil by March 2009		Limited to 300% of RR by 2007–8; IP/RR ratio to be in the range of 18–25%
12.	Punjab	May 2003	Growth of fiscal deficit to be less than 2% until 3% of GSDP target reached	Reduce RD–RR ratio by 5% points until RD reduced to zero	Cap guarantees on long-term debt to 80% of RR of the previous year	40% by 2006–7

Annexure 3.3 (cond...)

Annexure 3.3 (cond...)

S. No.	States	Year of enactment	Fiscal deficit target	Revenue deficit target	Cap on guarantees	Target liabilities
13.	Rajasthan	May 2005	3% of GSDP by March 2009	Nil by March 2009, average annual reduction of 3% points in RD–RR ratio		Debt plus risk-weighted guarantees not to exceed double of receipts in consolidated fund
14.	Tamil Nadu	2003, amended in 2005	3% of GSDP by March 2009	Nil by March 2009 and adhere to it thereafter	100% of RR of the previous year or 10% of GSDP whichever is lower	
15.	Tripura	June 2005	3% of GSDP by March 2010	Maintain revenue surplus and build up further surplus	Limit annual increment in risk-weighted guarantees to 1% of GSDP	40% of GSDP by 2010
16.	Uttar Pradesh	February 2004	3% of GSDP by March 2009	Nil by March 2009	Not exceeding any limit stipulated in any rule or law of the state government	25% by March 2018

Source: RBI (2005).

Notes

1. The relevant condition can be written as follows. For any state: $IP/RR = (i.B_{t-1})/(r.Y) = (i/r).(b_{t-1})/(1 + g) = (i/r).b^*/(1 + g)$ (when $b_{t-1} = b_t = b^*$)
2. This aggregate all-state target [= (IP_a/RR_a)] can be decomposed into targets for individual states.
   $(IP_a/RR_a) = [(RR_1/RR_a)*(IP_1/RR_1)+(RR_2/RR_a)*(IP_2/RR_2)+\ldots\ldots+(RR_n/RR_a)*(IP_n/RR_n)]$
   If states are indexed by subscript j, j = 1,2,…,n,
   we have, $n.IP_a = \Sigma IP_j$ and $n. RR_a = \Sigma RR_j$ and $\Sigma IP_j/\Sigma RR_j = (IP_a/RR_a)$
   The term (IP_a/RR_a) indicates the IP–RR ratio for the all-state average. The fiscal deficit and debt levels of individual states relative to their respective GSDP can be related to those for the 'average' state, consistent with the all-state sustainability requirements, under certain assumptions.

References

Chelliah, R.J. (2006). *A Tract on Reform of Federal Fiscal Relations in India*, Madras School of Economics, Monograph 1/2006.

Government of India (2004). *Report of the Twelfth Finance Commission.* New Delhi: Government of India.

Rajaraman, I., S. Bhide, and R.K. Pattnaik (2004). 'A Study of Debt Sustainability at the State level in India', Reserve Bank of India, mimeo.

Rangarajan, C. and D.K. Srivastava (2003). 'Dynamics of Debt Accumulation in India: Impact of Primary Deficit, Growth and Interest Rate', *Economic and Political Weekly*, 38(46), November.

________ (2005). 'Fiscal Deficits and Government Debt in India: Implications for Growth and Stabilization', *Economic and Political Weekly*, 40(27), July.

Reserve Bank of India (2006). *Monthly Bulletin*, August.

________ (2005). 'State Finances: A Study of Budgets of 2005–6', *RBI Bulletin.*

4

Anti-poverty Interventions under Cooperative Federalism

Early Experience of Implementing a Legal Rural Employment Guarantee in India

Pinaki Chakraborty and Partha Mukhopadhyay

This chapter presents the early experience of implementing an extensive anti-poverty initiative in the form of a legal guarantee of unskilled employment in rural areas in India. The initiative, known as the National Rural Employment Guarantee Act (NREGA), and its implementing scheme, differed in significant ways from existing centrally sponsored schemes (specific-purpose transfers) and, in particular, made resources available more easily, had less counterpart funding requirements from the sub-national governments, and a substantially higher level of transparency with respect to both physical and financial information. The initial evaluation of the initiative seems to indicate that the implementation has been better than for earlier schemes, but a number of questions remain, especially about the quality of works being constructed (about which little information is available) and the effect of the scheme on the implementation experience of other special-purpose transfers. In what follows, we briefly review the nature of anti-poverty initiatives under cooperative federalism, discuss the Indian experience with intergovernmental transfers, and then detail the nature of the National Rural Employment Guarantee Scheme (NREGS) and its implementation experience.

Cooperative Federalism

Under cooperative federalism, public goods are provided by sub-national governments moderated by inter-jurisdictional bargaining.[1]

In designing solutions to poverty alleviation in such a system, it is useful to distinguish between growth-focused initiatives, which can be undertaken by national governments, without significant jurisdictional considerations and redistributive or area-focused approaches, which have stronger jurisdictional implications. Within the principles of cooperative federalism, keeping the revenue collection side of redistribution at national level avoids excessive distortion of location decisions. However, on the expenditure side, the proximity of sub-national governments to the target population gives them with an advantage in implementation. Given this allocation of responsibilities, the role of intergovernmental transfers becomes critical. The usual approach has been to adopt a mix of general-purpose and special-purpose transfers.

General-purpose transfers are designed to offset the disabilities of certain jurisdictions with respect to their fiscal capacity and implementation cost. These transfers are proportionately more to jurisdictions that have low fiscal capacity, for example having a large portion of the activity in the agricultural or informal sector which is relatively harder to bring into the tax net, or high implementation cost, for example hilly terrain, which increases the cost of providing road connectivity. In principle, the general-purpose transfers should *enable* these jurisdictions to provide services at comparable levels to other jurisdictions with similar levels of local taxation.[2] Often, general-purpose transfers are based on a commonly accepted formula in order to retain a measure of fairness and objectivity that is important in insulating the allocation process from the day-to-day hurly burly of political negotiation that is likely to occur if the federal state is an engaged democracy like India with strong local political representation. If the underdevelopment of some jurisdictions is due to poor level of public services, then general-purpose transfers would help locate economic activity more efficiently by mitigating this difference across jurisdictions. However, if it is due to a more fundamental lack of economic potential in the region, such general-purpose transfers may diminish locational efficiency by reducing economically efficient migration from areas with low potential to those with more economic potential.[3]

Special-purpose transfers address issues of categorical equity, that is they try to *ensure* that certain levels of specific types of services are provided to everybody in all regions.[4] In part, this is done by specifying the nature of expenditures that will be undertaken by the recipient jurisdiction from these transfers. If every jurisdiction had similar preferences and the same level of incentive, usually reflected in the political discourse, to deliver services, the enabling nature of general-purpose transfers would have been sufficient to ensure categorical equity. This is because all citizens would demand similar bundles of categorical and non-categorical services, and since there would be no differences in inter-jurisdictional budgetary constraints, owing to the offsetting nature of general-purpose transfers, a government that had the incentive to deliver the desired level of categorical services would not be restrained by its fiscal inability to do so. Special-purpose transfers thus try to respond to different incentives across jurisdictions. This is difficult if the delivery mechanism is at the level of jurisdiction, since they are, in a sense, already pre-selected for preferences and/or incentives against the level of categorical equity thought necessary by the national government, and their enthusiasm to utilize the special-purpose transfers will thus be limited. Ensuring the delivery of categorical equity through special-purpose transfers may therefore need intensive monitoring by national government. However, this goes against the basic reason why delivery was decentralized[5] in the first place, where it was argued that proximity to the local population reduced the transaction cost in designing and implementing anti-poverty programmes. The familiarity of local jurisdictions with their specific conditions was supposed to help them design better schemes for targeting, leading to cost-efficient provision and better matching of services to demand. A divergence between the levels of service sought to be provided locally, based on presumably better and locally relevant information, and that thought appropriate by the central government opens up many questions relating to second-guessing and local capture.

While debating the relative merits of general- and special-purpose transfers,[6] it is important to remember the complementarity between generalized anti-poverty interventions such as better road infrastructure[7] and specific targeted interventions, such as wage-employment programmes. In many cases, more generalized interventions may be a precondition for the success of targeted interventions. Indeed, the East Asian experience shows (see, for example, Rao 1998) that public investment in infrastructure and human capital were critical in transforming rural areas by improving agricultural productivity and increasing rural non-farm activities. Creation of this base led to higher productivity, opened markets, transformed demographics, enhanced rural–urban linkages, and increased labour mobility. Together with land reforms, this created a shared basis for economic growth and reduction in poverty.

In sum, both general- and special-purpose transfers have a role in poverty alleviation, though the former is not often recognized as such. Furthermore, given the nature of specific-purpose transfers, reliance on service delivery through them would bring concomitant monitoring responsibilities on part of the national government, and these costs may overwhelm the relative benefits of better targeting that is sought to be achieved in specific-purpose transfers.

Intergovernmental Finance in India[8]

The Seventh Schedule to the Constitution of India outlines the division of legislative, executive, judicial, and fiscal functions into the domains of the union (national) and state (sub-national) governments. At the next jurisdictional level, below the states, there are nearly a quarter million local governments, statutorily recognized by the 73rd and 74th Amendments to the Constitution in 1992.[9] Of this about 3000 are considered urban, consisting of municipal corporations in large cities, municipalities in smaller cities and towns, and notified area committees in smaller towns. The remaining local governments are rural and can again be divided into district, block, and village levels.

States raise about a third of consolidated revenues and incur over half the expenditure. Their share of expenditure on administrative and economic services is about two-thirds; while they incur more than four-fifths of the expenditure on social services. Of this, their role in education, public health, and family welfare is particularly predominant. However, despite this, their effective manoeuverability in implementation is lower; since about 15 per cent of total expenditures are incurred on items requiring matching requirements from the states. Furthermore, in practice, the adoption of centralized planning in a mixed economy framework and the inclusion of 'economic and social planning' in the concurrent list meant that concentration of economic powers with the national government is substantial.[10] Recent economic and political events, however, have paved the way for a greater degree of decentralization. In the economic sphere, the transition to a market-oriented liberalization and more open economic environment has led to a greater degree of fiscal decentralization. On the political front, factors such as an end to single-party rule, the emergence of coalitions of parties in power at the centre, and increasing importance of regional parties in the political affairs of the country have provided a favourable environment for decentralized governance.

Intergovernmental transfers in India can be classified into a few broad categories: (i) tax-sharing transfers, mediated by the Finance Commission (ii) Plan assistance, mediated by the Planning Commission, and (iii) specific-purpose transfers mediated by different central ministries. The Finance Commission is a constitutional requirement, and is appointed by the President of India every five years or earlier to review the finances of the union and states and recommend devolution of taxes and grants-in aid of revenues to them for the ensuing five years. Each state government, in turn, is required to appoint a State Finance Commission to recommend tax devolution and grants to the local governments. The Planning Commission's assistance to states is based on a formula determined by the National Development Council (NDC, which is an institution where the Chief Minister of each state is represented). The specific-purpose transfers are governed by individual schemes that are administered by individual central ministries. In addition, states have the power to borrow from the market.

Tax-sharing Transfers

Over the years, the scope of the Finance Commission has become limited to meeting states' current expenditure requirements, with the Planning Commission providing resources for investment. The Finance Commission's determination of transfers comprises four steps:

> (i) assessment of overall budgetary requirements of the Center and States to determine the volume of resources that can be transferred during the period of their recommendation; (ii) forecasting States' own current revenues and non-plan current expenditures; (iii) determining the States' share in Central tax revenues and distributing between the states of these shareable proceeds; [and] (iv) filling the post-devolution projected gaps between non-plan current expenditures and revenues with the grants in aid.

This 'fiscal dentistry' obviously reduces the incentive for states to exert tax effort and has therefore been blamed for increasing the budgetary gaps at their level (see Rao 1998).

Plan Assistance

The assistance given by the Planning Commission comprises both grants and loans. In earlier years, both the volume and the loan–grant component was project based, but since 1969 assistance has been given on the basis of the Gadgil formula.[11] Thus plan transfers are actually determined independently of the required plan investments.

Specific-purpose Transfers

The third component of transfers is given for specified purposes. Grants for central-sector schemes are given to the states to execute central projects and are entirely funded by it. Centrally sponsored schemes, on the other hand, are shared-cost programmes falling within the states' ambit with matching ratios that vary across projects but are uniform across states. A number of central-sector and centrally sponsored schemes are implemented by local governments and the funds earmarked for the purpose are passed on to them by the state governments. Much of the budgeted funds under these schemes remain undisbursed. For example, the budgeted amount under 136 separate schemes in 2004–5 (FY05) was Rs 38,161.1 crore but the amount received by various states under centrally sponsored schemes in that year was only Rs 13,084.6 crore or 34.3 per cent or 16.3 per cent (25.6 per cent for non-special category states) of non-tax-sharing transfers from the centre.

Table 4.1 shows the shares of general- and special-purpose transfers across states in India. As shown in Figures 4.1 and 4.2, while the sharing of nationally collected tax revenues is progressive,[12] the distribution of the remaining transfers, namely grants and disbursements under centrally sponsored schemes, is unrelated to income.

While the number of schemes is large, the financial allocation is quite concentrated. As shown in Table 4.2, the top three schemes in 2004–5 had a share of 30.5 per cent while the same three schemes had a share of 29.5 per cent and 27.1 per cent in 2005–6 and 2006–7 respectively. Similarly, the top seven schemes in 2004–5 had a share of 53.7 per cent, while the same seven schemes had a share of 59.1 per cent and 60.5 per cent in 2005–6 and 2006–7 respectively while the top sixteen had shares of 75.8 per cent in 2004–5 and 77.6 per cent and 81.1 per cent in 2005–6 and 2006–7 respectively. There has been some change at the top. The top two and top five schemes in 2006–7 had a share of 31.4 per cent and 53.4 per cent respectively, but these schemes accounted for only 14.1 per cent and 33.3 per cent in 2004–5.[13] Table 4.3 shows the key schemes by budget allocation across the three years. As can be seen, while there are some changes in rank, as a set they are reasonably consistent across the years.

However, many of the schemes have relatively limited allocation, quite insufficient to make any kind of difference. As can be seen in Figure 4.3 and Table 4.4, nearly two-thirds of the schemes had an allocation of less than Rs 100 crore per year and nearly 90 per cent of

Table 4.1

Revenue Receipts of States, 2004–5

	Per capita total revenue (Rs)	Share of tax sharing (per cent)	State share (with share in central taxes) (per cent)	Central share (without share in central taxes) (per cent)	State share (without share in central taxes) (per cent)	Central share (with share in central taxes) (per cent)	Centrally sponsored schemes as a ratio of central share (per cent)
Andhra Pradesh	4347	19.2	84.8	15.2	65.6	34.4	18.6
Bihar	2027	54.3	76.8	23.2	22.6	77.4	–
Chhattisgarh	3665	25.7	81.1	18.9	55.4	44.6	11.4
Goa	14,634	8.6	91.8	8.2	83.2	16.8	17.5
Gujarat	4099	12.6	86.8	13.2	74.2	25.8	19.5
Haryana	5492	6.7	91.9	8.1	85.2	14.8	20.3
Jharkhand	2955	31.1	76.7	23.3	45.6	54.4	34.8
Karnataka	4970	13.2	87.6	12.4	74.5	25.5	27.4
Kerala	4674	16.9	85.7	14.3	68.8	31.2	26.9
Madhya Pradesh	3471	25.3	84.2	15.8	58.8	41.2	14.5
Maharashtra	4599	8.6	87.3	12.7	78.7	21.3	28.6
Orissa	3185	35.6	75.1	24.9	39.5	60.5	6.8
Punjab	6587	5.9	87.5	12.5	81.6	18.4	34.1
Rajasthan	3281	23.2	79.5	20.5	56.3	43.7	27.7
Tamil Nadu	4420	15.5	90.7	9.3	75.3	24.7	15.8
Uttar Pradesh	2417	39.2	83.6	16.4	44.4	55.6	25.7
West Bengal	2605	30.6	84.2	15.8	53.6	46.4	16.2
Delhi	5867		92.7	7.3	92.7	7.3	4.3

Table 4.1 (contd...)

Table 4.1 (contd...)

	Per capita total revenue (Rs)	Share of tax sharing (per cent)	State share (with share in central taxes) (per cent)	Central share (without share in central taxes) (per cent)	State share (without share in central taxes) (per cent)	Central share (with share in central taxes) (per cent)	Centrally sponsored schemes as a ratio of central share (per cent)
SPECIAL CATEGORY STATES							
Arunachal Pradesh	12,720	13.8	31.3	68.7	17.5	82.5	3.6
Assam	5606	18.1	59.4	40.6	41.3	58.7	14.8
Himachal Pradesh	7771	11.8	46.6	53.4	34.8	65.2	4.2
Jammu & Kashmir	10,044	9.9	30.5	69.5	20.6	79.4	5.0
Manipur	7396	17.0	26.4	73.6	9.3	90.7	4.4
Meghalaya	8142	13.0	31.5	68.5	18.5	81.5	12.1
Mizoram	17,950	9.7	16.0	6.3	84.0	93.7	8.9
Nagaland	10,154	7.9	15.7	7.7	84.3	92.3	–
Sikkim	40,454	5.8	55.9	50.1	44.1	49.9	13.5
Tripura	8266	15.2	30.6	69.4	15.4	84.6	11.4
Uttaranchal	6326	10.0	41.7	58.3	31.7	68.3	12.8
Share of Special Category States		**7.9**		**35.1**		**21.4**	**18.8**
All India	3917	20.4	80.2	19.8	59.8	40.2	16.7

Source: RBI Study on State Finances, 2006–7.

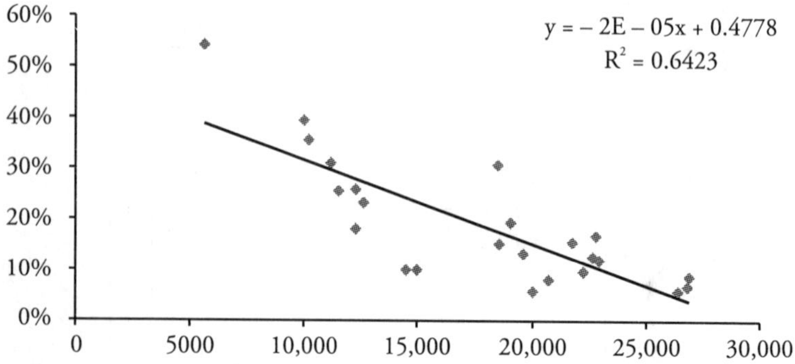

FIGURE 4.1: Share of Tax Sharing in Total Revenues vs Per Capita Income

Source: RBI Study on State Finances.

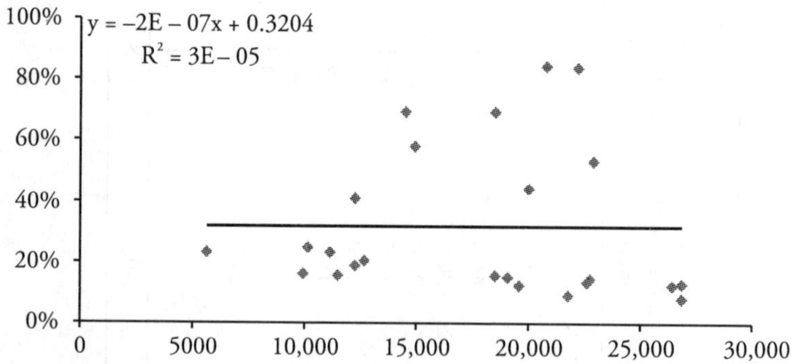

FIGURE 4.2: Central Transfers in Total Revenue vs Per Capita Income

Source: RBI Study on State Finances.

the schemes have an allocation of less than Rs 500 crore per year, or less than $5 million per state. This may be related to the need to display a token recognition of demands from different jurisdictions.

However, it does appear, from Figure 4.4, that there is an increasing tendency to concentrate on a few centrally sponsored schemes and on those with basic services rather than transfers. This is seen in the rising number of centrally sponsored schemes which have a large size, greater than Rs 2500 crore. This impression is reinforced when one looks at the ministry-wise allocations to centrally sponsored schemes in Table 4.5, which remain mostly unchanged, except that the top ten ministries are commanding a larger share of the budget.

TABLE 4.2

Stability of Share of Schemes

Ranked by 2004–5 allocation				Ranked by 2005–6 allocation				Ranked by 2006–7 allocation			
No.	FY05	FY06	FY07	No.	FY05	FY06	FY07	No.	FY05	FY06	FY07
3	30.5%	29.5%	27.1%	2	14.9%	25.8%	31.4%	2	14.9%	25.8%	31.4%
7	53.7%	59.1%	60.5%	6	47.1%	54.1%	56.4%	5	33.3%	46.7%	53.4%
16	75.8%	77.6%	81.0%	14	73.4%	76.0%	79.9%	11	67.8%	71.6%	76.1%
39	90.3%	89.2%	90.0%	36	87.2%	90.1%	91.5%	30	83.4%	86.8%	90.1%

Source: RBI Study on State Finances.

TABLE 4.3

Key Centrally Sponsored Schemes by Budget Allocation

	Rank FY07	Rank FY06	FY05
National Rural Employment Guarantee Scheme (Food For Work)	1	2	6
Sarva Shiksha Abhiyan	2	1	2
Mid-Day Meal Scheme	3	7	9
Pradhan Mantri Grameen Sadak Yojana	4	3	5
Accelerated Rural Water Supply Programme	5	4	3
Integrated Child Development Services	6	6	7
Sampoorn Grameen Rozgar Yojana	8	5	1
Indira Awas Yojana (Rural Housing Scheme)	9	9	4

Source: Union Budget Document 2006–7.

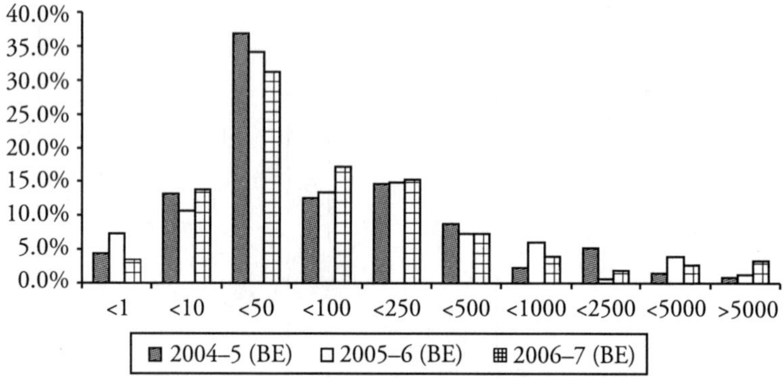

FIGURE 4.3: Size Distribution of Central Schemes

Source: Union Budget Documents.

TABLE 4.4
Size Distribution of Budgetary Allocation of Centrally Sponsored Schemes

Size class (Rs crore)	2004–5			2005–6			2006–7		
< 1	7	5.1%	5.1%	12	8.1%	8.1%	6	3.9%	3.9%
1–10	17	12.5%	17.6%	15	10.1%	18.1%	21	13.8%	17.8%
10–50	50	36.8%	54.4%	51	34.2%	52.3%	47	30.9%	48.7%
50–100	17	12.5%	66.9%	20	13.4%	65.8%	26	17.1%	65.8%
100–250	20	14.7%	81.6%	22	14.8%	80.5%	23	15.1%	80.9%
250–500	12	8.8%	90.4%	11	7.4%	87.9%	11	7.2%	88.2%
500–1000	3	2.2%	92.6%	9	6.0%	94.0%	6	3.9%	92.1%
1000–2500	7	5.1%	97.8%	1	0.7%	94.6%	3	2.0%	94.1%
2500–5000	2	1.5%	99.3%	6	4.0%	98.7%	4	2.6%	96.7%
> 5000	1	0.7%	100.0%	2	1.3%	100.0%	5	3.3%	100.0%

Source: Union Budget Document 2006–7.

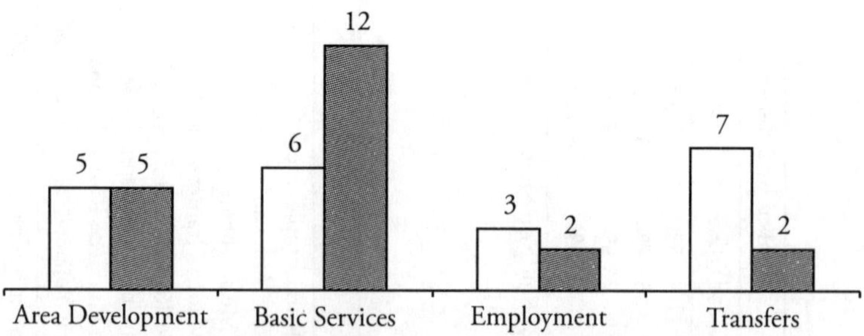

FIGURE 4.4: Change in Number of Key Centrally Sponsored Schemes (FY01–FY07)

Source: Union Budget Documents.

TABLE 4.5

Ministry-wise Shares of Budgeted Outlays on Centrally Sponsored Schemes

Sl No.	Ministry	2004–5		2005–6		2006–7	
		Share	Cumulative	Share	Cumulative	Share	Cumulative
1.	Rural Development	35.0%	35.0%	32.7%	32.7%	33.4%	33.4%
2.	Elementary Education and Literacy	15.3%	50.2%	22.2%	54.9%	23.8%	57.2%
3.	Family Welfare	13.9%	64.2%	10.3%	65.2%	10.3%	67.5%
4.	Drinking Water Supply	8.6%	72.8%	8.5%	73.7%	8.4%	75.9%
5.	Women and Child Development	5.7%	78.5%	6.7%	80.3%	6.4%	82.2%
6.	Agriculture and Co-operation	3.2%	81.8%	5.0%	85.3%	4.7%	87.0%
7.	Health	3.1%	84.9%	2.6%	87.9%	2.7%	89.6%
8.	Land Resources	2.5%	87.4%	2.5%	90.4%	1.9%	91.6%
9.	Environment and Forests	2.1%	89.5%	1.6%	92.0%	1.4%	92.9%
10.	Social Justice and Empowerment	1.5%	91.0%	1.1%	93.1%	1.0%	93.9%
11.	Commerce	1.1%	92.2%	0.9%	94.0%	0.8%	94.7%
12.	Animal Husbandry and Dairying	0.8%	92.9%	0.9%	94.9%	0.7%	95.4%
13.	Tourism	0.6%	93.5%	0.7%	95.6%	0.6%	96.0%
14.	Textiles	0.5%	94.0%	0.6%	96.2%	0.5%	96.5%
15.	Urban Employment and Poverty Alleviation*	1.1%	95.1%	0.8%	97.0%	0.5%	97.0%
16.	Urban Development	1.5%	96.6%	0.7%	97.7%	0.5%	97.5%
17.	Water Resources	0.6%	97.2%	0.6%	98.2%	0.5%	98.0%
18.	Road Transport and Highways	0.3%	97.5%	0.3%	98.6%	0.4%	98.4%
19.	Tribal Affairs	0.4%	97.9%	0.5%	99.0%	0.4%	98.8%

Table 4.5 (contd...)

Table 4.5 (contd...)

Sl No.	Ministry	2004–5		2005–6		2006–7	
		Share	Cumulative	Share	Cumulative	Share	Cumulative
20.	Secondary and Higher Education	0.7%	98.6%	0.4%	99.4%	0.4%	99.1%
21.	ISM&H (Now AYUSH)	0.1%	98.7%	0.2%	99.6%	0.2%	99.4%
22.	Non Conventional Energy Sources	0.3%	99.1%	0.1%	99.8%	0.2%	99.5%
23.	Labour	0.1%	99.1%	0.1%	99.8%	0.1%	99.7%
24.	Youth Affairs and Sports	0.2%	99.3%	0.1%	99.9%	0.1%	99.8%
25.	Panchayati Raj	0.0%	99.3%	0.0%	99.9%	0.1%	99.8%
26.	Law and Justice	0.4%	99.7%	0.0%	99.9%	0.1%	99.9%
27.	Industrial Policy and Promotion	0.2%	99.9%	0.0%	99.9%	0.1%	100.0%
28.	Culture	0.0%	99.9%	0.0%	100.0%	0.0%	100.0%
29.	Shipping	0.1%	100.0%	0.0%	100.0%	0.0%	100.0%
30.	Agro and Rural Industries	0.0%	100.0%	0.0%	100.0%	0.0%	100.0%
Total Budgeted Outlays (Rs crore)		38,161.1		55,770.2		71,610.4	

Note: *Does not include allocations to Jawaharlal Nehru National Urban Renewal Mission.

Source: Union Budget Document 2006–7.

Borrowing

From 1987–8, with increasing dis-savings at state level, borrowing is used not only to finance capital expenditures, but also a significant part of current expenditures. If a state is indebted to the centre, it has to take permission before borrowing from the market. As all the states are indebted to the centre, the Ministry of Finance, Planning Commission, and the Reserve Bank of India determine the market borrowing of the states. In determining the volume of market borrowings, repayments, plan investments, and the volume of indebtedness are taken into consideration. Figure 4.5 shows the distribution of the ratio of capital receipts to total revenues across states, which illustrates its significance.

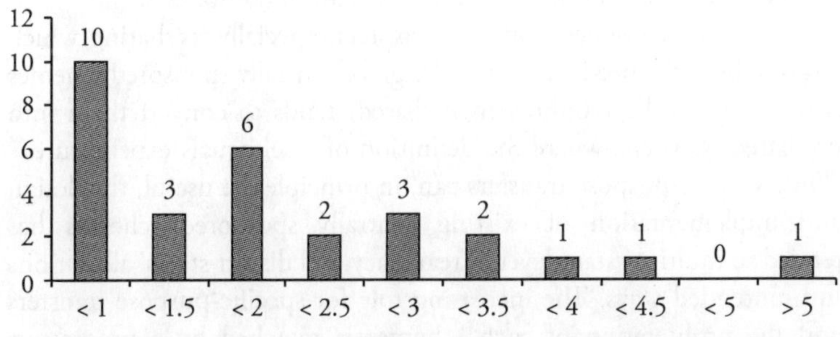

FIGURE 4.5: Ratio of Capital Receipts to Total Revenues
Source: RBI Study on State Finances.

At the next jurisdiction level, despite constitutional recognition, sub-state fiscal decentralization is negligible. While state governments have devolved powers to levy certain taxes and fees to local governments, these sources are limited. Instead, most of their revenue comes from sharing of revenues and grants, as determined by individual State Finance Commissions. However, they have very little flexibility in the use of these funds since very little is left after interceptions by the state governments, who deduct various charges owed to state government, such as the electricity utility, from these general-purpose transfers (see Rao et al. 2003). After expenditure on the administrative machinery, they have few resources left for executing developmental schemes. In part, this may be due to their size, with an average village panchayat, having a population of only 3000. In comparison, China has about 48,000 townships with average population size of about 25,000. At this size, it is possible to deliver public services in a viable manner (see

Rao 2003). In many provinces, townships are implementing agencies and fiscal decisions are taken at next (county) level where average population size is about 5,00,000. This system of sub-provincial intergovernmental finance reinforces the centre–provincial arrangements (Bahl and Wallace 2001) and has helped in the success of demand-driven decentralization.[14]

To sum up, the design and implementation of intergovernmental transfer schemes in India is complicated and progressively becoming more so. There are a number of agencies, with different objectives and transfer formulas. The design of the transfer system is not particularly targeted towards achieving equalization and ensuring minimum service levels in the states, even though a small weightage is currently given to an infrastructure index. In addition, the gap-filling approach has disincentive effects on the fiscal management in the states.

As compared to general-purpose transfers, especially tax sharing, which tends to be more need based, the design of centrally sponsored schemes (which tend to be reimbursement based) tends to convert them into use-based transfers, where the definition of 'use' equals expenditure.[15] While specific-purpose transfers can, in principle, be useful, the design and implementation of existing centrally sponsored schemes has tended to multiply state-level bureaucracy and distort states' allocations in unintended ways. The increasing role for specific-purpose transfers and the proliferation of such schemes is matched by a progressive erosion of administrative resources at the point of delivery, that is the district. Ex-ante, this would indicate that the chances of success of specific-purpose transfers are becoming progressively dimmer. States with more need for transfers do not have the capacity to use them and therefore transfers can flow more to states that can use them and who often may need it less. In particular, the administrative burden of delivering this diverse number of centrally sponsored schemes falls on the weakest administrative link.

An associated question is the continuing political support for such schemes, given the lack of outcomes. Here, it is possible that the growing influence of regional parties on the national government has converted the allocation of resources into something like a contest, where each region, and its representing party feel they have a better than fair chance of winning.[16] The growth in the size of the specific transfer pot only reinforces this feature, and may even be caused by this political situation.

National Rural Employment Guarantee Structure[17]

India has a long history of public works programmes, particularly in rural areas, as a poverty-reduction strategy. After India's Independence in 1947, there were many central government schemes for public employment, beginning with the rural manpower programme in 1960. It is argued[18] that this would not only increase the income of poor households directly, but the asset creation through the process of employment would generate much-needed productive infrastructure for poverty alleviation on a permanent basis.

The direct effect on poverty could be through multiple channels. The most straightforward is the increase in extent of employment of the rural poor, which, however, appears limited in its effect. The incidence of income poverty in rural areas is at least four times the incidence of unemployment as per the current daily status of the National Sample Survey (see Kannan 2005), which implies that the number of poor far outweighs the number of poor for want of work. This could imply that the quality of employment is so low that the wage income is inadequate to raise from even the limited notion of income poverty. Thus, if the NREGA has to make a perceptible dent on poverty, the applicable wage rate becomes important. The experience with the Maharashtra Employment Guarantee Scheme (EGS) provides no clear evidence of such an effect, although the possibility of the EGS resulting in upward pressure on agricultural wages has been indicated (see Acharya 1990; and Datt 1994). Another channel is by increasing the labour force participation of women, which we do not investigate in this chapter.

The National Rural Employment Guarantee Act 2005 was enacted by Indian Parliament to provide a minimum guaranteed wage employment to rural households with unemployed adult members prepared to do unskilled manual work. The NREGA goes beyond poverty alleviation and recognizes employment as a legal right.[19] While the expectation is that this will improve service delivery by strengthening the 'voice' of the poor, its implementation presents a formidable challenge. The important components involved in the implementation of the NREGA are (i) design of system and institutions for implementation of the scheme; (ii) provision of resources and the pattern of funding; (iii) fiscal impact; (iv) selection of beneficiaries and the wage rate; (v) capacity building for effective implementation of the scheme, including safeguards against corruption with regard to the use of fund and selection of beneficiaries.

In its structure, it differs from earlier centrally sponsored schemes in three critical aspects: (i) the funds are made available before expenditure, instead of being reimbursement based, (ii) the extent of counterpart funding required is relatively low, and (iii) a high degree of transparency with respect to physical and financial information is available in the public domain. It remains to be seen whether these changes have had substantive effect.

Design of System and Institutions for Implementation

The NREGA extends to all rural areas of India. Its key provisions are as follows:

1. Every household in the rural areas of India shall have a right to at least 100 days of guaranteed employment every year for at least one adult member, for doing casual manual labour at the wage rate specified by the state government.
2. Only '*productive works*' would be undertaken under the NREGA. The State Council shall prepare a list of permissible works as well as a list of 'preferred works', which is to be based on the economic, social, and environmental benefits of different types of works, their contribution to social equity, and their ability to create permanent assets. This circumscribes the freedom of the gram sabhas (village assemblies) to determine the nature of works undertaken as discussed later.
3. Wages may be paid in cash or in kind or both, taking into account the guidelines and recommendations of the State Council on this matter as far as possible.
4. Employment shall be provided within a 5-km radius of the village where the applicant resides at the time of applying. In cases where employment is provided outside such radius, it must be provided within the Block, and transport allowances and daily living allowances shall be paid in accordance with programme rules.
5. In cases where at least twenty women are employed on a worksite, provision shall be made for one of them to be deputed to look after any children under the age of six who may be brought to the worksite, if the need arises. The person deputed for child-minding shall be paid the statutory minimum wage.

6. A proportion of the wages, not exceeding 5 per cent, may be deducted as a contribution to welfare schemes organized for the benefit of labourers employed under the NREGA, such as health insurance, accident insurance, survivor benefits, maternity benefits, and social security schemes.
7. The NREGA also provides, as far as possible, for the training and upgradation of skills of unskilled labourers.
8. Finally, if '*an applicant under this act is not provided such employment within fifteen days of his application seeking employment*', s/he shall be entitled to a daily unemployment allowance, to be paid by the state government. This is an attempt to provide an incentive against non-performance by the state government, since there is no contribution from the centre towards the payment of unemployment allowance.

The NREGA provides for a multi-tier structure of authority for implementation and monitoring of the scheme with specified functions and duties for each authority. The agencies involved and the relevant sections of the Act where they are referred to are the central and state councils: 11(1) (a) and 12(3); district and intermediate panchayats: 13(2) (b), (3) (b); district programme coordinator: 14(2), (3) (f) (g); programme officer: 15(5) (a); and gram sabha: 17(1). The gram panchayats are responsible for the identification, execution, and supervision of projects as per the recommendations of gram sabhas. The gram sabhas are given the power to conduct regular social audit of individual schemes. Given this structure, the horizontal coordination across departments for programme identification and execution of work through the panchayat assumes critical importance.

Provision of Resources and the Pattern of Funding

To fund and implement the NREGA, the central government has established a National Employment Guarantee Fund and individual state governments have established similar State Employment Guarantee Funds for their contributions under this scheme. The centre is obligated to make payments of wages for unskilled manual workers under the scheme, and up to three-fourths of the material costs of the scheme, including wages to skilled and semi-skilled workers. The state government shall have to bear the remaining one-fourth of the material costs and administrative expenses of the State Council and, of course, the expenses related to the unemployment allowance, if required.

The release of funds is based on state proposals rather than on predetermined allocations. Under the Scheme, each state will formulate and submit a State Annual Work Plan and Budget Proposal (AWPB) to the Ministry of Rural Development, which will enable the Ministry to decide and sanction the budget likely to be used by the state in that year. The AWPB will be based on the demands for funds received from districts and reflected in the labour budgets approved by the district panchayats. The AWPB will also report on the use of the previous funds received by the state, as well as on the key performance indicators determined under the scheme. This will enable a qualitative assessment of the proposals received from a state government, to help decide the quantum of assistance likely to be released to it for a financial year. The actual release of funds to a state government will depend on its actual utilization of funds previously released. After utilizing 60 per cent of the funds earlier released, the District Programme Coordinator (on the recommendation of the state government) or the state government (in the event that a State Employment Guarantee Fund is established) may apply to the Ministry of Rural Development for the next instalment out of the Central Employment Guarantee Fund. The state share of funds will be released by the state government within fifteen days of the release of central funds. Thus, to make a success of this approach, state governments will have to evolve a well-coordinated approach to equate supply of employment with the demand. This requires in-depth understanding of region-specific labour demand and its seasonality so that a demand-based scheme of projects can be implemented at a frequency matching with the demand for work. Concomitantly, the flow of resources from the higher level of governments to panchayats needs to be ensured according to the demand. If the capacity to formulate AWPBs by states is low in some states, actual release may fall far short of potential demand for fund.

Budgetary Incidence

In order to understand the fiscal impact of NREGA implementation, we examined budgetary incidence of other self- and wage-employment programmes prior to the NREGA and compared them with the allocation to the NREGS. In term of budgetary incidence of rural employment programmes (REPs), as is evident from Figure 4.6, the expenditure on the NREGS as a percentage of total expenditure is still below the peak of 2.9 per cent achieved in 2002–3. While the share of the controlling ministry, namely, the Ministry of Rural Development, has

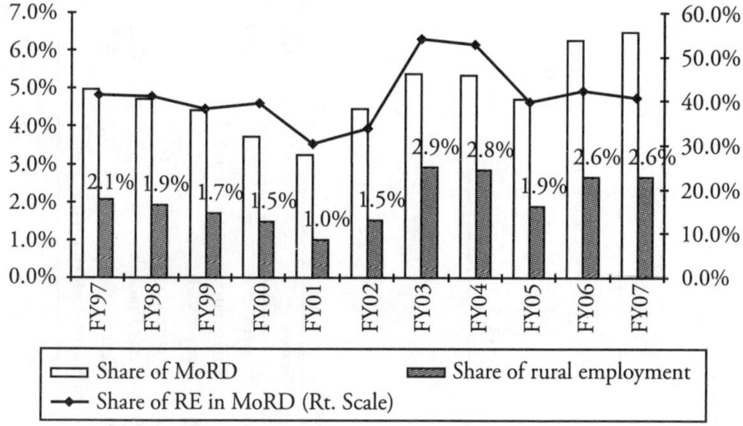

FIGURE 4.6: Budget for Rural Employment Programmes
Source: Union Budget Documents.

increased since then, the share of rural employment within the Ministry has dipped. This is because of the rising expenditure on the rural roads programme—the Pradhan Mantri Gramin Sadak Yojana (PMGSY). Despite introduction of the NREGA, there has been no spurt in the budgetary incidence of expenditure on employment programmes. As can be seen from Table 4.6, the allocation under the self-employment scheme—Sampoorn Gramin Swarozgar Yojana (SGSY)—declined secularly over the years, with a corresponding increase in the share of the wage employment programme—Sampoorn Gramin Rozgar Yojana (SGRY)—from 23.3 to 62.1 per cent between 1999–2000 and 2003–4. The SGRY allocation declined sharply thereafter with a corresponding increase in the allocation for the National Food for Work Programme (NFFW). The NFFW has been stopped in 2005–6 and its budget transferred to the NREGS. This, combined with a sharp reduction in the budget for SGRY, has enabled the NREGS to be financed without any increase in overall outlay for rural employment.

Selection of Beneficiaries and the Wage Rate

Wage employment under the NREGS is at the statutory minimum wage rate for agricultural labour. Table 4.7 makes a state-wise comparison of the average daily rural wages for casual workers and the statutory minimum wage rates in the respective states, which shows that in many of the states, the statutory minimum wage rate is much lower than the market wage rate. Given this large positive differential between

TABLE 4.6
Expenditure Distribution across Various Rural Employment Programmes

(percentage)

	FY00	FY01	FY02	FY03	FY04	FY05	FY06	FY07
Swaranjayanti Gram Swarozgar Yojana (SGSY)	13.1	4.2	4.5	4.3	4.6	6.5	4.2	4.5
Sampoorna Gramin Rozgar Yojana (SGRY)	23.3	15.1	32.2	56.9	62.1	33.1	35.8	11.2
National Food for Work Programme	28.2	16.4	7.5	5.7	0.0	13.1	19.0	0.0
National Rural Employment Guarantee Scheme	0.0	0.0	0.0	0.0	0.0	0.0	0.0	42.3
Other Expenditure	35.4	64.4	55.7	33.1	33.2	47.4	41.0	42.0

Source: Union Budget Documents.

TABLE 4.7
State-wise Comparison of Market and Minimum Wages

State	Mkt	Min.	Ratio	State	Mkt	Min.	Ratio	State	Mkt	Min.	Ratio
Andhra Pradesh	48.3	26.0	1.86	Jammu & Kashmir	94.8	30.0	3.16	Punjab	78.4	70.9	1.11
Assam	58.9	33.1	1.78	Jharkhand	53.5			Rajasthan	64.7	47.1	1.37
Bihar	44.3	41.0	1.08	Karnataka	50.6	40.6	1.25	Tamil Nadu	71.4	32.0	2.23
Chhattisgarh	35.4			Kerala	123.7	30.0	4.12	Uttaranchal	60.9		
Gujarat	49.2	46.8	1.05	Madhya Pradesh	46.6	51.8	0.90	Uttar Pradesh	58.8	58.0	1.01
Haryana	79.9	73.7	1.09	Maharashtra	51.5	8.5	6.09	West Bengal	50.0	48.2	1.04
Himachal Pradesh	83.2	51.0	1.63	Orissa	46.7	40.0	1.17	North-eastern States	66.2		

Source: Data from Ministrty of Labour, Government of India.

the market and statutory wage rates, the demand for work under the NREGS may not be high. Indeed, Figure 4.7 does indicate some relationship between the minimum wage of the state and the proportion of registered households demanding jobs.

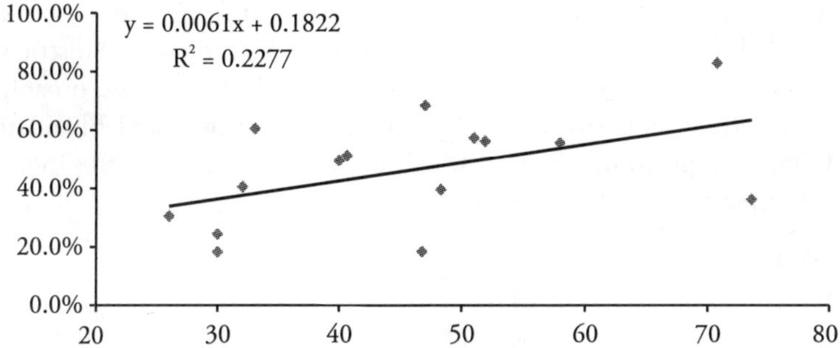

FIGURE 4.7: Minimum Wage vs Job Demand

Source: Ministry of Rural Development, Government of India, www.nrega.nic.in.

Capacity Building

Panchayats are proposed to be the principal agency through which the Act will be implemented. As mentioned earlier, panchayats will be responsible for the identification, execution, and supervision of projects as per the recommendations of gram sabhas and the gram sabhas are given the power to conduct regular social audit of individual schemes. A number of problems arise in this context. In many places panchayats do not have the necessary capacity to manage the schemes and capacity building ought to take place at panchayat level.[20] Another problem is the lack of regular and dedicated functionaries for many of the panchayats. Given these constraints, evolving a policy design and implementation strategy for the NREGA becomes extremely difficult and thus challenging.

Implementation Experience of the NREGA

Selection of Districts

As mentioned earlier, this scheme was initially implemented in 200 identified districts in the country spread over twenty-seven states. The first question is how these 200 districts compare to the rest of the districts in the country, though this is a temporary phenomenon since the Act is applicable to the entire country and all rural districts are to be included within its ambit in the near future, possibly from financial year 2007–8. Out of the 200 districts, 119 of them fall in seven states, namely Bihar, Chhattisgarh, Jharkhand, Madhya Pradesh, Orissa, Rajasthan, and Uttar Pradesh. These states are predominantly rural and 53.73 per cent of rural Indian households and 67.95 per cent of rural below poverty line (BPL) households reside in these 119 districts of seven states. Figure 4.8 shows that these 200 districts are broadly characterized by a low Index of Progress[21] (see Debroy and Bhandari 2003), though some districts, which are relatively high on the Index, also appear to have been included.

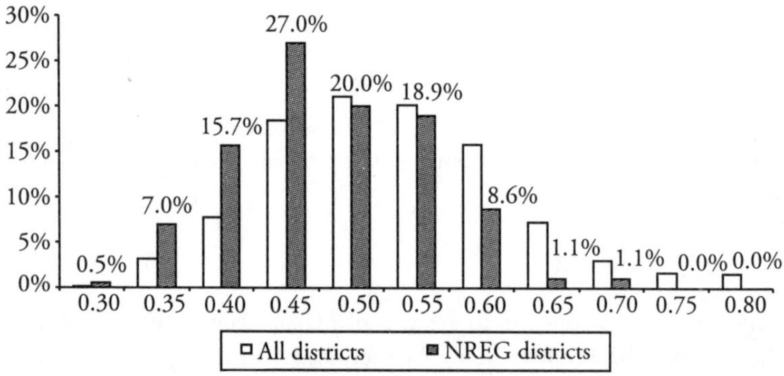

FIGURE 4.8: Comparative Profile of NREG Districts

Source: Ministry of Rural Development, Government of India, www.nrega.nic.in.

Outcome

In presenting the implementation experience of the NREGS, it is useful to first speculate on the desired outcomes of the Act. As already mentioned, since the level of actual unemployment in rural India is low, the direct provision of employment is not of significant additional benefit, except to the extent that it increases workforce participation by those currently out of the workforce. The increase in economic empowerment must therefore come from either increased or more stable wages. It could also be seen as providing a safety net.[22]

Another outcome is the creation and management of durable assets that are developed through work undertaken under the NREGS.[23] However, the Act itself is ambivalent on this, with the primary focus being on provision of unskilled work (see note 7 here). There is no provision within the Act for the management of assets, which the state is supposed to undertake. Furthermore, it is unclear whether the maintenance of existing assets can be part of the works undertaken under the NREGA. However, in the absence of information on this aspect, this issue is not explored further in this chapter.

There is a significant and commendable extent of transparency in information provided under the NREGS but neither of these outcomes is being measured in a systematic fashion so far. The mechanism for monitoring wages at a disaggregated level, discussed in the following section, is poorly developed, inconsistent, and thus an inappropriate baseline for measuring change. Furthermore, while there is a format for collecting information on the works created under the NREGS, this system is yet to become functional.

Rural Wages

There are a number of sources for rural wage rates in India. The comparability of wage rates from various sources depends to a large extent on their respective method of collection. Unfortunately, the available sources use different concepts and methodology of data collection and aggregation. This results in differences in the magnitude of reported wage rates as also in gender differential and growth rates, making it difficult to arrive at a definitive conclusion on the evolution of wage rates in rural India (see Himanshu 2005).[24]

In approaching the question of wage stabilization, we use the Wage Rates in Rural India series from the Ministry of Labour.[25] Tables 4.8

TABLE 4.8
Month-wise Inter-state Variation in Wages

	FY96	FY99	FY00	FY01	FY02	FY03	FY04	FY05
July	0.36	0.38	0.38	0.38	0.40	0.39	0.39	0.38
August	0.36	0.38	0.37	0.38	0.39	0.38	0.38	0.38
September	0.38	0.38	0.38	0.37	0.39	0.39	0.38	0.38
October	0.37	0.38	0.37	0.38	0.39	0.38	0.38	0.38
November	0.37	0.38	0.38	0.39	0.38	0.38	0.38	0.38
December	0.37	0.38	0.38	0.38	0.39	0.38	0.38	0.38
January	0.39	0.38	0.38	0.38	0.38	0.38	0.38	0.38
February	0.37	0.39	0.37	0.38	0.38	0.38	0.39	0.38
March	0.39	0.38	0.38	0.38	0.38	0.39	0.38	0.38
April	0.39	0.38	0.38	0.39	0.39	0.39	0.38	0.38
May	0.39	0.38	0.38	0.39	0.39	0.39	0.39	0.38
June	0.39	0.38	0.37	0.40	0.39	0.39	0.38	0.38

Source: Data from Ministry of Labour, Government of India.

TABLE 4.9
State-wise Intra-year Variation in Wages

	FY96	FY99	FY00	FY01	FY02	FY03	FY04	FY05
Andhra Pradesh	0.027	0.049	0.018	0.008	0.007	0.052	0.018	0.009
Assam	0.021	0.058	0.040	0.014	0.031	0.035	0.021	0.018
Bihar	0.016	0.044	0.009	0.022	0.026	0.008	0.013	0.007
Gujarat	0.035	0.047	0.008	0.037	0.019	0.009	0.005	0.014
Haryana	0.010	0.030	0.022	0.049	0.008	0.007	0.003	0.017
Himachal Pradesh	0.110	0.027	0.018	0.043	0.031	0.012	0.046	0.007
Jammu & Kashmir	0.069	0.026	0.029	0.018	0.021	0.025	0.007	0.019
Karnataka	0.034	0.021	0.029	0.031	0.014	0.003	0.007	0.011
Kerala	0.064	0.028	0.025	0.024	0.015	0.007	0.006	0.007
Madhya Pradesh	0.015	0.029	0.018	0.007	0.012	0.005	0.008	0.007
Maharashtra	0.022	0.034	0.012	0.011	0.013	0.012	0.012	0.009
Manipur	0.106	0.016	0.032	0.006	0.019	0.000	0.037	0.000
Meghalaya	0.011	0.025	0.023	0.014	0.052	0.011	0.013	0.093
Orissa	0.050	0.052	0.054	0.014	0.011	0.030	0.011	0.011
Punjab	0.010	0.026	0.020	0.020	0.024	0.014	0.025	0.015
Rajasthan	0.048	0.045	0.030	0.019	0.013	0.021	0.025	0.038
Tamil Nadu	0.059	0.044	0.030	0.033	0.016	0.010	0.012	0.018
Tripura	0.006	0.058	0.010	0.004	0.022	0.048	0.016	0.040
Uttar Pradesh	0.029	0.036	0.026	0.008	0.012	0.005	0.013	0.006
West Bengal	0.035	0.022	0.030	0.014	0.020	0.007	0.009	0.017
All-India	0.036	0.025	0.017	0.013	0.013	0.007	0.008	0.005

Source: Data from Ministry of Labour, Government of India.

and 4.9 present the month-wise variation in wages across states and the state-wise variation across months for different years respectively. As is evident, there is almost no change in the state-wise variation over time. Indeed, the extent of similarity makes the quality of the data suspect. The month-wise variation across states is somewhat larger and shows a declining pattern over time, as evident from Figure 4.9. However, the variation across months, as indicated by the data, is really small. However, it must be noted that even though the data is collected from 600 sample villages, this data source is not available centre-village-district-wise and only aggregate state-level figures (which are simple unweighted averages of district-level wage) are available. This aggregation can obscure variation across districts. If there are no significant problems with data quality then it is possible that this indicates that the earlier REPs have helped in many ways to stabilize wages and foodgrain prices in rural areas.[26] If so, then the scope for further stabilization of wages through the NREGA is limited.

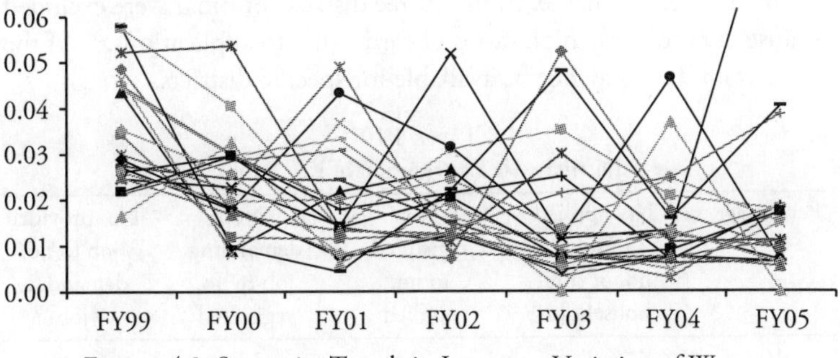

FIGURE 4.9: State-wise Trends in Intra-year Variation of Wages
Source: Ministry of Labour, Government of India.

Monitoring the NREGS

In order to examine the performance of NREGS implementation, the government has established a website (http://www.nrega.nic.in) where, inter alia, information on the following physical and financial indicators is provided for each of the districts in which the NREGS is being implemented:

1. Number of rural households (2001 Census)
2. Estimated number of BPL rural families (which is estimated by applying the state-wise poverty ratio to the number of rural households)[27]

3. Applications for registration for a job card, which is necessary to apply for a job under the NREGS
4. Number of job cards issued
5. Number of households demanding employment
6. Number of households provided employment
7. Cumulative number of households that have completed 100 days of employment, which is the maximum entitlement under the NREGA
8. Person-days of employment provided
9. Total availability of funds
10. Total expenditure under the NREGS
11. Expenditure on unskilled wage

This level of information differs sharply from that of other centrally sponsored scheme, where even the state-wise allocation and utilization data are not readily available. Table 4.10 shows the distribution of various ratios for the districts selected for analysis. From the 185 districts for which data were available, twenty-three districts of Bihar were excluded because of excessively high ratios of card issues to applications.[28] Of the rest, certain data may not be available for specific districts.

TABLE 4.10
District-wise Distribution of Key Ratios

Percentage	No. applied to total no. of rural households	No. registered to no. applied	No. demanding job to no. registered	No. provided job to no. demanding job
10	0	0	12	1
20	2	0	15	0
30	3	0	20	0
40	15	4	25	0
50	20	0	21	1
60	26	0	25	2
70	23	9	15	2
80	16	11	11	2
90	14	13	8	5
100	13	42	7	140
100+	30	82	1	7
N	162	161	160	160

Source: Ministry of Rural Development, Government of India, www.nrega.nic.in.

The first point of note is that in a number of districts, the number of households applying for a card is more than the number of households in the 2001 Census. There are many possible benign explanations for this, for example the growth of population, the formation of new households, and application by households belonging to neighbouring districts. The more sinister explanation would be a number of 'ghost' households, whose cards would later be used to divert funds under the NREGS. That said, more than half the rural households have applied for a job card in all but forty districts and only in five districts[29] have less than 30 per cent applied for them.

The case of eighty-two districts, where the number of registrations equal or exceed the number of applicants is harder to explain. None of the previously advanced explanations apply in this case. For purposes of detail, about 12 per cent of these (or ten districts) are those where the ratio is 100 per cent, another approximately 64 per cent is distributed nearly equally across districts where the over-registration is within 5 per cent, between 5 and 10 per cent, and 10 and 20 per cent (18, 18, and 16 respectively). In the twenty remaining districts, over-registration exceeds 20 per cent, with three districts, Hazaribagh (269 per cent) and Godda (189 per cent) in Jharkhand and Gorakhpur in Uttar Pradesh (150 per cent) exceeding 50 per cent. There would seem to be a prima facie case for re-examining these figures. Overall, the extent of enrolment is high on average, with only thirteen districts, comprising five from Maharashtra (experience of the EGS notwithstanding), two each from Uttaranchal, Jharkhand and Kerala, and one each from Tamil Nadu and West Bengal reporting a ratio of less than 70 per cent.

Given this high enrolment, the number demanding a job as a proportion of those enrolled is much more normally distributed, with 17 per cent of the districts, that is about twenty-seven districts each being less than 20 per cent or more than 70 per cent, with the remaining two-thirds between 20 and 70 per cent.[30]

Finally, once employment is demanded by a household, the NREGS seems to be highly successful in providing it, with only thirteen districts[31] reporting less than 90 per cent provision and 119 districts reporting more than 99 per cent. However, the weighted average demand for employment in these 119 districts is only 38.9 per cent as compared to 52.3 per cent in the other districts.

None of these ratios has any significant relationship with either the Index of Progress at district level or with per capita state domestic product (PCSDP) at state level. Table 4.11 reports the regression estimates for these ratios on the Index of Progress, with and without state dummies.

TABLE 4.11
Coefficient on Index of District-level Social Progress

	N	With dummies	t-value	Without dummies	t-value
Card issue	183	611.98	0.49	–1097.44	1.49
Job demand	152	18.37	0.51	17.33	0.71
Job provided	155	33.88	0.84	46.50	1.87
Card issue	149	910.43	0.54	–1684.00	–1.69
Job demand	149	16.19	0.45	13.17	0.53
Job provided	149	47.78	1.36	64.53	2.86

Source: Ministry of Rural Development, Government of India, www.nrega.nic.in.

In no case is any significance achieved. Similarly, regressing the state ratios on the PCSDP does not produce any result.[32]

To sum up, the variation in NREGS districts seems to be in the ratio of households demanding employment to registered households. From the other two ratios, that is enrolment, conditional on application, and provision, conditional on application, both of which are in part related to the efficacy of the district implementation machinery, appear quite high, maybe too high at times.

Expenditure under NREGS

Table 4.12 shows the distribution of availability and expenditure of funds per household across NREGS districts. From the distribution, there appears to be little reason to be worried about financial constraints as the expenditure distributions are much more left skewed as compared to the availability of funds. Given the observation in the previous section that the provision of employment, conditional on demand is almost complete, funds do not appear to be a constraint in enabling households to *participate* in NREGS.

If we look at the fund-utilization ratio defined as the actual expenditure to fund availability, there is no relationship to the demand for employment, as a ratio of those enrolled. However, there is a positive relationship between availability of funds per household enrolled and the demand for employment as a proportion of those enrolled, as shown in Figure 4.10. Thus it appears that more funds are being made available to those districts where proportionately more households are demanding employment, but district-level targeting could be improved further. Once the district administration has the funds, its ability to spend varies considerably across districts, as shown in Figure 4.11, but

TABLE 4.12

Distribution of Availability and Expenditure of Funds per Household

	Availability of funds per household			Expenditure per household			
	Applying	Registered	Demanding	Applying	Registered	Demanding	Provided
<500	1.9%	1.2%	0.0%	17.5%	14.9%	1.9%	0.0%
<1000	8.1%	6.2%	0.0%	21.9%	23.6%	3.8%	3.8%
<2000	21.9%	18.6%	3.8%	33.8%	36.0%	16.4%	17.0%
<3000	21.3%	26.1%	6.3%	16.3%	16.8%	26.4%	24.5%
<4000	15.0%	16.8%	6.9%	6.9%	5.0%	18.9%	19.5%
<5000	15.0%	18.0%	6.9%	1.9%	3.1%	11.3%	12.6%
<6000	6.9%	3.1%	13.2%	0.0%	0.0%	8.8%	8.8%
<7000	3.1%	4.3%	11.3%	0.6%	0.0%	3.8%	4.4%
<8000	1.3%	1.9%	13.2%	0.6%	0.0%	1.3%	1.9%
<9000	1.3%	0.6%	6.9%	0.6%	0.6%	0.6%	0.6%
>9000	4.4%	3.1%	31.4%	0.0%	0.0%	6.9%	6.9%
N	160	161	159	160	161	159	159

Source: Ministry of Rural Development, Government of India, www.nrega.nic.in.

there is still a robust relationship between availability and expenditure as seen in Figure 4.12, with a Re 1 increase in availability increasing expenditure by Rs 0.46.

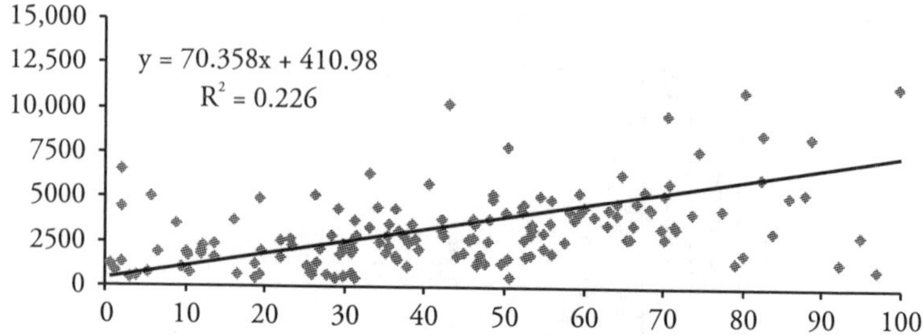

FIGURE 4.10: Demand for Employment and Fund Availability
Source: Ministry of Rural Development, Government of India.

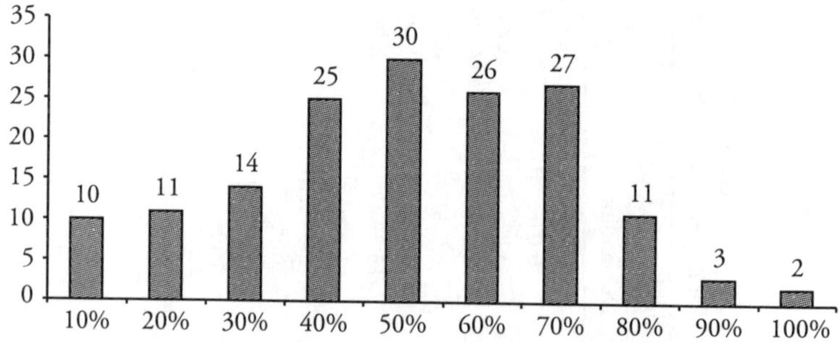

FIGURE 4.11: Ratio of Expenditure to Availability
Source: Ministry of Rural Development, Government of India, www.nrega.nic.in.

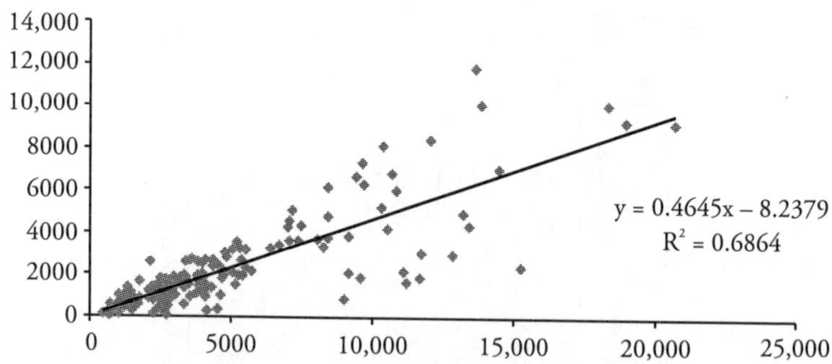

FIGURE 4.12: Availability to Expenditure
Source: Ministry of Rural Development, Government of India, www.nrega.nic.in.

Effect of Increased Availability of Funds

As mentioned earlier, there is little scope for either availability or expenditure of funds to make a difference at the margin since almost all households demanding employment are provided employment. However, it is possible that the availability and consequent expenditure of funds may lead to greater *intensity of employment*, that is a higher number of days per household. Figure 4.13 indicates support for this hypothesis, where greater availability of funds per household enrolled is associated with an increase in the number of days of employment provided per household employed. Figure 4.14 also indicates a robust relationship between district-wise expenditure and outcomes, as measured by days of employment. Wage expenditure per household provided employment rises with the days of employment provided per

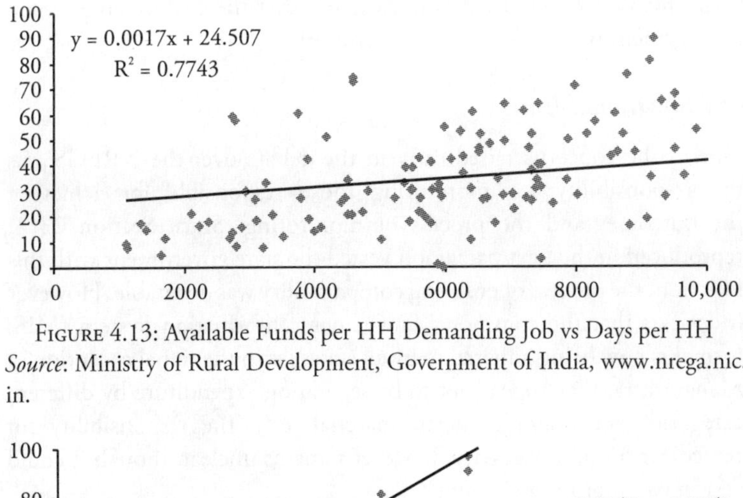

FIGURE 4.13: Available Funds per HH Demanding Job vs Days per HH
Source: Ministry of Rural Development, Government of India, www.nrega.nic.in.

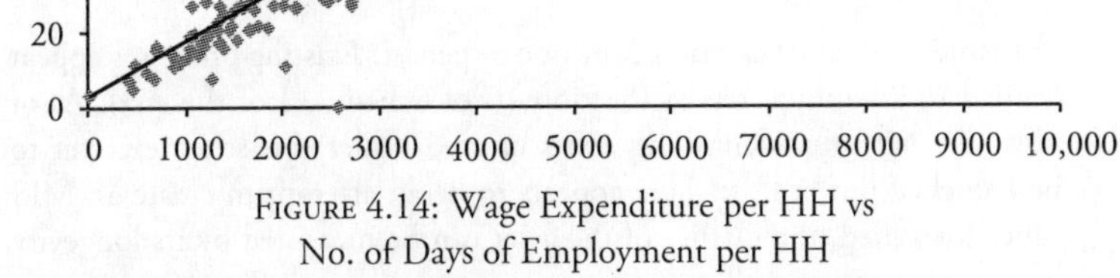

FIGURE 4.14: Wage Expenditure per HH vs No. of Days of Employment per HH
Source: Ministry of Rural Development, Government of India, www.nrega.nic.in.

household though there is significant variation with respect to non-wage expenditures (see Figure 4.15). The distribution of wage and non-wage expenditure per person-day (Figure 4.16) shows that there are some districts where it appears high, but overall, about 78 per cent of the districts (116 out of 148) have a wage between Rs 40 and Rs 80 per person-day.[33] Furthermore, as seen in Figure 4.17, the distribution of expenditure on unskilled labour wages to total expenditure, which is one of the critical features of the NREGA, given its prohibition against contractors and the use of excessive machinery, also appears reasonable.

Overall, 431 million person-days of employment have been provided so far[34] to 12.5 million households at the cost of roughly Rs 93 per person-day, of which Rs 60 is expenditure on wages. Each employed household has, on average, received Rs 2123. Of the remaining cost, Rs 23 (or 25 per cent) is on materials and another 4 per cent is on wages for skilled labour. It is unclear whether the cost of programme management is included in this expenditure.

Organizational Issues

One of the concerns raised early in the debate over the NREGS was the responsibility for monitoring those responsible for achieving the outcomes and the process of monitoring. Since Section 23(2), reproduced in the next paragraph vested the state government with this function, the process of ensuring comparability was debatable. However, it appears that the common Management Information System (MIS) format is now being adhered to by all states, with the signal exception of Maharashtra, that appear not to be separating expenditure by different categories, for example wages, material, etc. The responsibility for remedial action, if necessary, however remains unclear, though it could vest in the appropriate Council.

- 23 (2) 'The State Govt. may prescribe the manner of maintaining proper books and accounts of employment of labourers and the expenditure incurred in connection with the implementation of the provisions of this Act.'
- The issues with asset creation continue to persist. Existing processes appear limited to an annual report (Section 15 of Schedule I of the Act). As of now, the MIS for identifying assets created under this scheme is yet to be launched but at least there appears to be an attempt to create an MIS. Once identified, the quality of the asset can be measured by its longevity, but, as mentioned earlier, it is not clear whether the effort is to create a long-lasting asset. However, given that 25 per cent of the expenditure is on

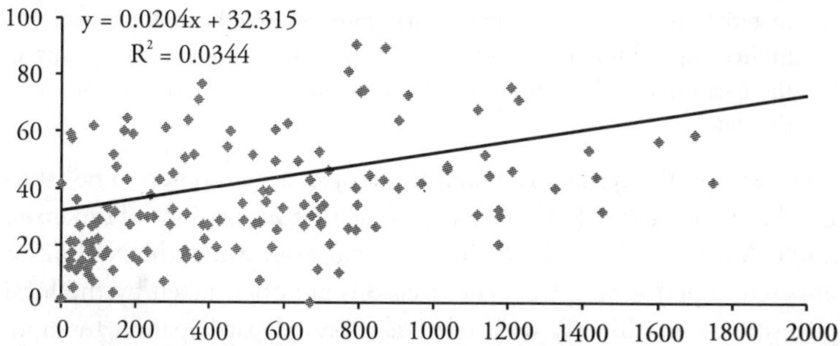

FIGURE 4.15: Non-wage Expenditure and Days per HH
Source: Ministry of Rural Development, Government of India, www.nrega.nic.in.

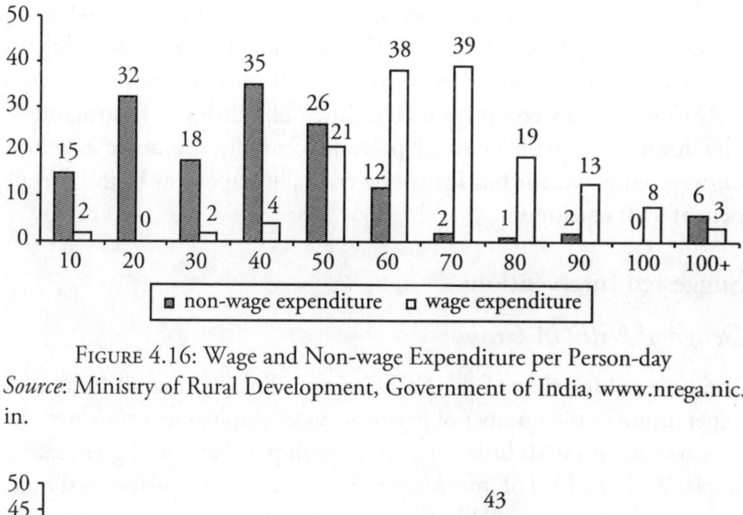

FIGURE 4.16: Wage and Non-wage Expenditure per Person-day
Source: Ministry of Rural Development, Government of India, www.nrega.nic.in.

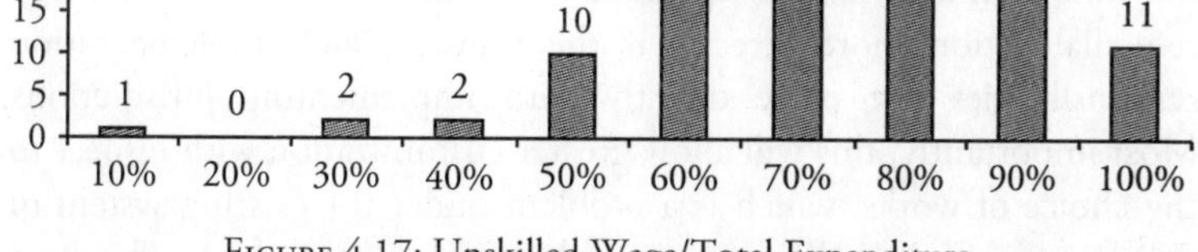

FIGURE 4.17: Unskilled Wage/Total Expenditure
Source: Ministry of Rural Development, Government of India, www.nrega.nic.in.

materials, it should be possible to maintain some of the assets, though the limited expenditure on skilled labour raises concerns about the quality of the asset (unless additional expenditure on skilled labour has been borne by the state).

Decisions on the type of asset and the project are supposed to be taken by the gram sabha. However, recent field investigations (Himanshu 2005; Aiyar and Samji 2006) indicate that even where the NREGS is apparently performing well, the decisions are often taken by the local government machinery, with relatively limited participation by gram sabhas. This is a chicken and egg problem, for the capacity of the gram sabha cannot be built in this fashion and until the capacity has been built the government machinery will continue to take these decisions. This is a critical area that needs to be addressed.

The Act specifies that '*Arrangements as may be laid down by the State Govt. ... for proper maintenance of the public assets created*' (Schedule I). This is still a relatively unaddressed area, including the question of whether NREG works can comprise maintenance of existing infrastructure.[35] This has been a weak point of previous centrally sponsored schemes on wage employment but it may be critically important in the overall benefit–cost equation.

Suggested Interventions

Design of NREGA Grants

The current fund flow of the NREG system links both availability and expenditure to the number of person-days of employment provided. In its structure, it builds little capacity at gram panchayat and gram sabha levels. With the level of information that is currently available, it should be possible to move to a block grant system for the implementing zila panchayats or even gram panchayats. The same level of reporting and MIS would enable monitoring at the same level as currently possible. Furthermore, while remedial action would necessarily have to go through the state in the current dispensation, it should be possible to exercise remedial action more directly if the transfers and implementation responsibilities rest more directly with implementing jurisdictions. Most importantly, this will allow greater customization with respect to the choice of works, which is a problem under the existing system of delivery. Given the MIS structure under development, this can be done without losing the ability to monitor the quality of implementation, though one hopes that such monitoring will also be undertaken by local political processes, perhaps utilizing the comparative information that is being provided in the public domain.

Outcome Monitoring Survey

In this chapter, we acknowledged that the evidence currently available indicates that two specific tasks, namely provision of employment to households seeking employment and linkage of expenditures with actual employment generation, seem to have been delivered by the existing administrative machinery. However, it remains to be seen whether this is an accomplishment on paper or in the field. To settle this question, one will have to go beyond the MIS systems of the NREGS and rely on related surveys.

In principle, surveys specific to the NREGA may be of limited usefulness, as they risk being turned into yet another evaluation exercise. Enhancement of existing surveys, for example by increasing the sample size of the NSS to enable it to discriminate by district and collecting information relevant for evaluation of centrally sponsored schemes like the NREGA, may be a more effective method, since there are a number of other neutral constituencies that have a vested interest in preserving the quality of the survey. It remains to be seen whether the person-days generated and the consequent income to the rural population is captured in these surveys.[36]

Administrative Traceability

The MIS system proposed for the NREGS can in principle identify each beneficiary, when fully implemented. This will facilitate randomized third-party audit of beneficiaries so that money is not being lost to corruption. Exception reports of the sort mentioned in this chapter can be used to select areas of intervention. This will permit greater delegation to the local jurisdictions subject to audit controls, similar to tax audits in most countries.

The NREGS thus provides a good opportunity to develop a digital personal biometric ID for each beneficiary. The beneficiaries aggregated to form 'soft-coded' households recognizing that households form and re-form. From a fund-allocation perspective, the digital IDs will permit funds to travel along with the beneficiary, if the beneficiary moves from one location to another in a different jurisdiction. Currently, the ability of an NREGS beneficiary to move across state boundaries is limited. The personal ID will assist in delivery of many other schemes, which require more targeting than the NREGS, which works on a self-targeting basis. A pilot initiative in this area has already begun in Andhra Pradesh.

A similar principle can create a Digital Asset register, using a unique project ID and inexpensive GIS 'fingerprint' for each project. This will also permit tracking of maintenance expenditures on the project after completion. Similar initiatives are now under way in many states.[37] The design of the NREGS's MIS system indicates that it may be used by the NREGS too.

A key reason for the poor performance of social programmes in India is the structural weakness of the delivery system. The Achilles heel of all such programmes is implementation. No matter how well programmes are designed and funded, in the end they all have to pass through the eye of the needle, namely local public administration. Social policy is increasingly being funded at one level of government (the national), implemented by another (local), which in turn is controlled by yet another level of government (state). In the less capable states, the state government has limited capacity to execute and this in turn affects the local governments. Recognizing this issue, the national government is trying to increase capacity of local governance by specifying a strong role for gram panchayats (village governments) and gram sabhas (village assemblies) in the NREGS. However, this is unlikely to be sustainable and produce long-lasting results unless a strong *demand* for effective services is articulated through the political system, which in turn will bring accountability into the government delivery system.

The evidence of the lack of accountability of government functionaries in implementing these schemes is overwhelming. The Indian state is unable to discipline its employees, take action against the corrupt ones, reduce their numbers, or make changes in their service conditions, leading to declining standards of performance and integrity among field officials and with it the ability to deliver. Normally we would expect voters to punish politicians for poor performance leading to retrospective accountability, spurring the latter to demand better performance from the bureaucracy (and prospective accountability). But this does not seem to occur in the Indian case. This appears puzzling, given the extent of deprivation and the strong participation of India's poor in elections.[38]

Based on the above analysis, it would appear that the existing institutional arrangement for implementing the NREGS has deficiencies that are similar to those of other social programmes. Despite this, it seems to have managed to deliver the employment provision objective in a passable manner. The relative success of the NREGS is perhaps in some measure due to its distinguishing features, namely, fund availability, low counterpart funding, and high transparency. It may also be due to its high profile and the consequent share of attention that it is receiving at implementation level, making sure it is one scheme that passes through the eye of the needle.

However, this may have led to reduced attention and consequent non-performance in other centrally sponsored schemes, for which the data are not so readily available. Moreover, in states with a strong administrative machinery, the state apparatus tends to replace the nascent elected bodies at local level and while there is an element of visible service delivery, it is much less demand driven than is envisaged under the NREGA. This affects the choice of projects relatively more than the employment provision aspect of the initiative. In order to obtain the full benefit of the NREGA, it is necessary to equip the gram sabhas and gram panchayats with skills for holistic and inter-sectoral planning and budgeting of projects.

The positive question is what kinds of public policy interventions will reinforce the articulation of demand from voters and the consequent increase in accountability. For example, will the recently passed Right to Information Act bring forth the stark difference between expenditures undertaken in the name of the poor and the limited benefits to the poor from such expenditure and, if so, will this foster a demand for greater accountability from the delivery system, as we suggest it, in some measure, has for NREGS? If so, it can be replicated for all centrally sponsored schemes without significant fiscal costs.

There are indications that such changes are in the offing, albeit slowly. Civil society actors, who have been pressing for delivery of social services, are becoming active in electoral politics.[39] Such participation is not only linked to an effort to alter existing relationships of patronage; it is also related to alternative priorities for public expenditure. New institutional mechanisms of service delivery that involve greater community participation, appear to hold promise for better service delivery and broad public good provision that can be accessed by the poor. Some of these, like the Rogi Kalyan Samiti, have begun as experiments at the level of state governments and have gone on to be adopted by the centre in their design of new centrally sponsored schemes. Such changes in design, leading to greater devolution of financial and administrative functions, are a necessary condition. However, coupled with a strong demand for accountability in service delivery from the beneficiaries, they may prove effective in transforming the efficacy of anti-poverty interventions in large democracies like India.

Notes

1. See Inman and Rubinfeld (1997). This is in contrast to democratic federalism which argues for a greater role for the national government. Of course, the quality of the outcome would depend on the relative political maturities and economic condition of the participating jurisdictions.
2. This difference across jurisdictions is often called the need–revenue gap (Ahmad 1996).
3. Oates (1982) has argued that since fiscal differentials are capitalised in property values, the rationale for equalizing transfers is reduced to that extent. It can also be argued that these transfers will enable these regions to make compensating investments in human capital to offset their resource disadvantages and enable the population to raise their productivity and income levels (Rao 2005).
4. See Feldstein (1975). For services in this category, the consumption levels should not be related to the individual's ability to pay.
5. There are three levels of decentralization, (i) delegation, where the local government carries out certain functions as agencies of government, (ii) deconcentration, where there is limited flexibility in the implementation of programmes, and (iii) the devolution of expenditure functions to local governments, where the design and implementation are with the local government, for example if they received an untied block grant.
6. Besides formal transfers there can be many other sources of inter-regional transfers. Important sources of such transfers include inter-state tax exportation, targeting investments in specific locations by the national government, lending to sub-national governments at below market rates of interest, and/or allowing them to borrow from the market under a financially repressive regime, and influencing the allocation of the resources by the banking system. These are not considered in this chapter. See Rao and Dasgupta (1995) for an excellent exposition.
7. According to Fan and Thorat (1999), roads lift six times more persons out of poverty, compared to rural development schemes, through their effect on non-farm employment and agricultural productivity. Investment in rural roads may prove to be the most powerful anti-poverty intervention, more so if these programmes are used as a part of an employment guarantee scheme (EGS). However, there seem to be many issues in combining these approaches. The trade-off seems to be in the perception that undertaking rural road works under EGS-like schemes will lead to use of excessively labour-intensive techniques that will compromise the quality of construction and, thereby, the durability of the asset. In India, therefore, the NREGS is kept separate from a major multi-billion dollar rural road works programme.
8. This section draws substantially on Rao (2004) and Rao (2005).

9. Although the Indian federation was a two-tier structure until 1992, corresponding local government units functioned both in urban and rural areas, but as agencies of the state governments. After 1992, each state government was required to pass legislation appointing Panchayati Raj institutions and urban local bodies, with elections to be held within a stipulated period. A separate list of twenty-nine functions for rural local bodies and eighteen for urban local bodies was placed in schedules for local governments to implement concurrently with the states. The sources of finance for the local bodies were also identified.
10. Besides the residuary powers that have been assigned to the national government; it also has overriding powers in respect of items placed in the concurrent list. Above all, it can alter the boundaries of a state and create new states by dividing the existing ones after informing the state government. This has been done relatively often, the latest instance being the creation of Jharkhand, Chhattisgarh, and Uttaranchal (since renamed Uttarakhand) by bifurcating Bihar, Madhya Pradesh, and Uttar Pradesh respectively.
11. At present, 30 per cent of the funds are kept apart for special category states and distributed (90 per cent of the assistance given by way of grants) on the basis of plan projects formulated by them. The remaining 70 per cent are distributed to the other states (only 30 per cent are given by way of grants to these states) with 60 per cent weight assigned to population, 25 per cent to per capita SDP, 7.5 per cent to fiscal management, and the remaining 7.5 per cent to special problems of these states.
12. The share of nationally collected taxes is distributed using a formula where 62.5 per cent of the weight is on distance of per capita income from that of the richest state, 10 per cent is on population, 7.5 per cent is on area, an index of infrastructure and a measure of fiscal discipline each, and the remaining 5 per cent is on tax effort.
13. The top three schemes in 2005–6 and 2006–7 were different and accounted for 33.4 per cent and 38.9 per cent of the budget respectively. These were the NREGS (erstwhile Food for Work), Sarva Siksha Abhiyan (Education for All), and the Midday Meal Scheme for schoolchildren (in 2006–7) and the Prime Minister's Grameen Sadak Yojana (Rural Roads Programme) in 2005–6.
14. Even though local governments do not determine the tax base and rates, local government in China up to township level has traditionally enjoyed economic power due to its hold over enterprises. This government–enterprise nexus helped develop administrative and fiscal capacity in local governments.
15. Achievement of physical outcomes is usually not used for anti-poverty schemes but there is now an incipient move to present outcome budgets for various ministries and centrally sponsored schemes.

16. In an evolving political situation, the expectations of the participating regional political parties need not be mutually consistent.
17. This section draws substantially on Chakraborty (2006).
18. There is a growing theoretical and empirical literature on the impact of public works programmes on poverty alleviation (see, for example Dreze and Sen 1989; Ravallion 1991; Besley and Coate 1992).
19. It is also seen as an initiative to operationalize the concept of the right to work enshrined in the constitution under the Directive Principles of State Policy (Papola 2005) by guaranteeing those who are demanding employment. The only example of guaranteed state-sponsored employment in India is the Maharashtra EGS, which was enacted and implemented under extraordinary circumstances of severe drought in the state during 1970–3 as an innovative anti-poverty intervention (Dev and Ranade 2001).
20. Out of these 200 districts, some are covered under the Scheduled Area Act. A proportion in Andhra Pradesh, Bihar, and Jharkhand are virtually under extremist control. There are also other districts where panchayats are simply non-existent and in many places non-functional.
21. For the purposes of analysis, in the absence of income indicators at district level, we have used the Index of Progress as an indicator of development.
22. Safety net requires a compression of the distribution at the bottom tail, while poverty reduction is more of a shift in the distribution.
23. Murgai and Ravallion (2005) argue that the benefit–cost ratio of the NREGS may depend on the durability and usefulness of the infrastructure built under the scheme, as the extent of income increase from the scheme will be limited as most workers will switch from existing lower paid employment to the NREGS.
24. Among the wage rate estimates, Agricultural Wages in India (AWI) and Wage Rates in Rural India (WRRI) both depend on collection of wage rates from local-level officials. The differences between these two sources puts a question mark on the whole modus operandi of collecting wages based on opinions of local officials The Committee on Agricultural Cost and Price (CACP) wages are not available to researchers for detailed scrutiny. While the wage estimates published by the Rural Labour Enquiry (RLE) uses National Statistical Survey (NSS) employment and unemployment surveys, the published estimates do not seem credible enough compared to the NSS estimates which use the same survey to arrive at wage estimates. Moreover, frequent changes in the definitions and concepts, as has been the case with the NSS surveys involving the 1999–2000 Employment Unemployment Status surveys affects the inter-temporal comparison.
25. This series is constructed for eleven agricultural and seven non-agricultural occupations based on the wage rate data collected every month as a part of the scheme of Rural Labour Enquiry, from 600 sample villages spread over sixty-six NSS regions of twenty states. Village functionaries like

the Panchayat Secretary, Progress Assistant, Patwari, and other Village or Block Officials are the primary informants for collection of data on wage rates.

26. However, many government audit and non-government evaluations have noted that the coverage of these schemes remained poor and more than 50 per cent of the beneficiaries were not from the most economically vulnerable sections in rural areas. Other than these, there were issues of corruption in the form of underpayment of wages, differential wage payment to males and females and proliferation of contractors in the implementation of the schemes.
27. A better approach would perhaps have been to use the poverty ratios from the relevant NSS region.
28. The ratio varied from 90 per cent to 98.36 per cent. Perhaps, the number of applicants was incorrectly reported.
29. These are Ranchi, Jharkhand; Jaunpur, Uttar Pradesh; Mohendergarh, Haryana; Palakkad, Kerala; and Hoshiarpur, Punjab.
30. Curiously, in the three districts with more than 150 per cent enrolment, demand is relatively low—less than 30 per cent and only 5.8 per cent in Hazaribagh.
31. These include three in Uttar Pradesh and West Bengal, two in Kerala, and one each in Himachal Pradesh, Madhya Pradesh, Jammu & Kashmir, Uttaranchal, and Orissa.
32. The maximum R^2 over the three ratios is 0.011 for the provision ratio.
33. Districts with a high component of non-wage expenditure per person-day are Waynad and Palakkad in Kerala, Lawngtlai in Mizoram, Bilaspur in Chhattisgarh, Lalitpur, Kushinagar and Jaunpur in Uttar Pradesh, Pakur and Sahebganj in Jharkhand, Bidar in Karnataka, and Banaskantha in Gujarat.
34. The data are as reported of November 2006. This is including Bihar (not considered in our analysis) and excluding Maharashtra (for which data are not provided).
35. Maintenance usually requires a higher proportion of skilled labour and this may prove a barrier.
36. The 12.5 million households that have received some kind of NREG employment form 25 per cent of the approximately 50 million rural households in these districts and should therefore be a large enough minority to show up in national surveys of these regions.
37. See for example www.egovernments.org
38. A reason sometimes offered is the strength of identity politics, as a result of which the political space is not seen as an arena for competing economic demands, but rather as a means to express a particular conception of identity. This is amplified by the ubiquitousness of clientelist politics, which reduces the incentives for politicians to press for programmatic policies. They perceive little correlation between the successful delivery of

social programmes and electoral success, which locks all players into a low-level equilibrium (see Kapur and Mukhopadhyay 2006).

39. A recent example is the participation in local elections by associates of the Mazdoor Kisan Sangarsh Samiti (MKSS), a Rajasthan-based rights group that played a pivotal role in the passage of the national Right to Information Act.

References

Acharya, S. (1990). *Maharashtra Employment Guarantee Scheme: A Study of Labour Market Intervention*. New Delhi: ILO-ARTEP.

Ahmad, Ehtisham (1996). *Financing Decentralized Expenditures: An International Comparison of Grants*. Cheltenham, UK: Edward Elgar.

Aiyar, Yamini and Salimah Samji (2006). 'Improving the effectiveness of National Rural Employment Guarantee Act', *Economic and Political Weekly*, 41(4), 28 January–3 February.

Bahl, Roy W. and Christine Wallace (2001). 'Fiscal Decentralization: The Provincial–Local Dimension', paper presented at seminar on Public Finance in Developing and Transition Countries, 4-6 April, Georgia State University, Atlanta.

Besley, T. and S. Coate (1992). 'Workfare vs. Welfare: Incentive Arguments for Work Requirements in Poverty Alleviation Programmes', *American Economic Review*, 82, pp. 249–61.

Chakraborty, Pinaki (2006). 'Implementation of National Rural Employment Guarantee Act In India: Spatial Dimension and Fiscal Implications', paper prepared and presented at conference on Employment Guarantee Policies: Theory and Practice organized by Levy Economics Institute of Bard College, New York, 13–14 October.

Datt, Gaurav (1994). 'Poverty Alleviation through Rural Public Works: The Experience of Maharashtra Employment Guarantee Scheme', *The Indian Journal of Labour Economics*, 37(4).

Debroy, Bibek and Laveesh Bhandari (eds) (2003). *District Level Deprivation in the New Millennium.* New Delhi: Konark Publishers.

Dev, Mahendra S. and Ajit K. Ranade (2001). 'Employment Guarantee Scheme and Employment Security', in Mahendra S. Dev, Piush Antony, V. Gayathri, and R.P. Mamgain (eds), *Social and Economic Security in India*. New Delhi: Institute of Human Development.

Dreze, Jean and Amartya Sen (1989). *Hunger and Public Action*. Oxford: Clarendon Press.

Fan, S., P. Hazell, and S. Thorat (1999). 'Linkages between Government Spending, Growth, and Poverty in Rural India', Research Report 110, International Food Policy Research Institute, Washington, D.C.

Feldstein, Martin, S. (1975). 'Wealth Neutrality and Local Choice in Public Education', *American Economic Review*, 65, pp. 75–89.

Himanshu (2005). 'Wages in Rural India: Sources, Trends and Comparability', *Indian Journal of Labour Economics*, 48(2), April–June 2005.

Inman, Robert P. and Daniel L. Rubinfeld (1997). 'Rethinking Federalism' *Journal of Economic Perspectives*, 11(4): 43–64.

Kannan, K.P. (2005). 'Linking Guarantee to Human Development', *Economic and Political Weekly*, October 2005.

Kapur, Devesh and Partha Mukhopadhyay (2006). 'Instruments Of Social Policy And Mechanisms Of Welfare Delivery In India', paper presented at the Conference on Welfare Regime and Social Actors, University of Texas, Austin, April.

Murgai R. and M. Ravallion (2005). 'Employment Guarantee in Rural India—What Would It Cost and How Much Would It Reduce Poverty?' *Economic and Political Weekly*, 40, pp. 3131, 3450–3455.

Oates Wallace E. (1982). 'The New Federalism: An Economist's View', *The Cato Journal* 2, Fall, pp. 473–88.

Papola T.S. (2005). 'A Universal Programme is Feasible', *Economic and Political Weekly*, 12 February.

Rao, M. Govinda (2005). 'Fiscal Decentralisation and Poverty Reduction', UNDP Primer November 2005, http://www.undp.org/governance/docs/DLGUD_Pub_FDPR.pdf.

________ (2004). 'Changing Contours in Federal Fiscal Arrangements in India', paper presented at the International Symposium on Fiscal Decentralisation in Asia Revisited, Hitotsubashi University.

________ (2003). 'Fiscal Decentralization in China and India: A Comparative Perspective', *Asia-Pacific Development Journal*, 10(1): 25–45.

________ (1998). 'Public Expenditure Policies in Fast Growing Asian Economies', *World Development*, 26(4): 673–94.

Rao, M. Govinda, H.K. Amar Nath, and B.P. Vani (2003). *Rural Fiscal Decentralisation in Karnataka*, Report Prepared for the World Bank. National Institute of Public Finance and Policy (Processed).

Rao, M. Govinda and Arindam Dasgupta (1995). 'Intergovernmental Transfers and Poverty Alleviation', *Environment and Policy C: Government and Policy*, 24, Fall, pp. 99–114.

Ravallion, Martin (1991). 'Reaching the Rural Poor through Public Employment: Arguments, Evidence, and Lessons from South Asia', *The World Bank Research Observer*, 6(2).

II

Fiscal Reforms for Balanced Regional Development

5

Reform of Intergovernmental Fiscal Arrangements for Balanced Regional Development in a Globalizing Environment

M. Govinda Rao

This chapter deals with the role of intergovernmental transfers in ensuring balanced regional development in India. Although theoretical formulations on intergovernmental transfers do not take equalizing inter-state per capita incomes per se as an explicit objective, the transfer system has significant inter-regional resource allocation implications. In an economy with significant differences in the institutions and structure of incentives, resource endowments, and infrastructure development, the transfer system has an important role in promoting cohesive and balanced development of the country. The transition from plan to market puts even greater burden on the transfer system to ensure the states a level playing field in their developmental effort. In addition, a globalizing environment requires creation of competitive levels of infrastructure and unless concerted efforts are made to ensure a level playing field through even spread of infrastructure, globalization can create highly skewed regional distribution of economic activities. In an environment where the population mobility is constrained by many factors including linguistic diversity, cultural differences, and education and skill levels, differences in economic activities could translate into differences in economic opportunities, employment, and income levels and this could pose serious threat to the stability of the federation itself.

It is in ensuring a level playing field among states that the transfer system has to play an important role. The theoretical literature advances rationale for intergovernmental transfers on horizontal equity grounds or merit goods reasons (Buchanan 1950, Boadway and Flatters 1982). The former are general-purpose transfers given from the central to regional (state) governments to offset fiscal disabilities arising from low-revenue-raising capacities of the poorer states or higher unit costs of providing public services for reasons beyond their control. The objective is to enable all the states to provide a normative level of public services at a given tax price. The transfers designed for merit good reasons are meant for specified purposes, and are made to ensure that every state spends the prescribed minimum outlay on meritorious services with significant inter-state spillovers. Providing these transfers is supposed to equalize the standards of social and physical infrastructure across different states and given their generalized externalities, provide a level playing field to the disadvantaged states.

Equalizing transfers could lead to convergence of incomes across states. The neoclassical growth model demonstrates that in closed economies with no differences in technology and preferences, the growth rate of per capita incomes tends to be inversely related to the initial levels of per capita incomes (Barro and Sala-i-Martin 1991). The principal force driving convergence is diminishing returns to reproducible capital. Thus economies with lower initial values of capital–labour ratios will have high marginal productivity of capital and, therefore, tend to grow at higher rates (Evans and Karras 1996). Given the low capital–labour ratio in poorer regions, equalizing transfers could accelerate the growth of the economy. Higher marginal productivity of capital in poorer regions attracts investments to these regions leading to convergence of incomes. Equalizing transfers, thus, are expected to hasten the process of convergence of inter-regional incomes. More importantly, by enabling the poorer states to provide a threshold level of infrastructure, transfers could help allocate resources according to comparative advantage of different regions.

Contrary to the predictions of neoclassical growth theory, there can be cases where marginal productivity of capital in poorer regions may be lower. In such cases, it is argued that population mobility can be a serious alternative to equalizing transfers. In fact, the latter, by constraining mobility of population from regions with low potential and productivity to higher productivity regions could reduce the income level in the economy. Free population mobility in response to fiscal differentials could be a preferred alternative from both equity and efficiency point of view. However, as mentioned earlier, neither is inter-regional mobility free due to institutional reasons nor is population mobility determined only by fiscal differentials. In such cases, equalizing transfers may be necessary even if it involves lower productivity. More importantly, transfer has a major non-economic objective of nation building and holding the country together.

This chapter analyses the implications of intergovernmental transfers for balanced regional development in India in an environment of economic reforms and globalization. When there are significant inequalities in physical and social infrastructure, market-based resource allocation could place poorer regions at a disadvantage and may not enable these regions to realize their potential growth. The chapter argues that although the Indian transfer system has equalizing elements, it is not adequate to offset fiscal disabilities of poorer states. Thus some of the low-income states, despite abundance of natural resources, have not been able to provide basic social and physical infrastructure, resulting in constraints to achieving their potential growth.

The chapter begins with the analysis of trends in inter-state disparities. In the next section, the role of regional policies, particularly the regional spread of central government investments in central enterprises, is discussed. The following section describes the prevailing transfer system in India and its equalizing impact is next analysed. The empirical analysis also shows that while the transfer system as a whole has been equalizing, there are still large and persisting differences in per capita expenditures on social and economic services among states. Along with the anecdotal evidence of poor standards of public service delivery in some of the low-income states, low expenditure levels indicate that the inequalities in public services are even larger than is indicated by expenditure inequalities.

Inter-state Differences in Per Capita Incomes in India

Comparable time series estimates of state domestic product in India are not available and inter-state comparisons are done on the basis of income estimated by individual states. These estimates are not strictly comparable, but as the states adopt the standard methodology for estimation, they can be taken to indicate a broad pattern. There are also problems of inter-temporal comparability as the base year is changed from time to time and changing structure of the economy over time is taken into account.

Figure 5.1 presents trends in inter-state inequalities as measured by the Gini coefficient since 1981–2. These are estimated for the large non-special category states that account for 6.36 per cent of the net state domestic product (NSDP) and 6.45 per cent of population. In the case of Bihar, Madhya Pradesh, and Uttar Pradesh, the NSDPs have been combined with the bifurcated states to make the measure comparable over time. The trend in Gini coefficient presented in Figure 5.1 gives interesting insights. First, much of the literature in India has asserted that there has been a sharp increase in inter-state inequalities after economic reforms were initiated in 1991. Indeed, much of the speculation was based on empirical evidence from the 1981 series per capita NSDP. The analysis of Gini coefficients estimated for the 1993 series of per capita NSDP in states shows that while inequalities have kept on increasing over time, this is merely a continuation of the trend from the 1980s and there hasn't been any acceleration in the increase after the economic reforms.

The deceleration in the Gini coefficient only shows that the inter-state inequalities in income levels have continued to widen, albeit at a slower rate. The growth rates of the gross state domestic product (GSDP) and per capita GSDP for the 1980s and the period after 1993–4 summarized in Table 5.1 show that, on the whole, the growth rate in the 1990s accelerated by about half a percentage point over that of the previous decade. Further, much of the acceleration was seen in the middle-income states of Andhra Pradesh, Karnataka, Kerala, Tamil Nadu, and West Bengal. In contrast, the growth rate decelerated in Bihar, Orissa, Rajasthan, and Uttar Pradesh. The analysis also shows a positive correlation between the level of per capita GSDP in the initial year and

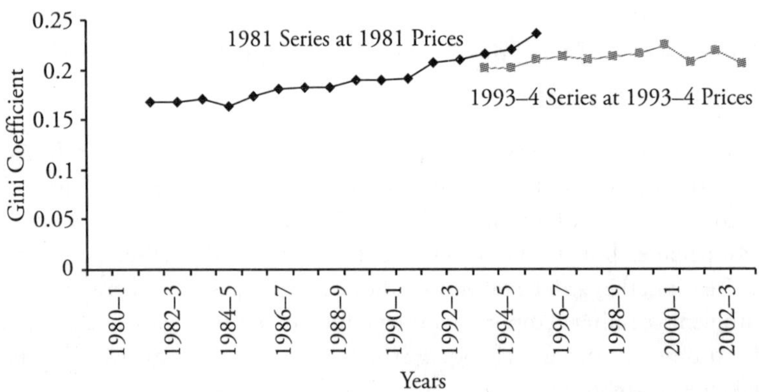

FIGURE 5.1: Inter-state Per Capita Income Inequalities in India

Source: Central Statistical Organisation, Ministry of Statistics and Programme Implementation, Government of India.

TABLE 5.1
Growth Performances of Major Indian States

(per cent per annum)

State	Growth rate of GSDP		Growth rate of per capita GSDP	
	1980–91 (1981 prices)	1993–2004 (1993 prices)	1980–91 (1981 prices)	1993–2004 (1993 prices)
Andhra Pradesh	5.65	6.02	3.39	4.65
Bihar	4.66	4.40	2.45	2.30
Gujarat	5.08	5.72	3.04	3.62
Haryana	6.43	6.03	3.89	3.82
Karnataka	5.29	7.24	3.25	5.73
Kerala	3.57	5.26	2.15	4.11
Madhya Pradesh	4.56	3.82	2.12	1.83
Maharashtra	6.02	4.72	3.63	2.77
Orissa	4.29	3.94	2.42	2.35
Punjab	5.32	4.28	3.35	2.47
Rajasthan	6.60	5.57	3.91	3.06
Tamil Nadu	5.38	4.69	3.88	3.68
Uttar Pradesh	4.95	3.70	2.57	2.17
West Bengal	4.71	6.94	2.44	5.59
All States	5.26	5.70	3.02	3.79

Source: Central Statistical Organisation, Government of India.

growth rates of per capita GSDP (Figure 5.2) and this indicates a steady increase in inter-state inequalities. The correlation coefficient between the level of per capita incomes and their growth rates was 0.472 during 1980–91, but declined to 0.331 during the next decade. The scatter also shows Punjab and Haryana as the outliers during 1990–2001 and when these two observations are omitted, the correlation coefficient increases to 0.721 for the period 1990–2001. The economic liberalization and opening up of the economy during the 1990s seems to have benefited states with a stronger industrial base and better access to markets more than states that are predominantly agricultural.

Thus, after the introduction of reforms, economic growth in the middle-income states has accelerated. Some of the high-income states with a predominant agricultural sector, particularly Punjab and Haryana, grew at low rates. This is also true of low-income states with predominant agricultural sectors and, not surprisingly, the growth of per capita NSDP in Bihar, Uttar Pradesh, Orissa, and Madhya Pradesh was very low. Thus economic liberalization has helped accelerate the growth of the service and, to a lesser extent, manufacturing sectors and,

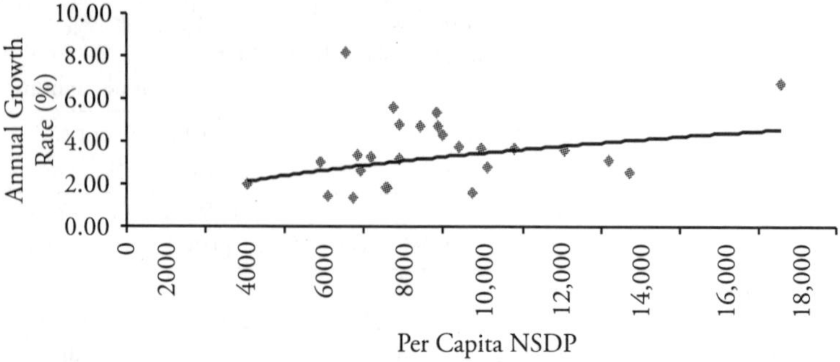

FIGURE 5.2: Level of Per Capita Incomes and Growth Rates in States
Note: Correlation Coefficient: 0.28.
Source: Central Statistical Organisation, Government of India.

consequently, middle-income states with high potential from these sectors benefited more than both low-income as well as high-income states. This has important implications for the nature of horizontal imbalance in the country, for the growth rates of middle-income states have significantly accelerated after economic liberalization. While the southern states have benefited from the boom in the services sector led by Information Technology (IT) and IT-enabled services, significant increase in agricultural productivity following land reforms has been cited as the reason for the growth acceleration in West Bengal.

REDRESSING INTER-STATE DISPARITIES: REGIONAL POLICIES

In a centrally planned economy, investment planning and its regional spread is determined by the government and, therefore, given the endowment of natural resources and nature of institutions, the pattern of regional growth and inter-regional distribution of incomes is largely determined according to regional policies. However, in a mixed economy the distribution of private-sector investment is also important.

In India, one of the important components of regional policies is the distribution of the central government's own investments and the direction to credit disbursal from the commercial banks. It is difficult to draw implications from the incidence of the central government's budgetary spending in the absence of a detailed empirical analysis. However, the spread of central investments in various enterprises is available. Clearly, the strategy of public-enterprise-dominated heavy-industry-based development directed considerable investments to the mineral-rich states of Bihar (including Jharkhand), Madhya Pradesh (including Chhattisgarh), and Orissa during the first three five year plans. Substantial investments were also made in heavy industries and this included heavy electrical industry in Bhopal and aircraft industry in Sunabeda in Orissa in the first three plans. However, the policy of taking over of sick private manufacturing units in the subsequent plans resulted in the spread of investments which is different from what was originally envisaged.

Despite pronouncements on regional equity, the spread of central government investment has not ensured balanced regional development. It can be seen from Table 5.2 that low per capita income states with population share of 45 per cent accounted for only 29 per cent of the total investments in central government enterprises and 41 per cent of the total employment generated in central enterprises. In fact, the income share of these states was equal to the investment share. Similarly, their share of employment in central enterprises was lower than their population shares by 4 percentage points. In contrast, the above-average-income states with 49 per cent of population accounted for 58 per cent of the investments and 65 per cent of the income generated in the country. Thus investments in central enterprises have not attempted to achieve balanced regional allocation. The story of Bihar is even more telling. The poorest state with about 8.2 per cent of population received only about 2 per cent of the accumulated central government investments until 2003–4 and these accounted for just about 1 per cent of employment in central enterprises.

Even the investments made in the poorer regions have not had the desired impact on their regional economies. The multiplier–accelerator effect that is supposed to activate the developmental process from these large investments was nullified by the freight equalization policy. Under this, basic raw materials such as steel and coal were made available at uniform prices throughout the country by the central government providing subsidy to offset freight charges. The consequence of the policy was to reduce the forward linkages from these investments besides bringing down the overall productivity of investments in the country. Investments in coal and steel were basically intended to promote both backward and forward linkages, and as poorer states like Bihar, Madhya Pradesh, and Orissa have a strong resource base, they had significant backward linkages to exploit their mineral resources. Although this policy has been given up, it is not possible to reverse the investment decisions that have already been made.

TABLE 5.2
Inter-state Allocation of Investments in
Central Government Enterprises, 2003–4

(per cent of total)

	Population share	GSDP share	Investment share	Employment share
Goa	0.14	0.44	0.07	0.12
Punjab	2.41	3.97	1.56	1.72
Maharashtra	9.57	15.09	19.38	12.80
Haryana	2.08	3.24	2.34	1.29
Kerala	3.15	4.09	2.75	2.77
Gujarat	5.00	6.86	7.04	3.26
Tamil Nadu	6.16	7.94	6.92	5.42
Karnataka	5.23	6.34	5.32	5.11
Andhra Pradesh	7.53	8.66	7.63	6.34
West Bengal	7.91	8.40	5.28	13.48
High-income States	**49.19**	**65.02**	**58.30**	**52.31**
Rajasthan	5.58	4.98	2.77	1.91
Chhattisgarh	2.05	1.71	2.17	6.40
Madhya Pradesh	5.97	4.67	4.97	6.77
Jharkhand	2.67	1.79	4.11	15.32
Orissa	3.64	2.42	5.65	4.18
Uttar Pradesh	16.42	10.38	7.18	5.48
Bihar	8.20	2.99	1.87	1.17
Low-income States	**44.53**	**28.94**	**28.72**	**41.23**
Arunachal Pradesh	0.11	0.11	0.39	0.12
Assam	2.63	1.89	4.73	3.26
Himachal Pradesh	0.60	0.91	2.93	0.68
Jammu & Kashmir	1.00	1.03	1.98	0.55
Manipur	0.23	0.23	0.04	0.06
Meghalaya	0.24	0.23	0.03	0.12
Mizoram	0.08	0.11	0.06	0.06
Nagaland	0.19	0.25	0.19	0.06
Sikkim	0.06	0.07	0.28	0.06
Tripura	0.32	0.39	0.27	0.12
Uttaranchal	0.84	0.83	2.07	1.35
Special Category States	**6.28**	**6.04**	**12.98**	**6.46**
Total	**100.00**	**100.00**	**100.00**	**100.00**

Source: TFC Report and Public Enterprise Survey, Vol. 1, 2003–4.

Another important initiative taken by the Government of India was to expand the network of bank branches to rural areas and poorer regions, particularly after the nationalization of the major commercial banks in 1969. However, the relative density of commercial banks in poorer regions continues to be lower than in middle- and high-income states. Furthermore, the expansion of banking network has served to transfer household savings of poorer states for investment in more affluent states. Table 5.3 shows the credit–deposit ratios in the fourteen major states in descending order of their ratios as seen in 2004–5. Interesting observations that can be made from the table are as follows: (i) By and large although credit–deposit ratios were higher in more developed states, there are important exceptions. Punjab, Haryana, and Gujarat are high-income states but the ratios in these states were much below average. (ii) The credit–deposit ratios were generally higher in states with relatively more manufacturing activity. Thus states such as Tamil Nadu and Maharashtra had much higher credit–deposit ratios as compared to Punjab, Haryana, Uttar Pradesh, and Bihar. The ratios in the last two states were abysmal and, in part, this reflects poor governance in these states. (iii) The relative position has changed very little from

TABLE 5.3
Credit–Deposit Ratios in Indian States

	1980	1995	2001	2004
Tamil Nadu	0.94	0.91	0.91	0.90
Maharashtra	0.79	0.70	0.85	0.81
Andhra Pradesh	0.74	0.76	0.63	0.68
Karnataka	0.75	0.68	0.59	0.63
Rajasthan	0.68	0.46	0.48	0.57
Gujarat	0.58	0.47	0.49	1.13
Madhya Pradesh	0.56	0.53	0.47	0.48
West Bengal	0.60	0.54	0.44	0.49
Kerala	0.68	0.45	0.43	0.47
Haryana	0.72	0.47	0.42	0.48
Orissa	0.59	0.54	0.41	0.54
Punjab	0.43	0.41	0.41	0.43
Uttar Pradesh	0.42	0.35	0.28	0.33
Bihar	0.41	0.33	0.24	0.26
Average	0.65	0.58	0.57	0.63
Coeff. of Var.	0.22	0.27	0.32	0.37
Coeff. of Var. (SDP)	0.32	0.40	0.36	0.41
Corr$^{n.}$ with per capita SDP	0.11	0.18	0.59	0.48

Sources: RBI Bulletins; National Accounts Statistics; and Census of India. Figures for Bihar, Madhya Pradesh, and Uttar Pradesh in 2001 include those from Jharkhand, Chhattisgarh, and Uttarakhand, respectively.

1980. Exception to this are Kerala, Gujarat, and West Bengal, which have moved down in their rankings substantially. (iv) The ratios have shown a steady decline in every state (except Maharashtra) indicating that commercial banks, as a policy, tend to employ their resources increasingly in other ways of earning income including investment in government securities. The decline has been particularly sharp in the two poorest states of Bihar and Uttar Pradesh. These states have the lowest credit–deposit ratios and they have been showing sharp declines.

INTERGOVERNMENTAL TRANSFERS[1]

Volume and Composition

Central transfers constitute a significant part of state finances as shown in Table 5.4. In per capita terms, at constant (1981–2) prices central transfers to states increased by over 2.5 times from Rs 77 in 1975–6 to Rs 194 in 1993–4 and declined marginally thereafter, owing to fiscal compression. It is also seen from the table that until 1993–4, growth of transfers was faster than both the centre's and states' own revenues. In the latter half of the 1990s, however, these transfers decelerated and the share of transfers in states' expenditures declined.

A notable feature of the transfer system in India is the existence of multiple channels. The constitutional body—the Finance Commission—recommends devolution of proceeds from central taxes to states and gives them grants for their non-plan requirements. Second, the Planning Commission gives assistance for implementing development plans. After the Twelfth Finance Commission's (TFC) recommendations, the assistance is confined to grants and central loans given to states for plan purposes have been discontinued since 2005–6. Finally, various ministries give their counterparts in the states grants for specified projects (central-sector and centrally sponsored schemes).

The trends in the relative shares of the three channels of central transfers[2] to states since the Fourth Five Year Plan, as presented in Table 5.5, show some interesting features. First, the share of Finance Commission transfers in the total declined from 65 per cent during the Fourth Plan (1969–74) to a little over 62 per cent during the Eighth Plan. Although it increased to 65 per cent in the Ninth Plan, in 2003–4 it was lower at 59 per cent. Second, the proportion of formula-based transfers given by the Finance Commission and the Planning Commission has declined and that of discretionary transfers has increased in recent years.

TABLE 5.4
Trends in Central Transfers to States

Years	Per capita transfers (1993–4 Rupees)	Percentage of transfers to GDP	Percentage of transfers to central revenues	Percentage of transfers to state revenues	Percentage of transfers to state expenditure
1975–6	198.2	3.67	31.8	38.64	44.8
1980–1	272.2	4.84	34.8	43.81	47.5
1985–6	381	5.55	40.98	45.62	46.42
1990–1	449.9	4.66	39.06	38.37	30.85
1995–6	465.3	4.28	35.55	38.60	31.06
1996–7	490.5	4.28	35.40	39.97	31.83
1997–8	570.7	4.86	38.90	44.91	35.33
1998–9	456.0	3.73	32.25	37.69	26.29
1999–2000	486.4	3.79	30.23	36.46	25.05
2000–1	562.7	4.29	34.89	40.41	29.22
2001–2	584.5	4.21	35.04	38.64	28.14
2002–3	533.0	4.07	32.48	37.95	27.63
2003–4	596.2	4.20	32.60	37.48	26.93
2004–5	628.6	4.26	33.43	37.24	28.82
2005–6	750.3	4.74	36.69	39.00	32.46
2006–7	840.1	5.06	37.85	39.13	32.06
2007–8*	1031.9	5.38	34.97	40.16	33.56

Note: * Revised estimates.
Source: Indian Economic Statistics/Public Finance Statistics, Ministry of Finance, Government of India.

The share of grants given under central-sector and centrally sponsored schemes increased from 12 per cent during the Fourth Plan to 17 per cent in 1990–1 before declining to about 15 per cent in 2003–4. However, there has been steady increase in assistance in state plan schemes from 13 per cent in the Fourth Plan period to 20 per cent in the Ninth Plan and 22 per cent in 2003–4. More importantly, until 1991–2, the assistance under state plan schemes was predominantly formula based as 80 per cent of the grants were given according to the formula devised by the National Development Council (NDC).[3] In subsequent years, however, the discretionary component of these transfers has shown steady increases with the introduction of assistance to schemes such as the accelerated irrigation programme, accelerated power development, Rashtriya Shram Vikas Yojana, Indira Vikas Yojana, Prime Minister's Gram Sadak Yojana, and advanced central assistance to externally aided projects. Thus the formula component of state plan grants declined from about 80 per cent in 1990–1 to 40 per cent in 2003–4 (Figure 5.3).

TABLE 5.5

Composition of Central Transfers to States

(Rs billion)

Plan periods/years	Finance Commission transfers			Plan grants			Other grants	Total
	Tax devolution	Grants	Total	State plan scheme	Central scheme	Total		
Fourth Plan	54.4	10.3	64.6	12.9	11.6	24.4	11.1	100.0
Fifth Plan (1974–9)	50.2	17.1	67.3	17.7	11.7	29.4	3.3	100.0
Sixth Plan (1980–5)	57.0	5.1	62.1	17.7	16.6	34.3	3.6	100.0
Seventh Plan (1985–90)	54.2	6.9	61.0	17.0	18.1	35.1	3.9	100.0
Annual Plan (1990–1)	52.2	10.5	62.7	17.4	16.8	34.2	3.1	100.0
Eighth Plan (1992–7)	55.6	6.2	61.8	20.4	15.4	35.8	2.5	100.0
Ninth Plan (1997–2001)	58.7	6.0	64.7	20.0	10.6	27.1	4.9	100.0
2002–3	55.4	8.3	63.7	19.4	10.4	29.7	6.6	100.0
2003–4	51.7	6.9	58.7	21.5	14.7	36.3	5.0	100.0

Source: State Finances: A Study of Budgets (various years), RBI.

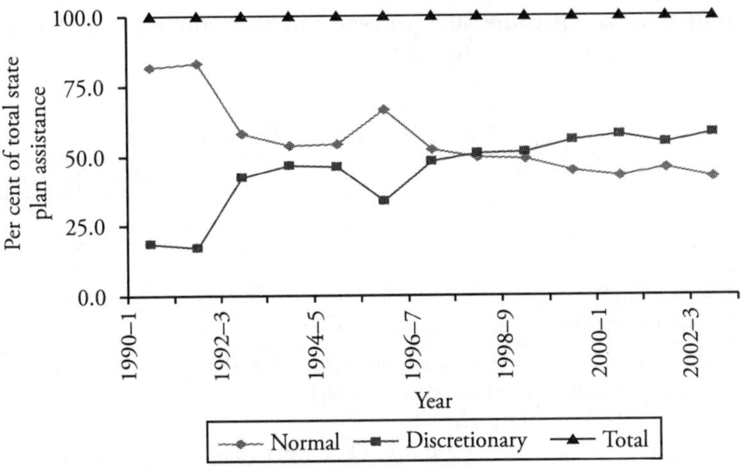

FIGURE 5.3: Components of State Plan Assistance

Source: Expenditure Budget, Vol. 1 (various years), Ministry of Finance, Government of India.

Finance Commission Transfers

Finance Commission transfers comprise tax devolution and grants given to meet non-plan expenditure requirements. With the emergence of the Planning Commission as a major dispenser of plan assistance, the Finance Commissions' role was restricted to meeting the non-plan current expenditure requirements of the states. The approach of the Finance Commissions to determining transfers consists of (i) assessing the overall budgetary requirements of the centre and states to determine the volume of resources that can be transferred during the period of their recommendation; (ii) forecasting states' own current revenues and non-plan current expenditures; (iii) determining the states' share in central tax revenues and distributing them between the states based on a formula; (iv) filling the post-devolution projected gaps between non-plan current expenditures and revenues with grants. This is known as the 'gap-filling' approach. The TFC has made the recommendations for the five years beginning April 2005.

The 80th Constitutional Amendment replaced the devolution of selective central taxes by general tax sharing; with the substitution of general tax sharing for sharing of individual taxes, separate assignment of additional excise duties has been discontinued. Thus the TFC has recommended the distribution of 30.5 per cent of the net proceeds of central taxes. The entire 30.5 per cent is to be distributed according to a uniform formula given in Table 5.6.

TABLE 5.6
Criteria and Relative Weights for Tax Devolution: TFC

Criterion	Weight (per cent)
1. Population	25
2. Income (distance method)*	50
3. Area	10
4. Tax Effort**	7.5
5. Fiscal Discipline***	7.5

Notes: * The distance method is given by: $(Y_h - Y_i)P_i/\Sigma_i (Y_h - Y_i)P_i$ where, Y_i and Y_h represent per capita SDP of the ith and the highest income state, respectively, and P_i is the population of the ith state.

** Tax Effort (η) is estimated as $(\eta) = (T_i/Y_i)/(0.5/Y_i)$ where, T_i is the per capita tax revenue collected by the ith state and Y_i is the per capita state domestic product of the ith state.

*** estimated as the improvement in the ratio of own revenue of a state to its revenue expenditures divided by a similar ratio for all states averaged for the period 1966–99 over 1991–3.

Sources: *Report of the Twelfth Finance Commission*, Ministry of Finance, Government of India. p. 133.

An important feature of tax devolution recommended by the Finance Commissions is that, while the criteria adopted for distribution are different from the principles of grants-in-aid, nowhere is it made clear that the economic objectives of the two instruments are different (Rao and Sen 1996: Ch. 6). Tax devolution is recommended mainly on the basis of general economic indicators (Table 5.6) and grants are given to offset the residuary fiscal disadvantages of the states as quantified by the Commissions. Further, assigning weights to contradictory factors like 'backwardness' and 'contribution' in the same formula has rendered the achievement of the overall objective of offsetting revenue and cost disabilities difficult.

Over the years, attempts have been made to improve the degree of equalization in the transfer scheme by assigning higher weight to per capita state domestic product (SDP) either in the 'inverse' or 'distance' form by successive Commissions. Yet population has continued to receive the largest implicit and explicit weights, though the last Commission has significantly reduced explicit weight to this factor. Equally important is the unreliability of tax effort and index of fiscal discipline. In a tax system that is predominantly origin based, there can be significant inter-state tax exportation and the tax effort indicator ignores this phenomenon. Besides, there are a number of other factors in addition to per capita SDP that determine taxable capacity of a state. The changes in the ratios of own revenues to revenue expenditures relative to all-state average and their changes over time can occur due to factors totally extraneous to states' own efforts at fiscal discipline. Equalization has been further blunted by the terms of reference, which require the Commissions to use the 1971 population figures wherever it is used in the transfer formula. This is because the Parliament has passed a resolution that wherever population is used for inter-state distribution, the 1971 figures should be used to provide the states incentive for population control. The important questions are first, whether the federal transfer mechanism should be employed as an instrument of population policy and second, even if it is, why states with high population growth not because of high fertility rate but due to migration should be penalized. Population is an important 'need' variable and not using current population can exaggerate horizontal equity.

This approach has been subjected to criticism. First, none of the Finance Commissions assessed the overall resource position and requirements of the centre on any objective basis. Second, the transfers made by the Finance Commissions were not designed specifically to offset fiscal disadvantages of states arising from lower revenue raising capacity and higher unit cost of public services. While tax devolution is determined on the basis of general economic indicators, grants are given on the basis of projected post-devolution budgetary gaps. The introduction of the backwardness factor in tax devolution has had the effect of equalization, but the transfer system is not specifically targeted towards fiscally disadvantaged states. Finally, it is argued that the 'gap-filling' methodology has led to both inequity and disincentives for fiscal management in states.

The critical element in the Finance Commissions' methodology is projections. This is done by taking base-year actual collections (or their estimates) of own revenues and non-plan revenue expenditures of the states, standardizing them, and projecting them using normative growth rates determined according to the fiscal restructuring plan. Some normative estimates of maintenance expenditures in the base-year estimates are used as well. Normative estimates are also taken for the return from investments in public enterprises. Indeed, the projections thus made were never realized. The gap thus estimated between projected revenue receipts and non-plan expenditures was first filled in by tax devolution and the remaining gap by grants.

This methodology has attracted two important criticisms, which impact on both incentives and equity in the transfer system. The first is that taking the base-year numbers, standardized non-plan expenditures did not take note of the differences in the existing level of services. The effect of the 'tyranny of base year' was to perpetuate the existing differences in expenditures on various public services. The poorer states with low resource base (even after the transfers), continued to have low gaps and, hence, low levels of transfers relative to their fiscal disability. In other words, the relevant base should have been 'fiscal capacity' and non-plan revenue expenditure 'needs' and not actual revenues and non-plan revenue expenditures. The sprinkling of norms by the Finance Commissions in the growth rates, maintenance expenditures, and public enterprises does not amount to estimating revenue capacities and needs. Therefore, it is argued that the methodology has failed to offset the fiscal disability of poorer states.

Equally important is the problem of incentives. The methodology is characterized as 'fiscal dentistry'—of filling in budgetary projected cavities between revenues and non-plan expenditures. It is argued that the methodology has no incentive for greater tax effort or fiscal austerity as more transfers will be received by the states with larger gaps. In fact, to a large extent, deterioration in state finances is attributed to the gap-filling approach followed by the Finance Commissions.

There has been considerable concern at the Finance Commissions following the 'gap-filling' approach and its possible disincentives for fiscal management in states. This was the reason for modifying the terms of reference of the Ninth Finance Commission to follow a 'normative approach'. The Commission estimated cost functions to measure expenditure needs of states. However, the subsequent Commissions thought the approach too difficult to adopt and reverted to the 'gap-filling' methodology. Concern about poor incentive was the reason behind the additional terms of reference to the Eleventh Finance Commission to 'draw a monitorable fiscal reforms program aimed at reduction of revenue deficit of the state and recommended the manner in which the grants to the States...may be linked to progress in implementing the program.' The Commission recommended a scheme of pooling 15 per cent of revenue-deficit grants and adding an equal amount to it to create an incentive fund and distributing the fund based on fulfilling the required reduction in the ratio of revenue deficits to total revenue receipts of the states.

The TFC, which examined the scheme, recommended its discontinuation due to design problems. It continued the 'gap-filling' approach and sought to incentivize the system by linking the debt restructuring scheme to passing of the fiscal responsibility acts (FRA) and write-off of loan repayable to the central government during the ensuing five years (2005–10) to reduction in revenue deficits. The equity built into the tax devolution formula, the assessment of revenues and expenditures along with upgradation grants for education and healthcare are supposed to take care of equity.[4]

Plan Transfers

The assistance given by the Planning Commission comprises both grants and loans. In earlier years, both the volume and the loan grant component was project based, but since 1969 assistance has been allocated on the basis of an NDC formula (Gadgil formula). At present, 30 per cent of the funds are kept apart for special category states and distributed among them on the basis of plan projects formulated by them, 90 per cent of the assistance is given by way of grants and the remainder as loans. The 70 per cent of the funds available to the major states are distributed with 60 per cent weight assigned to population, 25 per cent to per capita SDP, 7.5 per cent to fiscal management, and the remaining 7.5 per cent to special problems of these states (Table 5.7). Thus plan transfers are determined independently of the required plan investments, their sectoral composition, and the resources available to the states. Until 2004–5, 30 per cent of the resources were given as grants and the remainder as loans. The TFC, however, recommended the discontinuation of central loans to states and from 2005–6, central

TABLE 5.7
Formula for Distributing State Plan Assistance

Variable	Weight
Population (1971)	60.0
Per capita SDP, of which,	25.0
(i) Deviation from the average to the states below average per capita SDP	20.0
(ii) 'Distance' from the highest per capita SDP for all the general category states.	5.0
Fiscal performance, of which,	7.5
(i) Tax effort	2.5
(ii) Fiscal management	2.5
(iii) National objectives	2.5
(iv) Special problems	7.5
Total	100.0

Source: Planning Commission, Government of India.

assistance for plans consists of only grants and the states are required to raise balance resources from the market.

Assistance to Central-sector and Centrally Sponsored Schemes

This component of transfers is given for specified purposes with or without matching requirements. Grants for central-sector schemes are given to the states to execute central projects that are entirely funded by the centre. Centrally sponsored schemes, on the other hand, are shared cost programmes falling within the states' ambit with uniform matching ratios across the states, but varying with the projects. There are more than 200 schemes at present. These transfers have attracted the sharpest criticism due to their discretionary nature and the conditionality attached to them. They accounted for about 40 per cent of total plan assistance and about 15 per cent of total current transfers were given to these schemes in 2003–4 (Table 5.5).

Financing Infrastructure at State Level: The Loans

Borrowing is an important source of financing infrastructure. Until 1987–8, government savings at state level did contribute to financing of some capital expenditures. Since then, however, with increasing dissavings at state level, the borrowing is used not only to finance capital expenditures, but also a significant part of current expenditures of the states. In 1998–9 for example, almost one-half of the states' borrowing is used to finance capital expenditure.

The states' liabilities consist of central government loans, market borrowings, share of small savings collections, and provident funds, deposit accounts, etc. Central loans constitute 60 per cent of states' indebtedness. These loans were accumulated mainly for financing the plans under the Gadgil formula, under which 70 per cent of plan assistance to non-special category states and 10 per cent of assistance to special category states was given as loans. Since 2005–6, based on the recommendation of the TFC, the central government has discontinued the practice of advancing loans to states for plan purposes. Other central loans consist of ways and means advances (WMA) and share of small savings collections.[5]

The states can also borrow from the market. However, if a state is indebted to the centre, it has to take central permission before borrowing. As all the states are indebted to the centre, the Ministry of Finance, Planning Commission, and the Reserve Bank of India determine market borrowing of the states. In determining the volume of market borrowings, volume of repayments, the plan investments decided upon, and the volume of indebtedness of each state are taken into account. In 1998–9, market borrowings constituted 22 per cent of states' indebtedness.

Subscription to state government loans by the banking system constitutes a part of the statutory liquidity ratio (SLR) requirement. The commercial banks are required to maintain 24 per cent of their investible funds in government bonds including state government bonds. Thus the investible resources of the banking system are pre-empted for government consumption and investment. The interest rates on government bonds are significantly below market rates.

Shortcomings of Intergovernmental Transfers Summarized

The design and implementation of central transfer to states suffer from a number of shortcomings. First, multiple agencies with overlapping jurisdictions have blurred the overall objectives of transfers. Second, accommodating different interests has unduly complicated the transfer formula by Finance and Planning Commissions. Third, the transfer system is not well targeted to achieving equalization and ensuring minimum service levels in the states. Fourth, central transfers have disincentive effect on fiscal management in states. The design and implementation of centrally sponsored schemes have served the objectives and have tended to multiply state-level bureaucracy and distort states' own allocations. Most importantly, segregation of state budgets into plan and non-plan categories and a compartmentalized view has contributed to complexity in expenditure decisions. This has been further complicated by the eagerness to enhance plan spending, often by raising resources through indiscriminate means or by compressing more productive spending on social services and operation and maintenance of assets.

Central Transfers to States and Inter-state Equity

Degree of Equalization

Strict adherence to economic rationale would require that transfers be designed to offset revenue and cost disabilities. However, actual transfer systems fall short of this ideal, as historical and political factors are also important in determining them. However, the question of the extent to which the economic objectives of intergovernmental transfer policy are met is important and needs to be analysed. In what follows, an attempt is made to analyse the equity implications of central transfers to states in India.

Analysis of central transfers shows a fair degree of inter-state redistribution. Central transfers vary inversely with the level of per capita NSDP (Figure 5.4). The cross-section income elasticity of aggregate transfers in 2002–3 was –0.54 (Table 5.8). However, equalization in the transfer system was entirely due to redistribution in Finance Commission transfers. The elasticity of Finance Commission transfers with respect to the GSDP in 1997–8 was –0.80. In contrast, Plan grants and grants for centrally sponsored schemes did not achieve significant equalization. Although, by and large, the transfer system may be considered equitable, the absolute value of elasticity is low. On an average, per capita transfers were higher by 0.54 per cent when the per capita SDP was lower by 1 per cent. This shows that the transfer system on the whole has an equalizing impact, but is not entirely designed to offset fiscal disabilities.

Despite equalizing impact of intergovernmental transfers, per capita revenue accruals and, therefore, per capita expenditures across states continue to be significantly higher in states with higher per capita SDP as may be inferred from Figure 5.5. Thus the distribution of per capita revenue accruals as well as per capita expenditures across states has a positive slope when they are plotted against per capita SDP. It is also seen that the slope of revenue accruals, which includes central

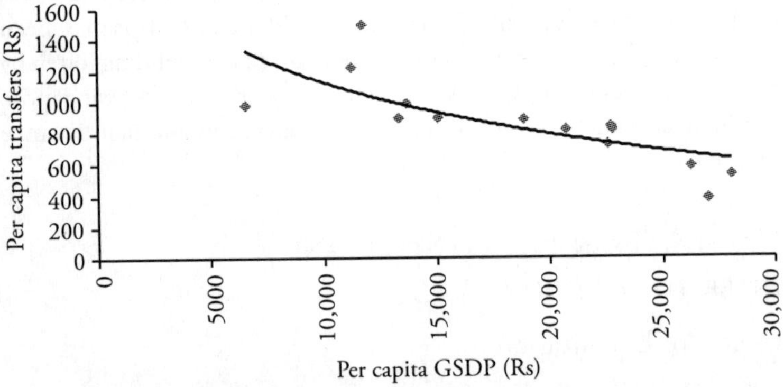

Figure 5.4: Equalization in Central Transfers to States, 2002–3
Source: NIPFP Databank.

Table 5.8
Equalization in Fiscal Transfer System in India, 2002–3

1. Major states	Finance Commission		Plan transfers			Total transfers
	Tax devolution	Total transfers	State plan schemes	Centrally sponsored schemes	Total plan transfers	
Intercept	13.9855*	13.9918*	7.3504*	8.1765*	8.7939*	11.9334*
	(9.5600)	(8.8145)	(3.3882)	(2.3465)	(3.4016)	(8.0616)
Coefficient	–0.7999*	–0.7960*	–0.2722	–0.3737	–0.3544	–0.5375*
	–(5.3244)	–(4.8829)	–(1.2217)	–(1.0444)	–(1.3348)	–(3.5356)
$\bar{R}^2$	0.669*	0.6300*	0.0060	0.0060	0.0495	0.4340*

Notes: Estimated by employing the functional form: $\text{Ln } G = \alpha + \beta \text{ Ln } Y + \in$ where, G denotes different types of per capita transfers, Y represents per capita GSDP, α and β represent parameter estimates, and $\in$ is the error term.

* Significant at 1 per cent level.

Source: NIPFP Databank.

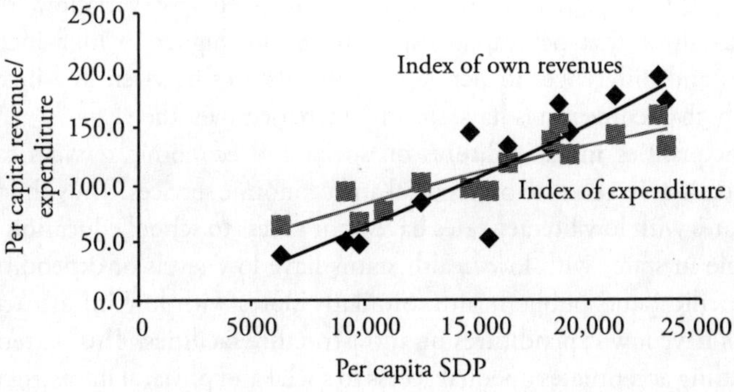

Figure 5.5(a): Equalization in Indian Fiscal Federalism, 1999–2000

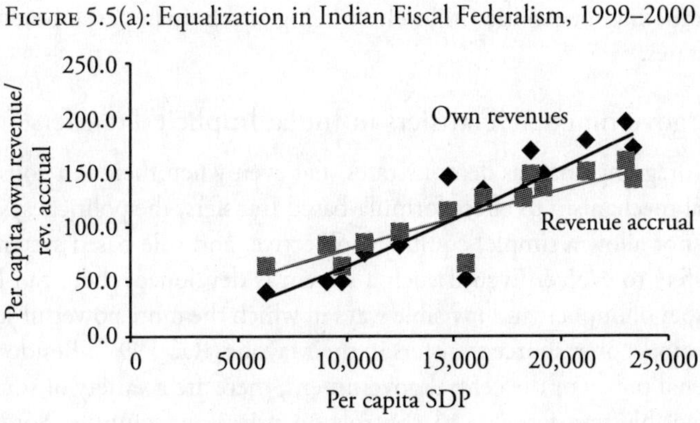

Figure 5.5(b): Equalization in Indian Federalism

Source: NIPFP Databank.

transfers, is only marginally different from that of states' own revenues. Thus although the transfer system as a whole is equalizing, the degree of equalization is not adequate to offset the fiscal disabilities arising from low revenue capacity of poorer states. As contradictory criteria are employed in the transfer system, fiscal disabilities are not entirely offset (Rao and Jena 2005).

The inability to offset fiscal disabilities has resulted in significant inter-state differences in spending on basic public services. The analysis of expenditures on basic social and economic services presented in Table 5.9 shows that inter-state differences in per capita expenditures are not only high but have increased. The coefficients of variation for per capita expenditures in education, health, as well as economic services have shown a steady increase during the last decade. It is also seen that per capita expenditures on education, health, total social services, economic services, as well as aggregate expenditures have always been high and significant. Together with increasing coefficients of variation, these results show that per capita expenditures are higher in high-income states and differences in per capita expenditures between low-income and high-income states have steadily increased over the years.

Inequalities in expenditures on social and economic services cause inequalities in access to basic social and economic services. Thus children in states with low literacy rates have poor access to school education and people in states with low health status have low levels of expenditures on medical and public health. Similarly states with low infrastructure levels have low expenditures on infrastructure facilities. This pattern of spending accentuates unequal access to social and physical infrastructure, exacerbating inequalities in levels of living and human development in the states.

Intergovernmental Transfers in India: Implicit Transfers

The foregoing analysis demonstrates that even when there is a constitutional mechanism to effect formula-based transfers, the political system may not allow a simple, equitable, objective, and rule-based system of transfers to evolve. Even if such a system is developed, there can be a number of implicit and invisible ways in which the more powerful states can impact on resource transfers in their favour (Rao 1997). Besides the regional policy of the central government, there are a variety of sources of invisible transfers due to controls on prices and outputs. Some of the important sources are: (i) inter-state tax exportation, (ii) subsidized lending by banking and financial institutions (this includes lending by

TABLE 5.9

Inter-state Differences in Expenditures on Public Services

Expenditure head	1995–6	2000–1	2001–2	2002–3	2003–4
1. Education					
a. Mean (Rs)	285.79	532.06	522.69	531.31	550.18
b. Coefficient of variation	0.35	0.45	0.40	0.47	0.48
c. Cor. coeff. with per capita NSDP	0.616	0.644	0.619	0.699	0.513
2. Medical and public health					
a. Mean	88.33	146.42	146.93	148.42	154.99
b. Coefficient of variation	0.27	0.45	0.36	0.34	0.35
c. Corr. coeff. with per capita NSDP	0.687	0.765	0.793	0.811	0.528
3. Social services					
a. Mean	575.48	1030.51	1033.23	1060.39	1136.11
b. Coefficient of variation	0.40	0.42	0.32	0.33	0.37
c. Corr. coeff. with per capita NSDP	0.841	0.763	0.812	0.852	0.716
4. Economic services					
a. Mean	514.74	827.85	821.69	854.21	1128.96
b. Coefficient of variation	0.38	0.58	0.49	0.42	0.34
c. Corr. coeff. with per capita NSDP	0.824	0.765	0.671	0.740	0.662
5. Development expenditure					
a. Mean	1090.23	1858.36	1854.92	1914.61	2265.07
b. Coefficient of variation	0.33	0.47	0.37	0.36	0.30
c. Corr. coeff. with per capita NSDP	0.872	0.794	0.791	0.828	0.865
6. Total expenditure					
a. Mean	1690.37	3059.30	3180.46	3348.41	3858.04
b. Coefficient of variation	0.37	0.45	0.34	0.36	0.31
c. Corr. coeff. with per capita NSDP	0.885	0.842	0.917	0.905	0.839

Source: Finance accounts of state governments, Comptroller and Auditor General, Government of India; Central Statistical Organisation, Government of Inida.

All-India Financial Institutions[6] (AIFIs) at below-market interest rates subsidized by the refinancing facility extended by the Reserve Bank of India, and priority-sector lending by commercial banks for specified activities like agriculture and rural development, industrial promotion, small-scale industry and exports); and (iii) subsidized borrowing by the states from the central government and the banking system. The main source of inter-regional transfers from lending to the governments comes from the stipulation to the banking system on the extent of their lendable resources to be held in government bonds at regulated interest rates (SLR), stipulation on the quantum of assistance to be given to the 'priority sector', and the distribution of seignorage or the profits of the Reserve Bank of India through the refinancing facilities given to the AIFI. I discuss the three sources of invisible transfers in some detail.

Inter-state Tax Exportation

Inter-state tax exportation arises from the levy of origin-based cascading-type sales taxation along with the taxation of inter-state sale of goods. The sales taxes levied by states are predominantly on the basis of origin, at the stage of manufacture or import. States also levy taxes on raw materials, intermediate inputs, and capital goods. In addition, inter-state sale is also taxed subject to the ceiling rate of 4 per cent.[7] In an economy where there is only limited internal and external competition, the tax is fully shifted forward, input taxes cascade on to inter-state sales tax, and, consequently, effective tax rate on inter-state sales is much higher than the 4 per cent nominally levied. This results in the exportation of the tax burden from more affluent producing states to consumers in poorer consuming states. When the exports of more developed states are larger than their imports, and the proportion of final goods in their exports too is higher, as in the Indian case (Rao and Singh 2005), the residents of poorer states end up paying taxes on larger volumes of imports and at higher effective rates.

Data on inter-state trade are not available and it is difficult to accurately arrive at the estimate of inter-state tax exportation. A comparison of consumption shares and sales tax shares, however, shows that the high-income states collect much higher share of sales taxes than their consumption shares.[8] While this cannot be entirely attributed to tax exportation and could partly indeed be due to lower tax effort in poorer states, the large and systematic difference points towards significant perverse transfer of resources through inter-state tax exportation.

Regional Transfers from Subsidized Lending by Financial Institutions

The pursuit of planned development strategy required the use of controls on prices and quantities. Important among these has been the distribution of credit to specified activities in the private sector by the banking and financial system at below-market interest rates. This includes credit given by the banking system to 'priority-sector' activities such as agriculture, small-scale enterprises, and exports, and refinancing facilities provided by the AIFI at subsidized rates. Priority-sector lending constituted about a third of total bank credit in 1995–6, and the subsidy element in these advances is significant. For example, interest rate on priority-sector borrowing in 1993–4 was 5.5 to 6.5 per cent as compared to the State Bank of India (SBI) long-term lending rate of 19 per cent. The quantum of subsidy implicit in the assistance given by the AIFI was significant in earlier years, as much of the profits of the Reserve Bank of India (RBI, seignorage) were used to provide a refinancing facility to these institutions, but the subsidy has declined since 1992–3 as the centre has been appropriating the profits of the RBI entirely.

A detailed analysis of priority-sector credit and financial assistance given by the AIFI shows that the distribution of both sources of lending is disproportionately in favour of high-income states. In the aggregate, these states with just about 19 per cent of population received 35 per cent of priority-sector lending given to agriculture, small enterprises, and exports and their share of assistance from the AIFI was 43 per cent. In contrast, the low-income states with almost 44 per cent of population received just about than 15 per cent of priority credit and 22 per cent of assistance from the AIFI. Thus the distribution of subsidized credit by the banking system and the AIFI has conferred disproportionate benefits to more advanced states.

Invisible Transfers from Subsidized Lending to States

The most important source of implicit transfers, however, is subsidized lending to the states. Loans from the central government alone contribute to almost 68 per cent of states' liabilities, the bulk of which was given for plan purposes under the Gadgil formula. Market borrowings constitute another 22 per cent, subscribed mainly by the banking system so as to fulfil the SLR requirements.[9] The extent and nature of intergovernmental transfers from this source depend upon the pattern of inter-state allocation of when loans to state governments or public enterprises run by the states are rescheduled and written off, implicit transfers do arise. Providing periodic relief such as the bail-out to the State Electricity Boards by providing a one-time settlement of their dues to central public-sector undertakings is a case in point. The states that gained from more from the scheme were the ones that had more accumulated defaults.

Implicit transfers are also involved in lending to states at below-market rates. In the past, this practice resulted in significant implicit inter-state transfers (Rao 1997). However, as the practice of central lending itself is being given up based on the TFC's recommendations, this source of implicit transfers is being phased out.

The sources of implicit transfer pointed out above are not the only ones and it is difficult to say whether they are the important ones. The transfers arise whenever there are controls on prices and quantities. The determination of procurement price, so long as it is higher than the market price enables resource transfers in favour of foodgrain-surplus states. The same is the case with cotton. So long as there are restrictions on imports and the prices are determined by government fiat rather than market forces, implicit transfers are inevitable.

Imbalance in regional development in India is a matter of serious concern and needs to be addressed not only to ensure balanced development of the country, but also to secure stability and progress of the federation. Unless this is addressed with a measure of urgency, the very federal fabric of the country could be threatened. While the equalization systems in place have helped to secure stability and integrity of the country so far, there poor access to even basic services, particularly in regions and for population groups with low levels of mobility.

Unequal access to social and physical infrastructure can be a serious source of inter-state inequalities in levels of living and human development. Private-sector investment tends to move to places where enabling environment is better and infrastructure availability is a major component of enabling environment. Even when these states are well-endowed with resources, these inequalities in infrastructure levels could threaten to lag them behind. Similarly, unequal access to quality public education and healthcare results in the more well-to-do sections quitting the public sector and only the poor clinging on to the publicly provided services. Given the low 'voice' of the poor, this threatens to deteriorate quality further and can be a cause of increasing educational and health inequalities. There is sufficient anecdotal evidence of low-quality social and economic services in poorer states. Combined with low expenditure levels, this could cause inequalities in service levels even more than the expenditure inequalities.

The analysis calls for reforms in the intergovernmental transfer system as well as further liberalizing reforms to minimize invisible transfers. It is also necessary to closely examine the allocative impact of various restrictions and controls on quantities and outputs to monitor the unintended consequences. It is important that invisible transfer arising from controls on quantities and outputs should not be a source of inequitable transfers.

Notes

1. A detailed analysis of the intergovernmental transfer system is available in Rao and Singh (2005).
2. There is a considerable amount of confusion in the term 'transfers'. In Indian fiscal literature, central loans to states are also considered transfers. Such transactions involve transfers only to the extent of any interest subsidy or write-off of loans. Here, I have only taken account of tax devolution and grants as transfers. Transfers arising from interest subsidy, guarantees, and loan write-off are not taken account of.
3. The formula and its modifications from time to time were adopted on the basis of consensus by the National Development Council (NDC). The NDC is constituted by the cabinet ministers at the centre, chief ministers of the states, and the members of the Planning Commission and is chaired by the Prime Minister.
4. For detailed evaluation of the Report of the TFC, see Rao and Jena (2005).
5. Small savings consist of post office savings in national saving certificates. The centre advances two-thirds of net collection of small savings to states on the basis of origin.
6. All-India financial institutions refer to all-India development banks (Industrial Development Bank of India, Industrial Finance Corporation of India, Industrial Credit and Investment Corporation of India, Small Industries Development Bank of India, Industrial Reconstruction Bank of India, SCICI) specialized financial institutions (RCTC, TDICI, TFCI), and investment institutions (LIC, UTI, GIC).
7. The ceiling rate is applicable only when the transaction takes place between registered dealers. If the sale is from a registered dealer in the exporting state to a non-registered dealer in the importing state, the ceiling rate applicable is 10 per cent.
8. For details, see Rao and Singh (2005: Ch. 9).

9. At present, the SLR stipulation requires commercial banks to keep 25 per cent of their demand and time liabilities in eligible assets like central and state government bonds. In fact, the financial-sector reforms brought down the SLR from 38.5 per cent in 1991–2 to 25 per cent in 1996–7.

References

Barro, Robert and Xavier Sala-i-Martin (1991). 'Convergence across States and Regions', *Brookings Papers on Economic Activity*, 1, pp. 107–81.

Boadway, R.W. and F. Flatters (1982). *Equalization in a Federal State: An Economic Analysis*. Economic Council of Canada, Ottawa: Canadian Government Publishing Center.

Buchanan, J.M. (1950). 'Federalism and Fiscal Equity', *American Economic Review*, September, 40(4): 421–32.

Evans, P. and G. Karras (1996). 'Do Economies Converge? Evidence from a Panel of U.S. States', *Review of Economics and Statistics*, 78, August, pp. 384–8.

Rao, M. Govinda (1997). 'Invisible Transfers in Indian Federalism', *Public Finances/Finances Publiques*, 52(3): 299–316.

Rao, M. Govinda and Pratap Jena (2005). 'Balancing Stability, Equity and Efficiency', *Economic and Political Weekly*, 40(31): 3405–12.

Rao, M. Govinda and Tapas Sen (1996). *Fiscal Federalism in India: Theory and Practice*. New Delhi: Macmillan Publishers.

Rao, M. Govinda and Nirvikar Singh (2005). *Political Economy of Federalism in India*. New Delhi: Oxford University Press.

6

Resource Endowment, Fiscal Flows, and Regional Equity in Indian Federalism

M. Govinda Rao and Subrata Mandal

Introduction

There has been considerable research over the years on what factors cause differences in the growth rate between regions and nations and why inequalities in the standards of living between persons, regions, and nations have continued to persist and even accentuated. In spite of this, the growth process remains to be understood better. The growth process is determined by the resources endowments and technological progress, and understanding the dynamics of the growth process requires analysing the impact of policies and institutions. Endowment of resources and volume of investments made can provide only a partial explanation for the differences in levels of incomes and their growth rates. The impact of the type of policies pursued and the responsiveness of the institutions are equally, if not more, important for they impact on the structure of incentives which in turn determines the volume of investments, efficient use of resources, and productivity growth.

Ironically, while the literature emphasizes the importance of natural resources in determining the levels of living and growth rates, history is replete with instances where the people in the regions and countries with abundant natural resources actually suffer low levels of living, whereas those in countries poorly endowed enjoy high levels of prosperity. Glaring examples of the former are the countries in sub-Saharan Africa; the examples of Israel and even some of the high performing Asian economies exemplify the latter. The phenomenon of a country or a region rich in natural resources and yet suffering from low level of income and growth rate is referred to as the 'Dutch disease' in literature. The rich endowment of mineral resources and its predominance in exports tends to overvalue the exchange rate, adversely impacting on the competitiveness of the manufacturing sector (Cordon and Neary 1982). At a more general level, resource abundance could cause complacency, low level of technical efficiency, and productivity. In particular, if the structure of incentives generated by the type of policies and institutions does not promote contestable competition, efficiency, and growth, the mere existence of resources would not lead to economic betterment of the population. Of course, generalizations on the phenomenon is inappropriate and there is no logical reason to show that abundance of natural resources can pose inherent disadvantages to the country, and the entire thing boils down to proper economic management, including exchange rate management.

The phenomenon of lagging regions with low level of incomes and growth rates and high concentration of poverty even with rich resource endowment is not uncommon even within a country. In India, for example, about 40 per cent of the population lives in the six states of Bihar, Chhattisgarh, Jharkhand, Madhya Pradesh, Orissa, and Uttar Pradesh but they account for only 20 per cent of income generation. It is also seen that while the economy has been registering high growth rates, these low income states have registered growth rates much lower than the average. Similar trends are seen in human development indicators. Thus, not only do these states have low incomes, but also disparities between them and the rest of the country have shown a divergent trend. Sustainable and inclusive growth acceleration in the country requires that constraints for growth in these states are identified and appropriate policy and institutional changes are brought about.

There are a number of factors determining the level of incomes and their growth rates in a country or regions within a country. These include the volume of capital including endowment of factors like natural resources, technical efficiency in combining the factors, level of technology used, and the nature of institutions. Also, the institutional environment determines the availability of capital, technical efficiency, and technological progress. This chapter attempts to analyse why despite abundance of natural resources, some of the states in India have remained poor and have registered low growth rates, what policy and institutional reforms are required to accelerate growth in the lagging regions and states and to promote balanced and inclusive growth in the country. The next section analyses inter-state disparities in the levels of living and growth rates and also the differences in social and human development indicators, and identifies the states well endowed with natural resources and yet poor. The section on 'Lagging Regions, Central Investments, and Intergovernmental Transfers' examines the various causes determining the growth rates in different factors such as resource endowments, infrastructure facilities, and volume of public and private investments. The section also speculates on the nature of institutions in these states and the constraints posed by them. The last section attempts to answer the question: Why are the people residing in well-endowed states poor?

Pattern of Regional Development in India

Table 6.1 presents select development indicators of the non-special category states in India for a recent year. Together, non-special category states have 93.7 per cent of population of the country and generate 94 per cent of the share of the total GSDP. The reason for not considering special category states in this analysis is that the problems of development in these states are different and in many ways unique from those of the non-special category states and need to be considered separately. More specifically, the constraints on development in special category states are from mountainous terrain, sparse population, low institutional capacity, poor infrastructure, lack of markets and, connectivity—different from the non-special category states.

The analysis of the per capita GSDP in non-special category states presented in Table 6.1 shows that in six states per capita GSDP was less than 20 per cent of the average. These states are Bihar (and its newly carved state of Jharkhand), Madhya Pradesh (and its newly carved state of Chhattisgarh), Orissa, and Uttar Pradesh. In other words, Chhattisgarh and Jharkhand, until they were created in 2001, were a part of Madhya Pradesh and Bihar, respectively, and therefore it is important to consider them along with their parent states. The population share in the six states is 40 per cent, but they generate less than 20 per cent of GSDP. Not only do these states have low per capita incomes, they also experienced low growth rates of GSDP during 1993–2004, causing divergence in per capita incomes between these states and others over the years. It is also seen that almost 56 per cent of the poor are concentrated in these states and their poverty ratio is significantly higher than the rest of the country. In terms of human development too, these states have lagged behind the rest. In fact, in terms of various components of human development, namely, literacy rate, life expectancy, and infant mortality, the performance of these states is far behind the others.

Table 6.1
Pattern of Regional Development in India

	Population (millions) 2002–3	Average per capita GSDP 1999–2002	Growth rate 1993–2004	Poverty ratio 1999	Human development ratio 1999
Bihar	86.4	6539	4.4	42.6	0.367
Uttar Pradesh	172.3	10,798	3.7	31.15	0.388
Orissa	37.6	11,234	3.94	47.15	0.404
Jharkhand	27.9	11,717	4.9	NA	0.367
Madhya Pradesh	62.4	13,340	3.99	37.43	0.394
Chhattisgarh	21.5	13,710	3.42	NA	0.394
Rajasthan	58.6	15,059	5.57	15.28	0.424
West Bengal	82.3	17,377	6.9	27.02	0.472
Andhra Pradesh	77.8	18,869	6.02	15.77	0.416
Karnataka	54.1	20,703	7.24	20.44	0.478
Kerala	32.3	22,824	5.26	12.72	0.638
Tamil Nadu	63.7	22,587	4.69	21.12	0.531
Gujarat	52.2	22,708	5.72	14.07	0.479
Haryana	22.1	26,256	6.03	8.74	0.509
Maharashtra	99.9	26,994	4.72	25.02	0.523
Punjab	25.0	28,030	4.28	6.16	0.537
Non-Special Category States	**977.7**	**17,022**	**5.13**	**25.97**	**0.467**
All States	**1043.62**	**16,978**	**5.7**	**26.1**	**0.469**

Sources: 1. Statistical Abstract of India, Central Statistical Organisation, Government of India.
2. Planning Commission, Government of India.

Interestingly, the six lagging states have abundance of natural resources. A large proportion of the undivided states of Uttar Pradesh and Bihar[1] is under the Indo-Gangetic plain and covered by fertile alluvial soil and has tremendous irrigation potential. The large river systems in Orissa and Madhya Pradesh have similarly provided livelihood systems to the majority of population. Both undivided states of Bihar and Madhya Pradesh and Orissa are rich in mineral deposits. The states of Orissa and Madhya Pradesh also have significant proportion of areas covered by forests.

The rich endowment of natural resources in the six lagging states is brought out in Table 6.2. Although the gross cropped area in these states is marginally lower than their population share, this is mainly due to the fact that more than proportionate share of their land area is covered by forests and deposits of major minerals such as coal and bauxite. Even so, states such as Madhya Pradesh and Orissa have gross cropped areas more than their shares of population. These states also have more than proportionate cropped area under irrigation. However, much of this is under natural irrigation from the perennial river systems. Not surprisingly, despite the high proportion of irrigated area, the productivity of land in these states is low. First, much of the irrigation in these states is natural and there have been very little investments in both agriculture and irrigation in these states. Second, a large proportion of land is under perennial flood, particularly in northern Bihar. Poor agricultural extension and poor input-use management are other reasons for low agricultural productivity.

TABLE 6.2

Natural Resource Endowment in Lagging States, 2004

	Population share (2004)	Share in gross cropped area	Share in irrigated area	Share of forest area	Share in coal deposits	Share in mineral output
Bihar	8.28	5.27	6.51	0.79	0.06	1.24
Jharkhand	2.67	*	*	3.25	29.17	8.59
Madhya Pradesh	5.98	10.29	8.50	10.9	7.80	5.79
Chhattisgarh	2.05	3.38	2.07	7.76	16.36	7.22
Orissa	3.6	4.13	3.47	7.46	24.48	5.75
Uttar Pradesh	16.51	12.48	22.89	2.06	0.42	4.02
Total–6 States	39.10	35.65	43.45	32.22	78.29	32.61
Other States	60.9	64.35	56.55	67.88	21.71	67.39
All India	100.0	100.0	100.0	100.0	100.0	100.0

Note: * Included in Bihar.

Source: Statistical Abstract, Central Statistical Organisation, Government of India.

Madhya Pradesh, Chhattisgarh, and Orissa are the states with more than proportionate share of forest area. These are also the states with large concentration of tribal population. Providing forest cover to the country is a national public good. Given the Supreme Court decision restricting the felling of the trees, the states have lost an important source of non-tax revenue. Furthermore, the restriction on logging has meant closure of significant economic activity related to major forest produce, particularly wood industries. Further, area under forests is not available for cultivation. Besides, state governments have to incur considerable amount of expenditure in maintaining forests. Thus, these states, particularly Madhya Pradesh, Chhattisgarh, Jharkhand,

and Orissa, have to maintain disproportionate area covered by forests within their jurisdictions for providing the national (and international) public good.

Almost 78 per cent of the coal deposits (including proved, indicated, and inferred deposits) in the country are concentrated in the six states. The state of Bihar (including Jharkhand) had over 29 per cent of the coal deposits. Similarly, the states of Madhya Pradesh (including Chhattisgarh) and Orissa accounted for about a quarter of coal deposits each in the country. Bihar, Madhya Pradesh, and Orissa also have significant deposits of iron ore, copper, and bauxite. In fact, almost 25 per cent of the iron ore comes from Madhya Pradesh, almost 42 per cent of the copper ore is produced in Orissa, and another 18 per cent in Bihar. Similarly, almost 42 per cent of the estimated deposit of bauxite is in Orissa, Bihar accounts for another 18 per cent, and Madhya Pradesh for 10 per cent. These states also have an overwhelming proportion of estimated deposits of other major minerals such as lead, zinc, and manganese.

The aforementioned analysis brings out some important features of regional development in India. First, the states with low level of per capita income are also the states growing at a slower rate, particularly since 1993. Thus, inter-state disparities have shown an increase. Second, the states lagging in development are also the states with large population (before bifurcation) and lagging in human development indicators as well. Third, these states have lagged behind others in development despite abundance of natural resources. This implies that the reasons for their lagging in development will have to be found in other factors. Fourth, these states have also borne the burden of providing the country significant volume of mineral resources and forest cover. The land cover for the minerals and the forest cover cannot be used for any other productive activity. The critical issue is whether the centre has adequately compensated these states for providing the national public goods.

The role of resources in development is only a part of the story. Besides resources, development of a region depends on both policies and institutions and interactions between them. It is the policies that determine the volume of investments and the nature of institutions determine the structure of incentives. Enabling policies include provision of competitive levels of infrastructure and creating enabling environment for attracting private economic activity. Creation of comparable competitive levels of infrastructure in lagging states requires a system of equalizing transfers to offset the fiscal disabilities arising from lower revenue raising capacity and higher unit cost of providing public services. In other words, the transfer system has to (i) offset the fiscal disabilities arising from lower revenue raising capacity and higher unit cost of providing public services to enable these states to provide comparable levels of physical and social infrastructure; (ii) ensure minimum standards of basic meritorious public services; (iii) compensate the states for the loss of economic activity due to banning of logging and additional spending required for maintenance of forests and higher unit cost of providing public services due to sparsity of population in forest areas; and (iv) compensate the states for the loss of economic opportunities due to the exploitation of mineral resources by the central government. Institutional reforms relate to creation of market institutions and creating the incentive structure through measures such as land reforms.

Offsetting Fiscal Disadvantages of Lagging Regions: Role of Central Transfers

In all multi-level fiscal systems, assignment of revenue and expenditure powers to different levels of government according to their comparative advantage necessarily results in vertical fiscal imbalances (Oates 1977, 1999). Furthermore, when there are differences in the capacity to raise revenues and in the unit cost of providing public services, there are horizontal imbalances. The intergovernmental transfer system is designed to offset the fiscal disabilities of the states to provide a level playing field for them in their developmental effort.

The theoretical rationale for equalization on horizontal equity grounds was advanced by Buchanan (1950) and later reformulated by Boadway and Flatters (1982). Taking comprehensive income as the index of well-being, it is argued that the income tax levied by the central government cannot ensure horizontal equity, for its base does not take into account the redistributive effect of states' fiscal operations. States' fiscal operations cannot be distributionally neutral except in the unlikely case of benefit taxes. When the states' quasi-public services are financed by resource rents or source-based taxes as against residence-based taxes, the net fiscal benefits (NFBs) will systematically vary. The residents in the resource rich (high income) regions will have higher NFBs and their higher public consumption will not be included in determining the tax base of the central government.

Boadway and Flatters (1982) define horizontal equity in two alternative ways. According to the broad view, the fiscal system should be equitable nation-wide vis-à-vis the actions of all governments. Two persons equally well off before central and state actions must also be so afterwards. To conform to this concept of horizontal equity, it is necessary to give transfers so that each province is enabled to provide the same level of public services at a given tax rate (like in a unitary state). In contrast, the narrow view of horizontal equity takes the level of real incomes attained by the individuals after a state's budgetary operation as the starting point and the central fiscal action will be directed to ensure horizontal equity after the state's fiscal system has been established. The central budget need not offset the inequalities introduced by the operation of the state budgets per se, but takes the income distribution effects of the states' fiscal operations as a given datum.

Fiscal equalization is argued on efficiency grounds as well. Boadway and Flatters (1982) following Buchanan (1950) argue that migration-induced differential NFBs could lead to lower efficiency in resource allocation. In other words, the low productivity of disadvantaged regions could be due to scarcity of public capital which generates generalized externalities (social and physical infrastructure) and providing capital to these regions could enhance productivity and income levels in the country. In such cases, equalization could be efficiency enhancing.

The neoclassical growth theory too takes a similar premise. Accordingly, in closed economies with no differences in technology and preferences, the growth rate of per capita income tends to be inversely related to the initial levels of per capita income (Barro and Sala-i-Martin 1991). The principal force driving convergence is diminishing returns to reproducible capital. Thus, economies with lower initial values of capital–labour ratios will have high marginal products of capital, and therefore tend to grow at higher rates (Evans and Karras 1996). Given the low capital–labour ratio in poorer regions, equalizing transfers could accelerate the growth of the economy. Higher marginal productivity of capital in poorer regions attracts investments to these regions leading to convergence of incomes. Equalizing transfers, thus, is expected to hasten the process of convergence of inter-regional incomes. More importantly, by enabling the poorer states to provide a threshold level of infrastructure, the transfers could help to allocate resources according to comparative advantage of different regions.

Contrary to the predictions of neoclassical growth theory, there can be cases where marginal productivity of capital in poorer regions may be lower. In a static sense, if the productivity of investments reflects endowment of resources, the transfers to poor regions reduce the overall productivity and, hence, would be efficiency reducing. In such cases, it is argued that population mobility can be a serious alternative to equalizing transfers and the latter, in fact, could constrain mobility and lower productivity in the economy. The free population mobility in response to fiscal differentials could be a preferred alternative from both equity and efficiency point of view. However, in India, neither is inter-regional mobility free for institutional reasons, nor is population mobility determined only by fiscal differentials. In such cases, equalizing transfers would be necessary even if it involves lower efficiency.

An important point to note is that mainstream fiscal federalism literature does not deal with some sources of inequity arising from controls on prices and outputs in planned economies. Also, the disadvantages arising from the assignment of natural resources and the issue of compensating the states for providing national public goods like forest cover are not discussed adequately in the literature. Invisible transfers can also arise from origin-based taxes levied by the state governments (Rao 1997). Another facet of planned economy with heavy emphasis on public sector dominated, heavy industry-based import substituting industrialization is central government's own investments in central enterprises different states. Although economic reforms since 1991 have reduced the role of central planning, the vestiges of planning continue and past investments continue to impact on the regional allocation of resources. There are also rationing of credit, credit allocation to 'priority' sectors at predetermined interest rates, and distribution of seignorage to refinancing institutions. The assignment of mineral resources to the central government and the responsibility of development of forestry and restrictions on the use of forest resources placed by the judiciary in the Indian case in particular, are additional disadvantages for the lagging states. It is important to see whether the intergovernmental transfer system takes account of these disadvantages and compensates these states adequately.

Lagging Regions, Central Investments, and Intergovernmental Transfers

In planned economies, central government can explicitly impact on regional allocation of resources either through regional spread of its own investments or through intergovernmental transfers. Distribution of central investments in different states impacts on the economic activity of the state and helps to determine the flow of inter-state distribution of private investments.

The analysis of central government's investments in public enterprises shows that in 2003–4, the six lagging states, with for over 39 per cent of the population, accounted for only 26 per cent of the capital stock of central government enterprises. Although the employment share of these states is broadly commensurate with population share, the indirect employment generation by these enterprises is not very high for two important reasons. First, most public enterprises in the lagging regions, such as steel and heavy electricals, are capital intensive and the highly skilled labour requirement has to be met from migrants as these states lack the same. Second, although these industries have a high degree of backward linkages as they depend on the resources of the states, they have very little forward linkages. Even as large investments were made in steel plants in states with large deposits of manganese and coal as in Bihar (including Jharkhand), Madhya Pradesh (including Chhattisgarh), and Orissa, the forward linkages from these large investments were nullified by having 'freight equalization policy'—policy of subsidizing freight charges to equalize the prices of steel across the country. In the event, the multiplier-accelerator interaction from these investments has, by and large, not been strong from the central government investments in these poorer states.

Another explicit method of impacting on regional resource allocation is through intergovernmental transfers. The problems with the intergovernmental transfer system in India are extensively discussed in literature (Rao and Singh 2005; Singh and Srinivasan 2006; Rao 2009). To summarize, multiple agencies making transfers from the centre, each working independently of the other, make it difficult to achieve overall objectives of the transfer system. It is seen that while the Finance Commission transfers have a strong equalizing element, the transfers given to the states for state plan schemes as well as discretionary transfers given by the Planning Commission and different central ministries are not equalizing. Furthermore, the equalization effected by the transfer system is not adequate to offset the fiscal disabilities of the low-income states and does not bring them to a level playing field in terms of public service provision (Rao 2009).

Thus, the transfer system in India has failed to offset the fiscal disabilities of poorer, particularly the lagging, states. These states, in general, had comparable tax–GSDP ratio. Despite this, per capita development expenditures as well as total expenditures in these states were less than the respective averages of non-special category states (Table 6.3). Of course, the transfer system was overall equalizing and the six states in general received higher per capita transfers than the average for non-special category states. However, a part of the higher per capita transfers in Chhattisgarh and Jharkhand were given for the creation of administrative infrastructure in these new states. Thus, per capita transfers in the states of Uttar Pradesh, Bihar, Madhya Pradesh, and Orissa were much lower than in the two new states. Consequently, per capita expenditures on developmental heads as well as per capita total expenditures were significantly lower than the average of non-special category states in Bihar, Orissa, Madhya Pradesh, and Uttar Pradesh. The shortfall was particularly significant in Bihar and Uttar Pradesh where the per capita expenditures were lower than the average by 47 per cent and 42 per cent, respectively. In other words, per capita development expenditure in Bihar was just about 53 per cent of the average. With shortfall of such a magnitude, the standards of services in these states would be significantly lower, and naturally these states have lagged behind in social and physical infrastructure. As the flow of private investment, inter alia, is a function of the standards of physical

Table 6.3
Central Transfers and State Expenditures

	Ratio of tax to GSDP 2003–4	Per capita royalties from minerals 2003–4	Per capita own revenues 2003–4	Per capita central transfer 2002–3	Per capita dev. exp. 2002–3	Per capita total exp. 2002–3
Bihar	5.1	8	359	982	1076	1912
Chhattisgarh	6.7	0	1697	992	2040	2904
Madhya Pradesh	6.7	0	1282	895	1859	2737
Jharkhand	4.8	139	1079	1493	2413	3437
Orissa	6.1	2	1146	1225	1703	3001
Uttar Pradesh	6.3	0	893	763	1187	2111
Low Income States	6.1	11.38	916	914	1511	2577
High Income States	7.7	60.70	2554	689	2705	4380
Non-Special Category States	7.3	38.68	1823	816	2034	3367
Special Category States		48.16	1467	3351	3475	5605
All States		39.82	1780	976	2125	3509

Source: State budgets.

and social infrastructure, these states receive much less in private investments as well.

As already mentioned, the six lagging states are rich in natural resources, but there are serious constraints in the use of natural resources for development. In particular, the states rich in forest resources cannot use these resources for development. The states have to spend considerable resources for the development of forestry and they face higher unit cost of providing public services in areas covered by forests. However, benefits from the development of forestry accrue to the entire country and there is no mechanism to compensate these states for providing the national public good. Although the Supreme Court, while delivering the judgment banning felling of trees has suggested that these states should be suitably compensated, no plans have been put in place to compensate them the opportunity cost of growing forests and the loss of revenues by not selling forest products. Similarly, the undivided states of Bihar and Madhya Pradesh as well as Orissa have large areas covered by major minerals like coal, copper, iron ore, and bauxite. The constitution assigns the right to exploit these major minerals to the central government and the centre pays royalty to the states for doing the same. However, fixing royalty at specific rates requires periodic revision to take account of price changes. Despite successive finance commissions recommending switching over to ad valorem rates, the central government has continued with specific royalty rates. More importantly, the royalty rates do not cover even a fraction of the opportunity cost of having mineral deposits in these states.

An important source of regional resource allocation in a planned economy arises from controls on prices and output. Although the pricing system has increasingly been liberalized to market discipline, historically these have impacted on regional resource allocation pattern. In fact, some prices continue to be determined by government fiat rather than market discipline either for strategic reasons or for reasons of political economy. The determination of support prices on foodgrains, for example, favours the states with food surplus at the cost of the national taxpayers. Similarly, pre-empting loans from the market at below market rates of interest benefits the states with larger borrowings than others. The predominance of origin-based tax system levied at the state level could result in significant inter-state tax exportation, particularly in a closed economy with price inelastic demand for commodities. An exercise quantifying invisible transfers from some sources for the period 1985–95 showed that when these are considered, a significant proportion of the equalization achieved through the explicit transfer system is negated by these invisible transfers (Rao 1997; Rao and Singh 2005).

The disequalizing effects of these invisible transfers particularly concern the six lagging states. The cascading type sales tax combined with the tax on inter-state sales have caused significant inter-state tax exportation from richer to poorer states. Generally, exports from the lagging states to others have been much less than their imports; the exports from these states are mainly the primary products whereas their imports are manufactured consumer goods bearing high effective rates. The recent reforms converting the cascading type sales tax into intra-state VAT has reduced the extent of tax exportation though the continued levy of tax on inter-state sales results in net tax exportation to the lagging states, though of a lesser magnitude. Complete switch over to destination-based tax is important not only to minimize resource distortions from the tax but also to minimize tax exportation to lagging states.

Concluding Remarks

This chapter tries to provide a partial explanation for a curious phenomenon of development in India. A close analysis of the development pattern in the country shows that the lagging states are the ones rich in natural resources. Endowed with rich alluvial soil, large river systems providing lifeline for the population, dense forest cover, and rich deposits of coal, manganese, iron, bauxite, and copper, these states have tremendous developmental potential, and yet they have continued to lag behind other states in both material progress and human development.

As mentioned earlier, regional growth pattern in any country is determined by a variety of policy-related and institutional factors. Institutional factors deal with the nature of governance and incentive structure. They deal with both the volume of investments and their productivity. There is considerable discussion on poor governance and inability of the lagging states to protect property rights. A recent study mapping the growth rates in different districts with the nature of land tenure system showed that the districts which had zamindari system of land tenure experienced lower growth rates (Banerjee and Iyer 2005). Not surprisingly, all the six lagging states were under the zamindari system of land tenure and in these states land reforms were not very successful. Related to the above is the overall governance in the states and protection, or lack of it, to property rights, particularly to the marginal landholders and the landless, poorer, and vulnerable sections of society. There are also serious problems with the nature and capacity of institutions to create enabling environment for private sector functioning. The lack of market development both for the commodities produced in these states and labour, low agricultural productivity due to poor extension services are other factors. In other words, considerable efforts at creating and enhancing the capacity of market institutions, governance system, and improving the structure of the incentives are extremely important.

Equally important are the problems created by the policies. While there are many policy reforms that are important to accelerate growth and enhance human development in these states, one of the most important to create enabling environment is the creation and maintenance of physical and social infrastructure. In a federal system where the states have a predominant role in the provision of social services and co-equal role with the central government in the provision of physical infrastructure, investments by the states in social and economic services is extremely important. Providing comparable levels of infrastructure is necessary not only to enable harmonious development, but also to ensure that all the regions in the economy realize their developmental potential.

Ensuring comparable levels of social and physical infrastructure is a necessary condition for the development of the lagging regions. The critical question is that despite all the pronouncements about balanced regional development for sixty years since independence, have the policymakers succeeded in providing comparable levels of infrastructure in all the states to ensure a level playing field for them in attracting private investment and ensuring development? This chapter attempted to show that besides other factors, poor developmental performance of lagging states is attributable to lower levels of public investment in social and economic services. Analysis shows that the share of lagging states in central government enterprise investments has been less than proportionate, and what is more, impact of these investments has been nullified to a considerable extent by the freight equalization policy.

Another major instrument to ensure comparable levels of public services in the lagging states is to offset their fiscal disabilities through federal transfers. The analysis of the intergovernmental transfer system in India shows that multiple agencies making transfers have blurred the objective of offsetting fiscal disabilities of these states. In addition, the methodology followed by the successive finance commissions has helped the states with larger base year expenditures to spend more on public services. Besides, there have been serious disincentives. Although on the whole the transfer system has been equalizing, it was inadequate to offset the shortfall in the fiscal capacity of the lagging states. In the event, per capita expenditure levels in the lagging states have been much below the average. In addition, there are several sources of invisible transfers arising from controls on prices and outputs and origin-based tax system which, to a considerable extent, nullifies the equalization done by the explicit transfer system.

The inability of the central government to adequately compensate the states for the opportunity cost of providing the much needed minerals and ensuring forest cover for the country is another important factor that has denied these states of legitimate compensation for their drain in resources. The Supreme Court decision banning the felling of trees in forests has robbed the states of significant economic activity and revenue. In other words, there is no mechanism in place to compensate these states for bearing the opportunity cost of providing the public good, namely, the forest cover. The transfer system does not take account of these costs to the states. While these states have to do much to improve governance, develop markets, and enhance institutional capacity, and also put in greater effort at raising revenues and improving efficiency in spending, it is important to re-evaluate the policies relating to transfers to ensure that these states are compensated for the costs they bear for the country in addition to offsetting their fiscal disabilities.

Note

1. The states of Uttar Pradesh, Bihar, and Madhya Pradesh were divided in 2001 to create Uttarakhand, Jharkhand, and Chhattisgarh, respectively.

References

Banerjee, Abhijit and Laxmi Iyer (2005). 'History, Institutions and Economic Performance: The Legacy of Colonial Land Tenure System in India', *The American Economic Review*, 95(4): 1190–1213.

Barro, Robert and Xavier Sala-i-Martin (1991). 'Convergence across States and Regions', *Brookings Papers on Economic Activity*, I, pp. 107–81.

Boadway, Robin and Frank Flatters (1982). *Equalization in a Federal State*. Ottawa: Economic Council of Canada.

Buchanan, James M. (1950). 'Federalism and Fiscal Equity', *American Economic Review*, 40(4): 583–99.

Cordon, W. Max and J. Peter Neary (1982). 'Booming Sector and De-Industrialisation in a Small Open Economy', *The Economic Journal*, 92: 829–31.

Evans, P. and G. Karras (1996). 'Do Economies Converge? Evidence from a Panel of U.S. States', *Review of Economics and Statistics*, 78 (August): 384–8.

Oates, W.E. (1999). 'An Essay on Fiscal Federalism', *Journal of Economic Literature*, XXXVII(3): 1120–49.

________ (1977). 'An Economist's Perspective of Fiscal Federalism', in W.E. Oates (ed.), *Political Economy of Fiscal Federalism*, pp. 3–20. Toronto: Lexington Books.

Rao, M. Govinda (2009). 'Reform of Intergovernmental Fiscal Arrangements for Balanced Regional Development in a Globalizing Environment' (this volume).

________ (1997). 'Invisible Transfers in Indian Federalism', *Public Finance/Finances Publiques*, 52(3–4): 429–48.

Rao, M. Govinda and Nirvikar Singh (2005). *Political Economy of Federalism in India*. New Delhi: Oxford University Press.

Rao, M. Govinda, Tapas K. Sen, and Pratap R. Jena (2008). 'Issues Before the Thirteenth Finance Commission', *Economic and Political Weekly*, XLIII(36): 41–53.

Singh, Nirvikar and T.N. Srinivasan (2006). 'Indian Federalism, Economic Reform and Globalisation', in Jessdica Wallack and T.N. Srinivasan (eds), *Federalism and Economic Reform*, pp. 301–63. Cambridge: Cambridge University Press.

7

Regional Disparities in Infrastructure and Urban Service Delivery

Policy Implications for India's Lagging Regions

Somik V. Lall

Even the most casual observer of the Indian situation knows that development outcomes in Bihar significantly lag behind the rest of the country. Bihar is the state with the highest poverty incidence, with 40 per cent of its population in 1999 being under the poverty line (World Bank 2004). Its net primary school enrolment ratio in 1999 was 52 per cent (compared to the all India average of 77 per cent); the female literacy rate of 33.6 per cent was far below the already low Indian average of 54.3 per cent; and only 10.3 per cent of households had access to electricity as a source of lighting (the Indian average was 55.8 per cent).

Average income in Bihar is about half the Indian average, which makes it close to or less than one-third of the averages of several leading states. Industrial capital formation in Bihar has gone down from almost 13 per cent of the national total to about 3.7 per cent in the post-reform period. Much of this was in a single district, Purbi Singbhum, which is no longer part of the state (having become part of the new state of Jharkhand). In short, Bihar, for long the poorest state in the union, is falling even further behind, perhaps at an even more rapid rate. This condition is not unique to Bihar. There are several states where per capita incomes are consistently lower than the national average. These include the states of Chhattisgarh, Jharkhand, Madhya Pradesh, Orissa, Rajasthan, Uttar Pradesh, and Uttaranchal.

In this chapter, I examine one issue that is closely linked to household welfare—that is access to public services such as water supply, sanitation, drainage, and electricity. This analysis complements considerable empirical work examining the impacts of policies for stimulating economic growth in lagging regions (Ahluwalia 2000; Chakravorty and Lall 2007) as well as sub-national fiscal reforms (Rao 2002, 2003). In a recent paper on infrastructure development, Lall (2007) shows that transport and communication infrastructures are the most significant drivers of regional growth in India. Further, while regional convergence in the growth of public infrastructure is possible, the short- to medium-term divergence in private capital formation between lagging and leading states suggests that infrastructure endowments, while possibly very important, are not sufficient to close the gap in private-sector growth.

There are two main questions that I address in this chapter. First, is there evidence to show that local governments in lagging states are doing worse than other states in providing basic services? Second, do public services improve with the size of transfers from higher levels of government, or do own source revenues have a considerable role to play in improving service provision? My analysis is limited to urban service delivery due to data availability issues, but the points raised here should apply more broadly. I find that service delivery and expenditures on basic public services are much lower in lagging states compared to the rest of the country. Much of the poor service delivery levels is explained by the cost of providing services and revenue composition of local bodies. The most important finding is that local service delivery responds to expansion in local revenue bases but is not sensitive to increases in general-purpose transfers from higher levels of government. From a policy perspective this raises an important concern about stimulating own source revenues in areas with limited administrative capacity and weak revenue bases.

The rest of the chapter is organized as follows. I first provide the basic facts on service delivery differentials across India's regions. In the next section, I develop a model of supply, demand, and finance of public services to examine the determinants of service delivery. The last section concludes with a discussion on policy implications.

Service Delivery across Regions

Local governments are responsible for delivering various public services, yet severe infrastructure shortages in water supply and sanitation, roads, transportation, housing, and waste management and poor planning and inefficient management have resulted in poor quality services with limited coverage. While inadequate service delivery is a nation-wide concern, these problems are particularly acute in India's lagging provinces. Figure 7.1 shows that Bihar, Uttar Pradesh, and Orissa have low rates of access to tap water for urban households in cities with more that 100,000 residents, and are systematically underperforming relative to other states. The situation is worse in smaller-sized cities. Other infrastructure service indicators such as access to electricity, networked sewerage, and sanitation facilities also exhibit similar trends.

Similarly, Figure 7.2 shows the share of households with access to electricity for urban areas with more than 100,000 people. The states of Bihar, West Bengal, UP, Orissa, and Chhattisgarh have lower access to electricity relative to the national average.

If infrastructure and service delivery is relatively poor in lagging regions, the relevant question to ask is why this is so and what can be done to improve service delivery. A starting point to answer this question is to look at expenditures made by (urban) local governments on infrastructure and service delivery. There have been various efforts in India to develop physical norms and standards for infrastructure services. One of these attempts is by the Zakaria Committee (1963) report on 'Augmentation of Financial Resources of Urban Local Bodies.' This report calculates per capita operations and maintenance (O&M) expenditure norms for four core infrastructure services: (i) water supply,

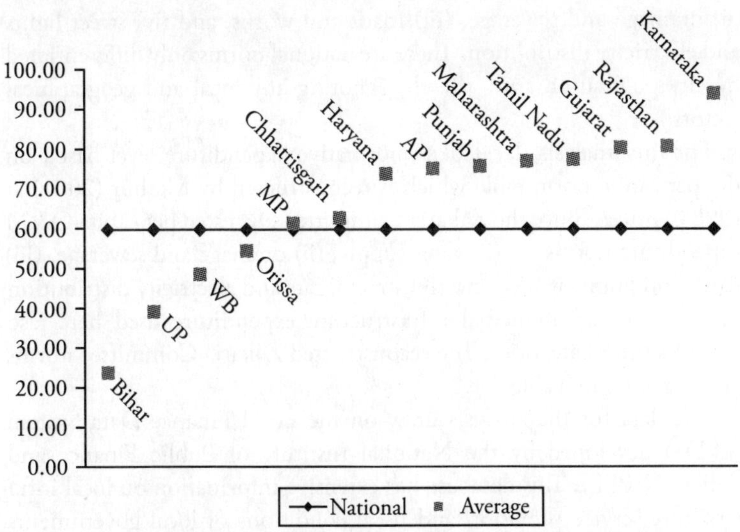

Figures 7.1: Share of Households with Access to Tap Water (Pop. > 100,000; 2001 Census data)

Source: Office of the Registrar General of India, Ministry of Home Affairs, Government of India.

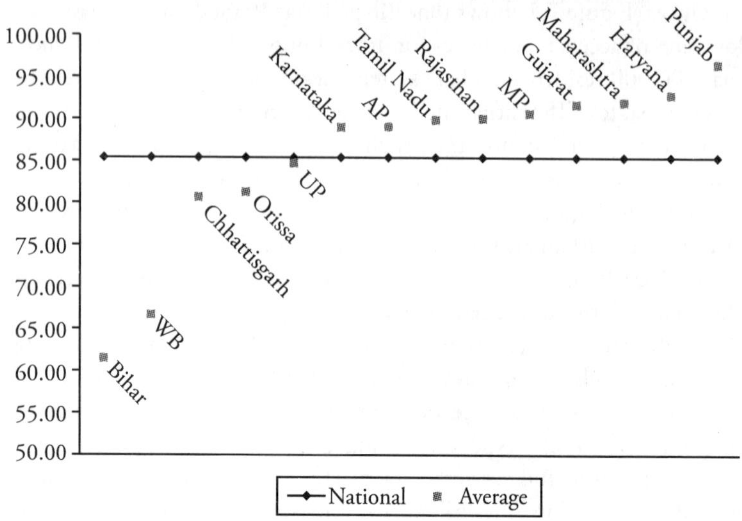

Figures 7.2: Share of Households with Electricity
(Pop. > 100,000; 2001 Census data)

Source: Office of the Registrar General of India, Ministry of Home Affairs, Government of India.

(ii) drainage and sewerage, (iii) roads and works, and (iv) street lights and electricity distribution. These are national norms only differentiated by city population sizes, thereby ignoring any local and geographical factors.

For this analysis, I calculate normative expenditure level based on the per capita norm table which is reconstructed by Mathur (2001) at 1998–9 prices. Since the Zakaria Committee suggested per capita O&M expenditure norms for (i) water supply, (ii) drainage and sewerage, (iii) roads and public works, and (iv) street lights and electricity distribution, the measure of municipal infrastructure expenditure used here also includes these categories. The reconstructed Zakaria Committee norms are presented in Table 7.1.[1]

The data for the analysis draw on the Local Finance Data System (LFDS) developed by the National Institute of Public Finance and Policy (NIPFP). This database has extensive information on local infrastructure service provision and fiscal conditions of local governments The final sample used in this analysis includes data for 151 Indian cities in 1992–3 and 1997–8. For the comparison, lagging states include Bihar, Chhattisgarh, Jharkhand, Madhya Pradesh, Orissa, Rajasthan, and Uttar Pradesh.

TABLE 7.1
Zakaria Committee Norms

	Water supply	Drainage & sewerage	Municipal roads & works	Street lights & electricity distribution	Overall
Pop. more than 500,000	189.95	217.98	42.51	53.00	503.44
Pop. between 100,000 and 500,000	177.28	195.37	32.56	45.23	450.44
Pop. between 50,000 and 100,000	156.30	168.24	24.42	41.61	390.56
Pop. between 20,000 and 50,000	135.68	157.38	21.71	38.89	353.66
Pop. less than 20,000	134.23	148.34	19.90	36.18	338.64

Notes: Reconstructed by Mathur (2001) at 1998–9 prices; Units: Rs 1000.

Table 7.2 provides a comparison of (population-) weighted means of various indicators in lagging and other states. Local bodies in lagging states spend less on local infrastructure services relative to normative levels in other states. The ratios of actual infrastructure expenditures of local governments in lagging states over the normative expenditure levels of the Zakaria Committee are disappointing. On average, expenditure on sewerage and drainage was just 12.2 per cent of the required level, that on water supply 7.3 per cent, roads 56.7 per cent, and street lights 13 per cent. The (weighted) mean of overall local infrastructure expenditures (relative the normative levels) in lagging states is 13.3 per cent which is considerably lower than that in other states (78 per cent). It is important to note here that these figures may somewhat overstate the extent of the gap as many local infrastructure services are provided by state governments or parastatal agencies.

Table 7.2 also reveals a troubling trend, that of expenditures on service delivery falling in lagging states. Relative to the Zakaria Committee norms, spending on infrastructure went down from an already low 14.6 per cent to 12.3 per cent. The drop in spending is seen across services for lagging areas.

An important policy question is whether the current revenue base of local governments is adequate to finance local infrastructure needs. This resource gap can be measured by the difference between the normative infrastructure expenditure level and the municipal revenue base. We compute two measures of local infrastructure resource gap in a city: the ratios of combined total expenditure requirement of the

TABLE 7.2

Expenditure Relative to Zakaria Committee Norms for Lagging and Other States

Dummy for lagging states (=1)	Weighted mean (weight=city population)			1992			1997		
	0	1	Total	0	1	Total	0	1	Total
All services	0.780	0.133	0.721	0.743	0.146	0.688	0.813	0.123	0.750
Water supply	0.812	0.073	0.744	0.76 9	0.082	0.706	0.849	0.065	0.777
Sewerage	0.448	0.122	0.418	0.396	0.123	0.371	0.493	0.121	0.459
Roads	2.549	0.567	2.367	2.483	0.628	2.313	2.607	0.514	2.415
Street lights	0.709	0.130	0.656	0.751	0.165	0.697	0.673	0.100	0.620

Source: Report of the Committee of Ministers on the Augmentation of Financial Resources of Urban Local Bodies (Chairman: Zakaria), 1963, constituted by the Central Council of Local Self-government.

Zakaria Committee over (i) total revenue incomes and (ii) own revenue receipts. Considering expenditures for other municipal public services, such as public education, public health, and various administrative and regulatory functions, this ratio needs to be greater than 1.

Table 7.3 presents these ratios as a measure of the local infrastructure resource gap. Surprisingly, the average ratio of own revenue receipts relative to the required expenditure level was just 53.9 per cent. Own revenue receipts can finance only half the required expenditure level. The average ratio of total revenue incomes including various transfers from higher levels of governments was 90.8 per cent. Considering other municipal public service expenditures for which local governments are responsible, the revenue base of local governments should be increased significantly.

Comparing the resource gap between municipal corporations and municipalities, municipal corporations emerge in a more favourable position. The own revenue receipts of municipal corporations were

TABLE 7.3
Municipal Resource Gap

Own revenue receipts/required level			
	Observation	Mean	Coefficient of variation
1992	243	0.504	1.220
1997	243	0.574	1.852
Total	486	0.539	1.585
Municipalities	442	0.490	1.506
Municipal corporations	44	1.029	1.143
Total	486	0.539	1.585
	(a)	(b)	(share, b/a, %)
≥ Required level	486	64	13.17
Total revenue incomes/required level			
	Observation	Mean	Coefficient of variation
1992	244	0.839	0.610
1997	244	0.976	0.866
Total	488	0.908	0.766
Municipalities	444	0.854	0.725
Municipal corporations	44	1.451	0.651
Total	488	0.908	0.766
	(a)	(b)	(share, b/a, %)
≥ Required level	488	146	29.92

Source: Author's estimates.

enough to meet the required local core infrastructure expenditure level, but those of municipalities were less than half of the required level (102.9 per cent vs 49.0 per cent). In the case of total revenue incomes, the ratios of municipal corporations and municipalities were 145.1 per cent and 85.4 per cent, respectively.

In summary, only 13 per cent of the cities in our sample can afford to meet local core infrastructure needs from their own revenue sources, and 30 per cent of cities from their total revenue receipts.

Supply, Demand, and Finance of Public Services

In this section, I develop a model of service provision, demand and financing to identify determinants of the shortfall in public services across Indian cities and cities in lagging regions in particular. In this model, the equilibrium level of local infrastructure provision is endogenously determined through the interaction of supply and demand:

$$\ln g^D = a_0 - a_1 \ln P + a_2 \ln y + \Omega \quad (1)$$

$$\ln g^S = b_0 - b_1 \ln P - b_2 \ln (\text{cost}) + b_3 \ln (tax) + \ln (transfer) + \Omega \quad (2)$$

$$g^D = \theta . g^S$$

where a_i, $b_i \geq 0$ and per capita infrastructure demand (g^D) is distinguished from infrastructure supply (g^S). Following Roller and Waverman (2001), we consider 'effective' demand rather than 'observed' demand for infrastructure services. The effective demand takes into account the unmet demand which cannot be observed due to supply constraints. More formally, the unmet demand can be defined by the gap between normative infrastructure usage requirement and the actual infrastructure service provision. In my model, $\theta = g^D/g^S$ measures the size of unmet demand relative to the observed level of infrastructure service provision.

The price of infrastructure can be defined by how much consumers pay for one unit of infrastructure service consumption (in the form of user charges and tariffs). In this regard, (per capita) infrastructure demand (g^D) depends on the price and income elasticities of infrastructure demand. As user charges or tariffs are revenue sources to the service providers, the supply of infrastructure (g^S) also responds to the price (P) of infrastructure, the average cost of infrastructure service provision (*cost*), and the revenue income of local governments in forms of municipal tax receipts (*tax*) and transfers from higher levels of governments (*transfer*).

These receipts will be allocated to cover the infrastructure provision costs. The b_3 and b_4 coefficients measure how much of local governments' fiscal resources responds to increase local infrastructure supply in addition to revenues from user charges and tariffs. I assume infrastructure supply costs are determined by various local physical attributes such as technological and topographical/geographical factors. Finally, various observed and unobserved local characteristics (Ω) influence the supply and demand of local infrastructure.

The supply of overall local infrastructure services, $\ln g^S$, is measured by the first principal component of (i) ln(water supply released, per capita), (ii) ln(drainage length, per capita), (iii) ln(solid waste collection, per capita), (iv) ln(surface municipal road length, per capita), and (v) ln(street lights, per capita). The scoring coefficients are 0.296, 0.480, 0.348, 0.536, and 0.524.[2]

The demand for local infrastructure services takes into account excess demand, such that

$\ln g^D \equiv \ln(\theta \times g^S)$ and

$$\theta \equiv \frac{\text{normative expenditure level of the Zakaria Committee}}{\text{municipal infrastructure expenditure}}$$

Specifically,

$\ln g^D = \ln(g^S \times \theta)$,
if $\theta \geq 1$
$\ln g^D = \ln g^S$,
otherwise

The local infrastructure price, $\ln P$, can be measured by how much local residents pay for their local infrastructure service consumption. I assume local governments' (per capita) receipts of user charges/tariffs (from local infrastructure services) to be the same as (per capita) non-tax revenue receipts, or proportional to them. Then the price of local infrastructure can be proxied such that

$$\ln P = \ln\left(P \cdot g^S\right) - \ln g^S = \ln\left(\begin{matrix}\text{per capita}\\ \text{infra purchase}\end{matrix}\right) - \ln g^S$$

$$= \ln\left(\frac{\text{non-tax revenue receipts / city population}}{\text{CPI/100}}\right) - \ln g^S$$

The figures are deflated by the all-India consumer price index (CPI) for urban non-manual employees with 1984–5 base. The average (per capita) cost of local infrastructure service provision, deflated by the all-India CPI for urban non-manual employees is defined as

$$\ln ac = \ln\left(\frac{\text{municipal infrastructure expenditure / city population}}{\text{CPI / 1000}}\right) - \ln g^{S}$$

Average per capita city income, ln*y*, is measured by the first (unrotated) principal component of (i) ln(per capita net state domestic product at factor cost, at constant price), (ii)ln (municipal total tax revenue receipts, per capita, real), and (iii) ln(per capita waste generated). The scoring coefficients are 0.688, 0.698, and 0.200. Another measure of city per capita income is per worker wage income:

$$\ln(w) = \ln(\text{wages and salary + bonus, per worker, real})$$

The per worker wage income is deflated by the state-level CPI for industrial workers (state urban prices, base year 1973–4) to control for state-level cost-of-living differences. The wage information is from the Annual Survey of Industry (ASI).

The net value-added per employee is a measure of labour productivity, which will be used to estimate the local wage equation. It is converted to real terms using the all-India CPI for urban non-manual employees. We also have a measure of local business service jobs relative to city population, as a local intermediate input to firm production.

Expenditures of local governments including local public service provision are financed by local taxes or transfers from higher levels of governments. We construct these variables such that ln*tax* = ln(municipal tax receipts, per capita, real), and ln*transfer* = ln(total transfers from higher levels of governments, per capita, real), both of which are deflated by the all-India CPI for urban non-manual employees. I also endogenize two main revenue sources of local governments: own municipal tax receipts and transfers from higher levels of government. Since these two come from different sources (local residents vs higher levels of government), the factors that influence these revenue generations will differ. I model these two financing mechanisms such that

$$\ln(tax) = c_0 + c_1 \ln y + \Omega \tag{3}$$

$$\ln(transfer) = d_0 + d_1 \ln y + \Omega \tag{4}$$

I assume that these revenue sources of local governments are influenced by per capita local income levels (y) and various other local characteristics (Ω).

Estimation Results

In Table 7.4, I present estimates of local infrastructure supply and demand using ordinary least squares (OLS). I also add state dummies and a year dummy to control for unobserved attributes. Column 1 provides estimates for local infrastructure demand and Columns 2 and 3 provide estimates for supply. The only difference between Columns 2 and 3 is the introduction of a dummy for municipal corporations in Column 3.

TABLE 7.4
The Supply and Demand of Local Infrastructure Services: OLS
(standard errors in parentheses)

	(1)	(2)	(3)
Dependent variable:	ln (local infrastructure demand)$_t$ OLS	ln (local infrastructure supply)$_t$ OLS	ln (local infrastructure supply)$_t$ OLS
ln (local infrastructure price)$_t$	–0.659*** (0.032)	–0.268*** (0.039)	–0.275*** (0.039)
ln (local avg. income)$_t$	–0.120 (0.089)		
ln (avg. cost)$_t$		–0.572*** (0.045)	–0.559*** (0.045)
ln (local tax revenue, per capita, real)$_t$		0.493*** (0.045)	0.443*** (0.046)
ln (transfers, per capita, real)$_t$		0.189*** (0.052)	0.203*** (0.051)
a dummy for municipal corporations			0.476*** (0.133)
a year dummy	Yes	Yes	Yes
state dummies	Yes	Yes	Yes
Constant	Yes	Yes	Yes
Observations	296	300	300
R^2	0.658	0.822	0.830

Note: *** significant at 1 per cent level.
Source: Author's estimates.

The coefficient estimate of the price elasticity of local infrastructure demand is statistically significant with an expected sign. However, the supply elasticity estimates have wrong signs, and the income elasticity of local infrastructure demand is not statistically significant. As expected, the cost of infrastructure has a negative effect on supply. The OLS estimates also show that both local own source tax revenues and transfers from higher levels of government have positive effects on infrastructure supply. The parameter estimate for own source revenue is higher than that for transfers. The results for the municipal corporation dummy are statistically significant and positive, suggesting that cities with municipal corporations, that is, cities with higher degrees of political responsibility and fiscal autonomy, do a better job of supplying local infrastructure.

In Table 7.5, I report generalized method of moments (GMM) estimations for local infrastructure supply and demand to correct for bias introduced by omitted variables and measurement error.

The GMM estimates are from the two-step efficient GMM in the presence of arbitrary heteroskedasticity and arbitrary intra-group (within-state) correlation. Instruments are strong with high average partial R^2s (average Fs).[3] The instruments for the demand equation readily pass the Sargan (Hansen J) overidentification tests suggesting instruments are orthogonal to error terms, with a p-value of 0.968. The supply-side equation is exactly identified. All coefficient estimates have expected signs. In Column 1, price and income elasticities of local infrastructure demand are statistically significant and with expected signs.

Column 2 presents supply-side determinants. The price elasticity of local infrastructure supply has the expected positive sign, but is not statistically significant. This may imply that local governments provide infrastructure services on a non-market pricing basis, emphasizing the role of governments as public good providers. Local infrastructure provision costs have a negative effect on supply, as expected.

Interestingly, municipal tax receipts (per capita, real) have a statistically significant and positive effect on local infrastructure supply, but the effect of transfers from higher levels of governments is not significant. In summary, 'raising municipal taxes' is a more effective way of financing and increasing local infrastructure service supply.

I also estimate equations 1–4 as a system of regression equations, and estimate the model of local infrastructure supply, demand, and financing using three stage least squares (3SLS). Compared to the single equation GMM estimators, 3SLS is asymptotically efficient. For normally distributed error terms, the 3SLS has the same asymptotic distribution as the full-information maximum likelihood estimator, which is asymptotically efficient among all estimators (Greene 2003). In this system, local infrastructure finance is also endogenized.

The system consists of local infrastructure demand, supply, and two financing equations of local governments (municipal taxes and transfers

TABLE 7.5
The Supply and Demand of Local Infrastructure Services: GMM
(robust standard errors in parentheses)

	(1)	(2)
Dependent variable:	ln(local infrastructure demand)$_t$ GMM	ln(local infrastructure supply)$_t$ GMM
ln(local infrastructure price)$_t$	–1.308***	–0.167
	(0.155)	(0.492)
ln(local avg. income)$_t$	2.267*	
	(1.215)	
ln(avg. cost)$_t$		–0.838**
		(0.357)
ln(local tax revenue, per capita, real)$_t$		1.308**
		(0.634)
ln(transfers, per capita, real)$_t$		–0.398
		(0.520)
a year dummy	yes	yes
state dummies	yes	yes
constant	yes	yes
Observations	296	294
Hansen J statistic (overidentification test)	0.002	–
(p-value)	(0.968)	–
Avg. partial R^2	0.336	0.245
Avg. partial Fs	149.7	41.7

Notes: *** significant at 1 per cent level; ** significant at 5 per cent level; * significant at 10 per cent level.

a. The instruments are (i) the average (real) cost of local infrastructure service provision, ln (avg. cost), which is assumed to be exogenously determined by technological and topographical/geographical factors, (ii) a dummy for port cities (distances to ports by roads or rails are less than five hours), (iii) a dummy for state capitals, (iv) a year dummy and state dummies, and (v) various state characteristics in year 1970. The 1970 state characteristics include population size; population density; per capita total state government revenue; the share of manufacturing sector in the total net state domestic product (NSDP); per capita NSDP; the share of the number of seats won by Congress Party, hard left parties, and soft left parties; a dummy for President's (state) rule.

b. The local infrastructure supply equation is exactly identified.

Source: Author's estimates.

from higher levels of governments). I use the same instruments as in Table 7.5.

Columns 1 and 2 in Table 7.6 show the 3SLS estimation results of the local infrastructure supply and demand equations. When compared with the OLS results in Table 7.4, higher price elasticity of local infrastructure demand (0.7 → 1.7) can be observed, and the income elasticity becomes statistically significant with an expected sign. Local governments' own source tax revenues have a statistically significant and positive effect on local infrastructure supply, but the effect of transfers is not statistically significant.

TABLE 7.6
The Local Infrastructure Service Supply, Demand, and Financing: 3SLS
(standard errors in parentheses)

	(1)	(2)	(3)	(4)
Dependent variable:	ln(local infrastructure demand)$_t$ 3SLS	ln(local infrastructure supply)$_t$ 3SLS	ln(local tax rev., per capita, real)$_t$ 3SLS	ln(transfers, per capita, real)$_t$ 3SLS
ln (local infra. price)$_t$	−1.670***	−0.374		
	(0.144)	(0.440)		
ln (local avg. income)$_t$	4.839***		2.035***	0.167
	(1.262)		(0.175)	(0.295)
ln (avg. cost)$_t$		−0.760**		
		(0.330)		
ln (local tax revenue, per capita, real)$_t$		1.772***		
		(0.631)		
ln (transfers, per capita, real)$_t$		−0.771		
		(0.539)		
A year dummy	Yes	Yes	Yes	Yes
State dummies	Yes	Yes	Yes	Yes
Constant	Yes	Yes	Yes	Yes
Observations	294	294	294	294
RMSE	2.659	1.174	0.371	0.625

Notes: *** significant at 1 per cent level; ** significant at 5 per cent level.
a. Instruments are the same as in Table 7.5.
Source: Author's estimates.

Columns 3 and 4 endogenize local infrastructure-financing mechanisms. These two equations are added to the system to get consistent parameter estimates of local infrastructure supply and demand in equations (1) and (2). While own tax revenues increase with city incomes, transfers do not show such a relationship.

Policy Implications

In this chapter, I examined if states in India that are lagging in terms of economic performance also lag in terms of service delivery. I looked at service delivery as it is a quasi-public good that has direct implications for household-level welfare. As lagging states are home to a large number of poor people (as in Bihar), access to basic public services becomes a key component of improving local quality of life.

I found that there is systematic underprovision of public services in lagging regions. For example, data from the 2001 Census tell us that less than 30 per cent of urban households in these regions in cities with more than 100,000 people have access to tap water, compared to over 90 per cent for Karnataka. These statistics are consistently worse in lagging regions for a broad range of public services.

One of the main factors contributing to the lower provision of public services is inadequate spending on service delivery—both in terms of new investments and operation and maintenance expenditures. Urban areas in lagging states (for which data are available) have considerably lower spending on basic services relative to the norms set up by the Zakaria Committee and compared to spending by better-off states. Of course, this statement is likely to be tautological as states in lagging regions do not have the fiscal capacity (both the base and the administrative capacity) to stimulate local resource generation.

To provide robust links between local infrastructure supply and revenue generation, I empirically tested a model of service provision, demand, and financing. My main finding confirmed the basic intuition that local service delivery responds significantly to local revenue generation efforts of local governments. On the other hand non-dedicated or general-purpose transfers from higher levels of government do not have any clear effects on stimulating local service delivery.

The policy implication for improving local service delivery is to find mechanisms that would expand the local revenue base in poor regions. However, this is not an easy task as local tax bases in these regions are not buoyant and local governments do not have the autonomy to change local tax rates or the administrative capacity to improve collection efficiency.

In the short run, there may be need to increase the scale of transfers that are dedicated for service delivery (as in ring-fenced operations). This is likely to stimulate economic benefits, both in terms of improvements in household welfare and willingness to pay for services via direct user charges (as households see visible improvements in service performance) and stimulate new economic activity—thereby increasing the tax base.

In the medium to long run, efforts should be focused at improving local revenue capacity using a combination of new valuation methods and enhanced administrative capacity. If an area-based system is adopted, as is used now in some of the larger urban local bodies in the country, then a method of updating the guidance values on a regular basis is necessary (see Lall and Deichmann 2006). This will require not only reliable values from the Stamp Office, and from the state ministries of construction, but also a set of procedures for updating these values. It will also require trained staff, capable of valuing real property, and perhaps a central valuation unit in each state should be considered. There is much to be done to implement such a system. Most local governments do not have a cadre of trained assessors to evaluate property values and regularly update them. A capital value system is even more difficult, because valuation of individual units will be required. In either case, a method of requiring updating of any new construction or major renovations, subdivisions, etc. will need to be put in place. A capital value system will be difficult and costly to implement. Its introduction will require much careful planning and will take considerable time.

Notes

1. A caveat is that in several states some local infrastructure services, such as water supply and sewerage, are taken over by state governments, parastatal agencies, or are under shared responsibility. Therefore, actual infrastructure expenditure of a local government does not necessarily represent overall public-sector expenditure in a city.
2. Since the focus is on making a proxy or a synthetic index of local infrastructure stock rather than factor analysis, factor loading and rotation are irrelevant in this analysis.
3. Partial R^2 is a squared partial correlation between the excluded instruments and the endogenous regressor in question, and the *F*-test of the excluded instruments corresponds to this partial R^2.

References

Ahluwalia, M.S. (2000). 'Economic Performance of States in the Post-Reform Period', *Economic and Political Weekly*, 5 May.

Chakravorty, S. and S.V. Lall (2007). *Made in India: The Economic Geography and Political Economy of Industrialization*. New Delhi: Oxford University Press.

Greene, W. (2003). *Econometric Analysis*, fifth edition. Upper Saddle River, New Jersey: Pearson Education.

Lall, S.V. (2007). 'Infrastructure and Regional Growth: Growth Dynamics and Policy Relevance for India', *Annals of Regional Science*, 41(3): 581–99.

Lall, S.V. and U. Deichmann (2006). 'Fiscal and Distributional Implications of Property Tax Reforms in Indian Cities', *Economic and Political Weekly*, 22 July, pp. 3209–20.

Mathur, O.P. (2001). *Approach to State-Municipal Fiscal Relations*. New Delhi: National Institute of Public Finance and Policy.

Rao, M.G. (2003). 'Incentivising Fiscal Transfers in Indian Federation', *Publius: Journal of Federalism*, 33(4): 43–62.

________ (2002). 'Sub-national Fiscal Reforms in India', Paper presented at conference on Indian Economic Reforms, Cornell University, 19–20 April.

Roller, Lars-Hendrik and Leonard Waverman (2001). 'Telecommunications Infrastructure and Economic Development: A Simultaneous Approach', *American Economic Review*, 91(4): 909–23.

World Bank (2004). *Bihar: Towards a Development Strategy*. World Bank Report, Processed.

8

Regional Development Policies and Regional Inequality in a Developing Country

India as a Case Study

Raja Shankar and Anwar Shah

Reduction in regional disparities is a major concern for governments in most countries. Large regional inequalities represent serious threat to the unity of a country and, in extreme cases, lead to calls for separation both by the richest and poorest regions. While the poorest may consider such inequalities as manifestation of regional injustice, the richest may view a union with the poorest as holding them back in their drive to prosperity. The centrifugal effect of regional disparities is often exacerbated by the fact that regions in most countries also differ ethnically, culturally, linguistically, or religiously. These differences are a barrier to the flow of labour from the poorer to the richer regions. As regional disparities cannot be reduced through the large-scale movement of people from the poorer to the richer regions, each region has to develop on its own. Even if mass migration were possible, it may not be desirable because it may lead to congestion in the richer regions. Further, the migration of labour to the richer regions does not automatically lead to wage increases in the poorer regions. It is often the better educated and more skilled who migrate, leaving the poorer region even worse off.

Therefore, it is not surprising that reduction in regional disparities has been a major policy objective of most governments, especially in developing countries, where these disparities are two to six times more than in the developed countries (Shankar and Shah 2001). In this chapter, we discuss different regional development policies that have been pursued in developing countries to address regional disparities. Using India as a case, we show that most of these policies have not been effective in reducing regional inequality. Specifically, we look at explicit centre–state transfers and implicit inter-state transfers of productive resources and investments. We find that the failure of these policies is due to two major factors. First, the strong centralized and paternalistic bias of explicit centre–state transfers creates incentives for sub-national governments to abdicate their responsibility for development and become dependent on central aid. Second, the more productive implicit transfers of resources and investments flow disproportionately to the richer states, helping them widen their lead over the poorer states. Our findings suggest that contrary to conventional wisdom that calls for a central role in reducing regional inequality, strong sub-national governments, accountable to their constituents for raising and spending resources, could be pivotal to the catch-up process in poorer regions.

In the next section we briefly summarize the theory and evidence on regional convergence/divergence and theoretically discuss the relationship between regional development policies and regional inequality. While increasing regional disparities might be affected by factors other than government policies, we focus on the policies in this chapter. Next, we present regional inequality trends in India, and in the following section we discuss regional development policies pursued to reduce such disparities and evaluate their success. Finally, we present a summary of the Indian experience and suggest areas for future research.

Regional Inequality and Regional Development Policies

There is wide-ranging academic literature on trends in regional inequalities. This literature follows two strands—one explores the relationship between income inequality and the level of economic development, and the second looks at convergence/divergence between regional or national economies. The first strand explores Kuznets' (1955) hypothesis that the relationship between income inequality and the level of economic development is likely to be U-shaped, with increasing inequality during the take-off period followed by decreasing inequality as a country becomes more developed. Williamson's (1965) study extended the U-shaped theory of the behaviour of inequality to regional incomes and found that the data generally support the hypothesis for non-socialist economies. A more recent study by Shankar and Shah (2001) also finds that developed economies tend to have lower regional disparities than developing ones.

The second strand, which has been at the forefront of economic research more recently, looks at convergence/divergence between economic regions. More specifically, this research has investigated whether there is evidence to support the prediction of the neoclassical growth model (Solow 1956) that with similar preferences and technology, poor economies tend to grow faster than rich ones. Barro and Sala-i-Martin (1991, 1992) analyse a cross-section of countries, US states, and European regions to conclude that convergence occurs at the very slow rate of 2 per cent per year. However, the gap between the rich and the poor nations has been increasing not just over the past few decades but over the longer period of centuries (Pritchett 1997; Easterly 2001a, 2001b; Easterly and Levine 2001). Canova and Marcet (1995) find that the steady state is different for different cross-sectional economic units—both regions and countries. They also say that while convergence to respective steady states happens faster than the Barro and Sala-i-Martin rate of 2 per cent, poor regions tend to stay poor.

While convergence across countries may be slow or non-existent due to cross-country differences in preferences, varying technology levels, and barriers to factor movements, one could reasonably expect regions within countries to converge faster. However, the evidence on this is mixed. Barro and Sala-i-Martin (1992) find evidence of convergence in the US states. Boldrin (2001) finds that poorer European Union countries and, to some extent, poorer regions had a tendency to catch up from 1950 to about 1973–4. From the late 1970s or early 1980s onwards, the evidence for convergence weakens. Shankar and Shah (2001) present evidence on regional inequality trends for Canada, US, and fourteen developing countries. The US states converged in the 1990s and regional inequality in Canada remained stable. However, regional inequality in most of the other countries increased in most of the time periods studied. Several authors have looked at regional inequality trends in some of the bigger developing countries such as Indonesia and China, and have found mixed evidence for income convergence.[1]

Theoretically, strong convergence hypothesis suggests that equality in factor productivity and income levels will be achieved regardless of initial conditions, provided diffusion and adoption of technological change is unrestrained. A weak convergence hypothesis, on the other hand, requires competitive market structures to send the right signals for allocation of productive factors (Boldrin 2001). Under the weak convergence hypothesis, differences in technology alone do not explain the differences in factor productivity. Lack of competitive price signals such as those observed with regional incentives and subsidies, infant industry protection, and barriers to trade may perpetuate regional differences in factor productivity and income.

At conceptual level, regional convergence is assured under perfect competition, constant returns to scale with no external effects, and free and costless mobility of factors across relatively homogeneous (with respect to resource endowment, topography, composition of population, human capital, political and legal environment, informal culture, etc.) regions within the nation state. This requires that political units are commensurate with reasonably large geographic areas with reasonably diverse endowments so that regional income differentials are attributable to policy and institutional considerations rather than simply to irreversible acts of nature. For example, one should not necessarily expect to have convergence among three completely heterogeneous regions comprising solely desert, mountainous, and arable lands.

Regional convergence becomes more difficult to achieve under increasing returns to scale and with externalities of investment and growth. Strong non-convergence (divergence) hypothesis places greater emphasis on path dependency (initial conditions matter), increasing returns to scale, and externalities of investment as sources of differences in factor productivity and growth (Krugman 1991; Romer 1990). Realization of increasing returns to scale and/or agglomeration economies under perfect mobility in one of the regions and not others would accentuate regional divergence. Divergence would also happen if factors are either unable (due to impediments) or unwilling (say age and ethnicity considerations) to move. Under strong divergence hypothesis, inequality in levels of income and resource endowments will prevent convergence in regional growth rates. Under a weak divergence hypothesis, attainment of a minimum threshold of physical and knowledge capital in the leading regions is necessary for persistence in the divergence of growth paths. Thus some regions that attain the minimum thresholds in these factors may form 'clubs' or 'growth poles' and may grow faster than others and achieve 'club convergence'.

To break regional concentration of income, most developing countries have followed regional development policies that have involved redistribution from the richer to poorer regions through central government transfers. These transfers are based on the same Harrod-Domar model that international aid to poorer countries has been based upon—poorer regions can grow faster by raising investment levels. Central transfers seek to bridge the gap between regional savings and the investment required for faster growth. Easterly (2001b) calls this the 'financing-gap approach'. A similar but more limited concept in the public finance literature is that of fiscal balance, where transfers are used to reduce both vertical imbalances between the centre and the regions and horizontal imbalances between the regions. These imbalances arise from a mismatch between the spending needs of and revenues that accrue to regional governments. Poorer regions tend to have larger gaps between the revenues they can raise and the expenditures needed to provide public services. However, as we shall show in the case of India, central transfers are used not only to correct for fiscal imbalances but also to redistribute more funds to poorer regions for development. And, as Easterly (2001b) shows in the case of aid to poor countries, we shall also show that central aid to poor regions in India has not contributed to higher per capita regional GDP growth. Conversely, Chen and Fleisher (1996) point out that reduced central government control over existing enterprises in China has given local government incentives to create a better social and economic environment for local economies, led to better resource allocation, and thus contributed to regional equality. Kanbur and Zhang (2005) find that greater decentralization in China increases rural–urban polarization but reduces inland–coastal polarization. They say that the negative effect of decentralization on inland–coastal inequality goes against the argument that giving provinces greater power has necessarily had detrimental effects on all components of inequality.

In this chapter, we show that while central transfers flow to the poorer states, investments in productive capacity flow to the richer ones. While the former create a moral hazard problem as discussed, leading to inefficient state government policies, the latter help states already ahead to increase their lead. This disproportionate flow of investments in productive capacity to richer regions has also been observed in other countries. Markusen (1994) states that regional policies in Japan, Brazil, and Korea were only moderately successful in directing investment to smaller cities and underdeveloped regions. Even when they were successful, the smaller cities tended to be near the existing dominant ones. Although public investment has been more decentralized, private investment has continued to be concentrated. Even the building of communications and transport infrastructure has tended to reinforce the agglomeration economies of relatively developed regions. With world market integration, there is greater tension between regional and industrial policy, and in the countries that Markusen studied, she found that industrial policy dominates.

Divergence of Regional Incomes in India

In this section, we present trends on regional inequality in India, and show that Indian regional development policies have not been successful in reducing regional disparities. For the purposes of this study, we chose fourteen major states[2] in India. These states contain close to 93 per cent of the country's population and generate 85 per cent of the country's gross domestic product (GDP). Any study of convergence or divergence has to compare units that are reasonably large and reasonably heterogeneous in factor endowments. Therefore, we did not include the other states that were too small in population. Moreover, most of the excluded states (in north-east India) are considered 'special category' by the Planning Commission of India. In most of these states, the only important source of income is governmental activity (Rao et al. 1999).

India has seen a constant and unambiguous rise in regional disparity from 1980 to 1999, the period of our study. Its level of inequality has risen from about twice that of the United States in 1990 to more than three times in 1997 (Shankar and Shah 2001). Two statistical concepts are helpful in looking at the dynamics of regional inequalities. First, a reduction in the dispersion of regional income over time is termed as sigma convergence. Second, any catching up in incomes by relatively poorer regions through faster growth is called beta convergence (Barro and Sala-I-Martin 1995: 383). Analysis of Indian GRDP data shows the absence of both sigma and beta convergence.

Regional Inequality Trends in India—Sigma Convergence

Table 8.1 presents our calculations of different measures of regional inequality from 1980 to 1999. These measures are most widely used in the inequality literature. Shankar and Shah (2001) present a detailed discussion of the calculation of these measures. Other sources for the description and relative merits of these measures include Williamson (1965), Kakwani (1980, 1990), and Atkinson and Bourguignon (2000). The measures include both unweighted measures as well as measures weighted by population. The latter gives greater weight to per capita state domestic products (SDP) differences of states with larger populations.

If larger states lie close to the mean, then the weighted measures will be lower than the unweighted ones and vice versa.

TABLE 8.1
Regional Disparity Trends in India

Year	Max/ Min (MMR)	Simple coefficient of variation (CVu)	Weighted coefficient of variation (CVw)	Relative mean deviation (Rw)	Unweighted gini index (Gu)	Weighted gini index (Gw)	Theil index (T)
1980	2.548	0.276	0.250	0.190	0.158	0.134	0.030
1981	2.642	0.286	0.256	0.196	0.163	0.138	0.031
1982	2.694	0.293	0.255	0.186	0.166	0.135	0.031
1983	2.545	0.274	0.250	0.183	0.152	0.131	0.030
1984	2.531	0.290	0.256	0.203	0.164	0.137	0.031
1985	2.661	0.310	0.268	0.208	0.173	0.140	0.033
1986	2.587	0.306	0.263	0.205	0.170	0.136	0.032
1987	2.836	0.306	0.266	0.202	0.172	0.142	0.033
1988	2.678	0.301	0.269	0.205	0.170	0.144	0.034
1989	2.934	0.314	0.295	0.229	0.179	0.158	0.041
1990	2.704	0.313	0.288	0.220	0.180	0.157	0.039
1991	2.945	0.313	0.289	0.231	0.181	0.159	0.040
1992	3.206	0.335	0.333	0.263	0.195	0.183	0.053
1993	3.246	0.337	0.345	0.276	0.198	0.191	0.057
1994	3.075	0.332	0.343	0.279	0.196	0.191	0.057
1995	3.517	0.345	0.367	0.296	0.203	0.205	0.066
1996	3.355	0.356	0.368	0.295	0.208	0.204	0.066
1997	3.351	0.349	0.373	0.303	0.205	0.208	0.068
1998	3.328	0.346	0.367	0.298	0.204	0.206	0.066
1999	3.413	0.350	0.378	0.313	0.208	0.213	0.070

Source: Calculations based on data from Reserve Bank of India (RBI) and the World Bank's database on state domestic products in India.

On all the different measures, we find that regional inequality has been rising from 1980 till 1999. The ratio of per capita SDP of the richest to the poorest state has risen from 2.5 in 1980 to almost 3.5 in 1989. This is not simply an outlier effect as all the other measures have shown similar increases, suggesting that the regional income distribution has changed over time. Figure 8.1 graphically presents the changes in the different measures of inequality over time. The weighted measures are lower than the corresponding unweighted ones from 1980 till the mid-1990s, when the weighted ones overtake the unweighted ones. This is due to larger states like Maharashtra, Karnataka, and Tamil Nadu moving further away from large and poor states of Bihar and Uttar Pradesh (Figure 8.2).

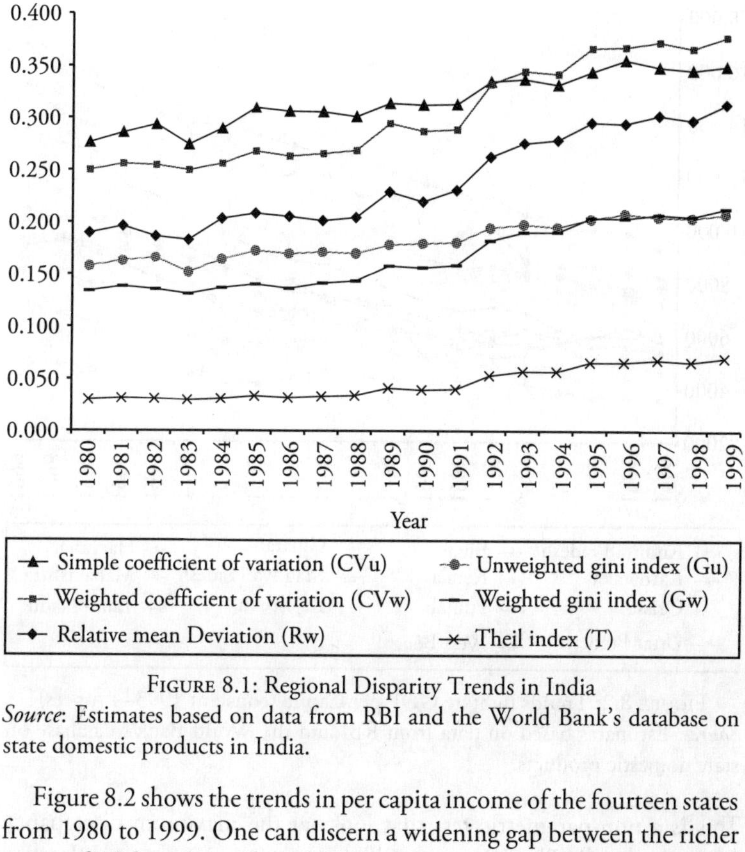

FIGURE 8.1: Regional Disparity Trends in India
Source: Estimates based on data from RBI and the World Bank's database on state domestic products in India.

Figure 8.2 shows the trends in per capita income of the fourteen states from 1980 to 1999. One can discern a widening gap between the richer states of Maharashtra, Punjab, Haryana, and Gujarat and the poorer states of Orissa, Bihar, and Uttar Pradesh. In fact, there seem to be three relatively distinct categories of states in terms of economic performance. The high-performing states are Punjab, Haryana, Maharashtra, Gujarat, and Tamil Nadu (especially in the 1990s). The middle-performing states are Karnataka, Kerala, Andhra Pradesh, West Bengal, Rajasthan, and Madhya Pradesh. The lowest performing states are Bihar, Orissa, and Uttar Pradesh. One might almost be tempted to say that there are three steady states in India towards which these three groups are converging. But before one makes such a leap, one should look at the sharp upward movements of states like Karnataka and Andhra Pradesh in the late 1990s, driven possibly by the information technology services revolution in these states.

We also performed the Kolmogorov–Smirnov test on the hypothesis that the initial and final distributions of per capita SDP are the same.

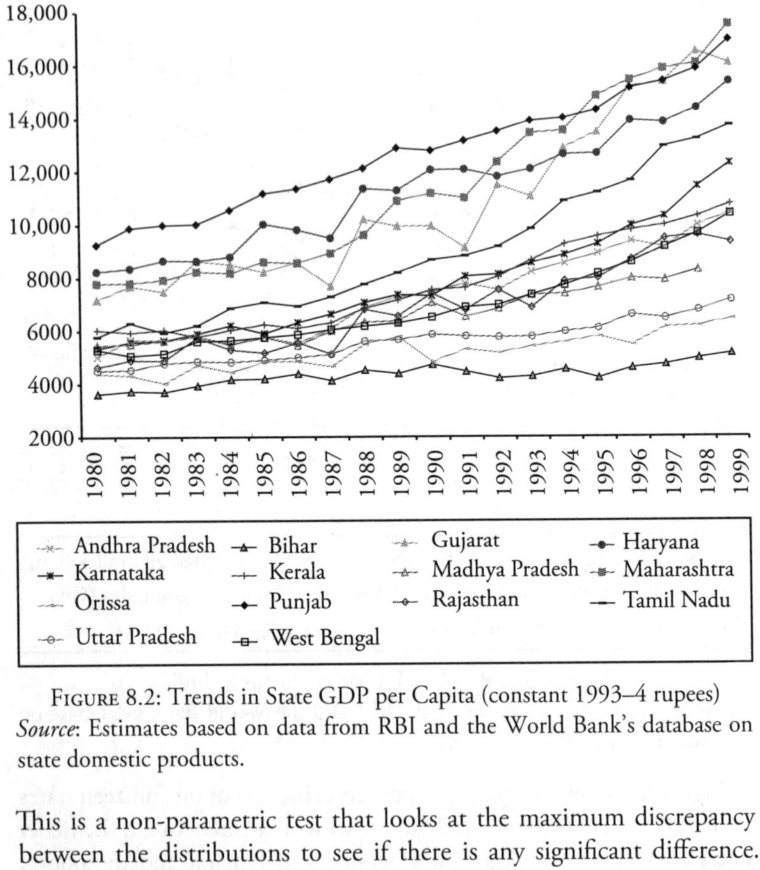

FIGURE 8.2: Trends in State GDP per Capita (constant 1993–4 rupees)
Source: Estimates based on data from RBI and the World Bank's database on state domestic products.

This is a non-parametric test that looks at the maximum discrepancy between the distributions to see if there is any significant difference. Table 8.2 presents the results of this test for different year groups. When the years selected for the test are ten or more years apart, the statistic rejects the null that the distributions are the same. The test-statistic is significant at the 1 per cent level for the 1980–98 comparison. It is significant at the 5 per cent level for the 1980–95 and 1985–98 comparisons. Finally, the statistic is significant at the 10 per cent level for the 1980–90 and 1985–95 comparisons. The results of this test provide further evidence of divergence between per capita SDPs.

The rising income inequality between states is also mirrored by other indices. For example, Figure 8.3 shows that inter-state inequality of the poverty level as measured by the headcount index has been rising since the mid-1970s. As expected, there is an inverse relationship between per capita SDP and poverty levels in states. The rich states of Punjab and Haryana also had the lowest poverty levels, while poor Bihar had the

TABLE 8.2
Kolmogorov–Smirnov Statistics

Years of comparison	K-S statistic	p-value
1980–8	1.89	0.002***
1980–95	1.512	0.021**
1980–90	1.323	0.06*
1980–5	0.756	0.617
1985–98	1.512	0.021**
1985–95	1.323	0.06*
1985–90	1.134	0.153
1990–8	1.134	0.153
1990–5	1.134	0.153
1995–8	0.945	0.334

Notes: * significant at 10 per cent level
** significant at 5 per cent level
*** significant at 1 per cent level
Source: Analysis based on SDP data from RBI and the World Bank.

highest poverty level. However, this inverse relationship is not perfect as rich Maharashtra had higher poverty levels than poor Orissa.[3] In fact the Pearson correlation coefficient between the headcount index and per capita SDP in 1993 was –0.66, which shows a high but not

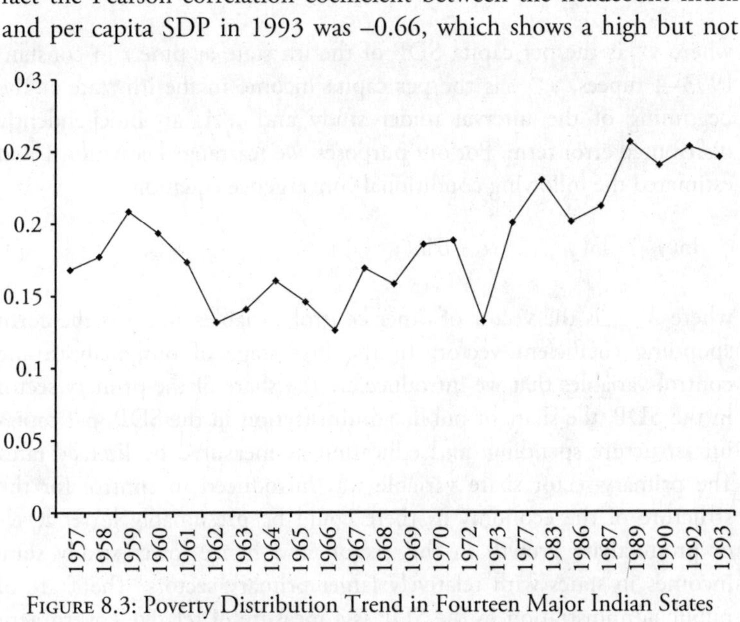

FIGURE 8.3: Poverty Distribution Trend in Fourteen Major Indian States (Coefficient of Variation of Headcount Index)
Source: Database on Poverty and Growth in India, Poverty and Human Resources Division Policy, Research Department, the World Bank.

perfect negative association. Our findings are supported by Jha (2000), who also finds that the coefficient of variation of the rural headcount ratio between the fourteen major states has been rising over time, especially since the mid-1970s. There are also widening disparities in other measures of welfare including sex ratio, female literacy, share of urban population, infant mortality, and life expectancy. Kurian (2000) presents a synopsis of disparities in these indicators.

Regional Inequality Trends in India—Beta Convergence

In general, our analysis does not support the hypothesis of beta convergence among the states of India. For this analysis, we have estimated a growth equation based on a log-linear approximation around the steady state of the Solow growth model. This is similar to the one suggested in Barro and Sala-i-Martin (1992 and 1995). The model is as follows:

$$\frac{1}{T}\ln\left(\frac{y_{i,t}}{y_{i,t-T}}\right) = \alpha_i - \left(\frac{1-e^{-\beta T}}{T}\right)\ln(y_{i,t-T}) + u_{i,t} \qquad (1)$$

where $y_{i,t}$ is the per capita SDP of the ith state at time t in constant 1993–4 rupees, $y_{i,t-T}$ is the per capita income in the ith state at the beginning of the interval under study and u_i is an independently distributed error term. For our purposes, we rearranged equation 1 and estimated the following conditional convergence equation:

$$\ln(y_{i,t}) - \ln(y_{i,t-T}) = \alpha_i + \beta\ln(y_{i,t-T}) + \bar{\gamma}X_{i,t-T} + u_{i,t} \qquad (2)$$

where $X_{i,t-T}$ is the vector of other control variables and $\bar{\gamma}$ is the corresponding coefficient vector. In the first stage of our analysis, the control variables that we introduce are the share of the primary sector in the SDP, the share of public administration in the SDP, per capita infrastructure spending, and education as measured by literacy rates. The primary-sector share variable was introduced to control for the structure of the economy as there could be presumably lower levels of productivity growth in this sector, and hence lower steady state incomes in states with relatively larger primary sectors. The share of public administration in the SDP is a measure of relative government size. Presumably, states with relatively larger public administration components have lower productivity growth. This is just a first cut at effect of the role of government intervention in the economy. Public administration as a share of the SDP varies from 2.5 to 5 per cent in the Indian states. This understimates the role of the government in the economy. In the next section, we have a more detailed treatment of the government's role. The per capita infrastructure component of the SDP was calculated by adding the per capita contributions to the SDP of the transport, communication, and electricity, gas and water sectors in the states' SDP sectoral distribution table. Presumably, states with larger infrastructure production grow faster, especially if the levels of infrastructure are low as is the case in India. Finally, one would expect education to have a positive effect on growth, and states with different educational levels presumably have different steady state incomes.

We carried out the regression analysis over different time periods so that we could build a 'periodization' of convergence phases as Boldrin (2001) puts it. Table 8.3 shows the results of a cross-sectional least-squares regression for the period 1980–99. The coefficient on the initial income level variable is positive in four of the five regressions. It is significant at the 10 per cent level in equation 1 and at the 5 per cent level in equation 3. These results show the absence of convergence, either unconditional or conditional, with the control variables used. The primary-sector share has the expected negative sign and is significant at the 1 per cent level. The coefficients on the public administration and literacy variables are not significant, while the infrastructure variable has the expected positive sign and is significant at 10 per cent level.

Table 8.4 shows the results of a mixed panel and cross-sectional least-squares regression where two time periods, 1981–90 and 1990–9, are pooled together. Again, the coefficient on the initial income variable is positive in all regressions and is significant at 5 per cent level with no control variables. The primary-sector share is negative and significant at 1 per cent level in all the regressions. The other variables are not significant in any of the regressions.

Tables 8.5 and 8.6 show the results separately over the periods 1981–90 and 1990–9. Again, the coefficient on the initial income variable is almost always positive and it is significant in equation 3 in Table 8.6 at 5 per cent level. No other variable in Table 8.5 shows up any statistically significant relationship. However, over the time period 1990–9 (Table 8.6), the primary-sector share has the expected negative effect and is significant at 1 per cent level. This could be the effect of liberelization reforms during this period, which might have helped states with relatively large manufacturing and services sectors to grow

Table 8.3

Regression Equations on Convergence, 1980–99

N = 14	Initial income level	Share of primary sector in SDP	Share of public administration in SDP	Per capita spending on infrastructure	Literacy rate	R-square	Adj R-square	F
Equation 1	0.312					0.226	0.161	3.502
t-statistic	1.871							
p-value	0.086*							0.086*
Equation 2	0.125	–1.209				0.672	0.612	11.269
t-statistic	1.017	–3.868						
p-value	0.331	0.003***						0.002***
Equation 3	0.393		12.506			0.386	0.275	3.459
t-statistic	2.423		1.694					
p-value	.034**		0.118					0.068*
Equation 4	–0.074			0.41		0.399	0.279	3.318
t-statistic	–0.302			1.877				
p-value	0.769			0.09*				0.078*
Equation 5	0.255				0.233	0.251	0.115	1.843
t-statistic	1.309				0.607			
p-value	0.217				0.556			0.204

Notes: * significant at 10 per cent level

** significant at 5 per cent level

*** significant at 1 per cent level

Source: Author's estimates.

Table 8.4

Regression Equations on Convergence, 1981–9

N = 28	Initial income level	Share of primary sector in SDP	Share of public administration in SDP	Per capita spending on infrastructure	Literacy rate	R-square	Adj R-square	F
Equation 1	0.135					0.158	0.126	4.886
t-statistic	2.21							
p-value	0.036**							0.036**
Equation 2	0.042	–0.63				0.426	0.38	9.267
t-statistic	0.712	–3.413						
p-value	0.483	0.002***						0.001***
Equation 3	0.026	–0.688	–1.157			0.433	0.362	6.105
t-statistic	0.398	–3.198	–0.547					
p-value	0.694	0.004***	0.589					0.003***
Equation 4	0.088	–0.715		–0.055		0.432	0.361	6.088
t-statistic	0.823	–2.869		–0.52				
p-value	0.419	0.008***		0.608				0.003***
Equation 5	0.05	–0.677			–0.068	0.43	0.359	6.034
t-statistic	0.796	–3.095			–0.422			
p-value	0.434	0.005***			0.677			0.003***

Notes: * significant at 10 per cent level

** significant at 5 per cent level

*** significant at 1 per cent level

Source: Author's estimates.

TABLE 8.5

Regression Equations on Convergence, 1981–90

Year	Initial income level	Share of primary sector in SDP	Share of public administration in SDP	Per capita spending on infrastructure	Literacy rate	R-square	Adj R-square	F
1981–90								
Equation 1	0.102					0.148	0.077	2.08
t-statistic	1.442							
p-value	0.175							0.175
Equation 2	0.066	–0.281				0.279	0.148	2.127
t-statistic	0.917	–1.484						
p-value	0.379	0.185						0.166
Equation 3	0.08		–1.99			0.188	0.04	1.273
t-statistic	1.02		–0.738					
p-value	0.329		0.476					0.318
Equation 4	0.061			0.047		0.163	0.011	1.069
t-statistic	0.515			0.444				
p-value	0.617			0.665				0.376
Equation 5	0.132				–0.146	0.208	0.064	1.445
t-statistic	1.686				–0.916			
p-value	0.12				0.38			0.277

Notes: * significant at 10 per cent level
** significant at 5 per cent level
*** significant at 1 per cent level

Source: Author's estimates.

TABLE 8.6
Regression Equations on Convergence, 1990–9

N = 14	Initial income level	Share of primary sector in SDP	Share of public administration in SDP	Per capita spending on infrastructure	Literacy rate	R-square	Adj R-square	F
Equation 1	0.16					0.133	0.061	1.847
t-statistic	1.359							
p-value	0.199							0.199
Equation 2	0.04	–1.267				0.682	0.625	11.818
t-statistic	0.502	–.361						
p-value	0.625	0.001***						0.002***
Equation 3	0.337		10.106			0.4	0.291	3.663
t-statistic	2.59		2.209					
p-value	0.025**		0.049**					0.060*
Equation 4	–0.135			0.31		0.324	0.201	2.633
t-statistic	–0.673			1.76				
p-value	0.515			0.106				0.116
Equation 5	0.061				0.525	0.36	0.243	3.089
t-statistic	0.523				1.971			
p-value	0.612				0.074*			0.086*

Notes: * significant at 10 per cent level
** significant at 5 per cent level
*** significant at 1 per cent level

Source: Author's estimates.

faster. The share of public administration is surpisingly positive and significant at 5 per cent level in equation 3, while the literacy rate has an expected positive coefficient significant at 10 per cent level. Again, this could be because liberalization helped the more educated states to grow faster.

Table 8.7 presents the regression results over 1985–95. The initial income coefficient is almost always positive and it is significant at 5 per cent level in equation 3. The primary-sector share has the expected negative and significant coefficient. Surprisingly, again the public administration share has a positive and significant effect. The infrastructure variable is also significant at 1 per cent level with the expected sign.

Table 8.8 presents the results when four time periods 1980–5, 1985–90, 1990–5, and 1995–9 are pooled together. The coefficient on the initial income variable is positive and significant in equation 1, but it becomes insignificant when the primary-sector share variable is added in equation 2. The primary-sector share variable again has the expected negative effect, significant at 1 per cent level.

Tables 8.9, 8.10, and 8.11 pool three different sets of five-year time periods together contiguously. The coefficient on the initial income variable is again mostly positive, and it becomes significant when the public administration share variable is added in Tables 8.9 and 8.11. The coefficient on the public administration variable itself is positive and significant in Table 8.11. The coefficient on the primary-sector share is again negative and significant in all the three Tables. The infrastructure variable did not have any significant effect and is hence not included in these Tables. The literacy variable has a positive and significant effect during 1990, 1995, and 1999.

Finally Tables 8.12 through 8.15 present separate cross-sectional regression results over the four time periods 1980–5, 1985–90, 1990–5, and 1995–9. For the time period 1980–5, the initial income variable coefficient has positive signs and is only significant in equation 3. During 1985–90, no variable shows a significant effect.

Table 8.14 shows the most interesting results as this captures the period before and after the liberalization reforms. The initial income variable mostly shows up with a positive coefficient, which is significant when the public administration variable is added in equation 3. The coefficient on the primary-sector share is again negative and significant. The coefficients on the infrastructure and literacy variables are also positive and significant. Table 8.15 shows no significant effects in the period 1995–9.

TABLE 8.7

Regression Equations on Convergence, 1985–95

N = 14	Initial income level	Share of primary sector in SDP	Share of public administration in SDP	Per capita spending on infrastructure	Literacy rate	R-square	Adj R-square	F
Equation 1	0.181					0.12	0.047	1.638
t-statistic	1.28							
p-value	0.225							0.225
Equation 2	0.024	–1.205				0.697	0.642	12.64
t-statistic	0.261	–4.574						
p-value	0.799	0.001***						0.001***
Equation 3	0.355		15.689			0.46	0.362	4.688
t-statistic	2.665		2.632					
p-value	0.022**		0.023**					0.034**
Equation 4	–0.228			0.428		0.528	0.442	6.152
t-statistic	–1.333			3.083				
p-value	0.21			0.01***				0.016**

Notes: * significant at 10 per cent level

** significant at 5 per cent level

*** significant at 1 per cent level

Source: Author's estimates.

TABLE 8.8

Regression Equations on Convergence, Pooled Observations for 1980–5, 1990–5, and 1995–9

N = 56	Initial income level	Share of primary sector in SDP	Share of public administration in SDP	Per capita spending on infrastructure	Literacy rate	R-square	Adj R-square	F
Equation 1	0.059					0.065	0.047	3.73
t-statistic	1.931							
p-value	0.059*							0.059*
Equation 2	0.001	–0.361				0.212	0.182	7.132
t-statistic	0.039	–3.149						
p-value	0.969	0.003***						0.002***

Notes: * significant at 10 per cent level

** significant at 5 per cent level

*** significant at 1 per cent level

Source: Author's estimates.

TABLE 8.9

Regression Equations on Convergence, Pooled Observations for 1980, 1985, and 1990

N = 28	Initial income level	Share of primary sector in SDP	Share of public administration in SDP	Per capita spending on infrastructure	Literacy rate	R-square	Adj R-square	F
Equation 1	0.075					0.077	0.041	2.157
t-statistic	1.469							
p-value	0.154							0.154
Equation 2	0.037	–0.249				0.174	0.108	2.642
t-statistic	0.685	–1.722						
p-value	0.5	0.097*						0.091*
Equation 3	0.095		2.918			0.132	0.063	1.903
t-statistic	1.796		1.264					
p-value	0.085*		0.218					0.17

Notes: * significant at 10 per cent level

** significant at 5 per cent level

*** significant at 1 per cent level

Source: Author's estimates.

Table 8.10

Regression Equations on Convergence, Pooled Observations for 1980–5, 1985–90, and 1990–95

N = 28	Initial income level	Share of primary sector in SDP	Share of public administration in SDP	Per capita spending on infrastructure	Literacy rate	R-square	Adj R-square	F
Equation 1	0.065					0.039	0.002	1.052
t-statistic	1.026							
p-value	0.315							0.315
Equation 2	–0.014	–0.64				0.342	0.289	6.497
t-statistic	–0.248	–3.394						
p-value	0.806	0.002***						0.005***
Equation 3	–0.131	0.196				0.203	0.139	3.188
t-statistic	–1.257	2.271						
p-value	0.22	0.032**						0.058*

Notes: * significant at 10 per cent level
** significant at 5 per cent level
*** significant at 1 per cent level

Source: Author's estimates.

TABLE 8.11

Regression Equations on Convergence, Pooled Observations for 1990, 1995, and 1999

N = 28	Initial income level	Share of primary sector in SDP	Share of public administration in SDP	Per capita spending on infrastructure	Literacy rate	R-square	Adj R-square	F
Equation 1	0.07					0.074	0.038	2.075
t-statistic	1.44							
p-value	0.162							0.162
Equation 2	–0.007	–0.657				0.377	0.328	7.579
t-statistic	–0.157	–3.491						
p-value	0.876	0.002***						0.003***
Equation 3	0.168		5.619			0.23	0.168	3.73
t-statistic	2.675		2.25					
p-value	0.013**		0.034**					0.038**
Equation 4	0.07	–0.574	3.888			0.447	0.378	6.476
t-statistic	1.113	–3.074	1.742					
p-value	0.277	0.005***	0.094*					0.002***
Equation 5	0.01				0.287	0.206	0.142	3.242
t-statistic	0.19				2.039			
p-value	0.851				0.052*			0.056*

Notes: * significant at 10 per cent level
** significant at 5 per cent level
*** significant at 1 per cent level

Source: Author's estimates.

TABLE 8.12
Regression Equations on Convergence, 1980–5

N = 14	Initial income level	Share of primary sector in SDP	Share of public administration in SDP	Per capita spending on infrastructure	Literacy rate	R-square	Adj R-square	F
Equation 1	0.07					0.132	0.06	1.828
t-statistic	1.352							
p-value	0.201							0.201
Equation 2	0.068	–0.013				0.133	–0.025	0.842
t-statistic	1.157	–0.088						
p-value	0.272	0.932						0.457
Equation 3	0.112				–0.174	0.295	0.167	2.301
t-statistic	2.024				–1.593			
p-value	0.068*				0.139			0.146

Notes: * significant at 10 per cent level
** significant at 5 per cent level
*** significant at 1 per cent level

Source: Author's estimates.

TABLE 8.13

Regression Equations on Convergence, 1985–90

N = 14	Initial income level	Share of primary sector in SDP	Share of public administration in SDP	Per capita spending on infrastructure	Literacy rate	R-square	Adj R-square	F
Equation 1	0.035					0.015	–0.067	0.181
t-statistic	0.425							
p-value	0.678							0.678
Equation 2	–0.017	–0.398				0.222	0.081	1.57
t-statistic	–0.203	–1.712						
p-value	0.843	0.115						0.251

Notes: * significant at 10 per cent level
** significant at 5 per cent level
*** significant at 1 per cent level

Source: Author's estimates.

Table 8.14

Regression Equations on Convergence, 1990–5

N = 14	Initial income level	Share of primary sector in SDP	Share of public administration in SDP	Per capita spending on infrastructure	Literacy rate	R-square	Adj R-square	F
Equation 1	0.137					0.132	0.059	1.821
t-statistic	1.348							
p-value	0.202							0.202
Equation 2	0.029	−1.134				0.726	0.676	14.548
t-statistic	0.462	−4.88						
p-value	0.653	0.000***						0.001***
Equation 3	0.267		7.453			0.327	0.205	2.677
t-statistic	2.257		1.789					
p-value	0.045**		0.101					0.113
Equation 4	−0.222			0.377		0.512	0.423	5.772
t-statistic	−1.516			2.928				
p-value	0.158			0.014**				0.019**
Equation 5	0.038				0.525	0.436	0.334	4.255
t-statistic	0.404				2.437			
p-value	0.694				0.033**			0.043**

Notes: * significant at 10 per cent level
** significant at 5 per cent level
*** significant at 1 per cent level

Source: Author's estimates.

TABLE 8.15

Regression Equations on Convergence, 1995–9

N = 14	Initial income level	Share of primary sector in SDP	Share of public administration in SDP	Per capita spending on infrastructure	Literacy rate	R-square	Adj R-square	F
Equation 1	0.025					0.033	–0.047	0.415
t-statistic	0.644							
p-value	0.532							0.532
Equation 2	0.011	–0.111				0.057	–0.114	0.335
t-statistic	0.235	–0.529						
p-value	0.818	0.608						0.723

Notes: * significant at 10 per cent level
** significant at 5 per cent level
*** significant at 1 per cent level

Source: Author's estimates.

Summarizing the evidence so far, there is no convergence in incomes across the Indian states, not even when several different control variables are added. In fact, there has been significant divergence after 1990, when the liberalization reforms started. These reforms allowed states with larger manufacturing and service sectors as well as stronger educational and infrastructure base to grow faster and widen differences compared to the other states. This is seen by negative and significant coefficients on the primary-sector share variable and positive and significant coefficients on the infrastructure and literacy variables after 1990. This reinforces the evidence of sharp increases in the inequality measures presented in the previous section after 1991.

Our findings, which show that per capita state domestic product is diverging, are consistent with those of other authors who have looked at regional inequalities in India. Bajpai and Sachs (1996) find evidence of divergence of state domestic products in the time period 1971–93. Cashin and Sahay (1996) also find a widening in the dispersion of the net domestic products of Indian states from 1971–91. Das and Barua (1996), Nagaraj et al. (2000), Rao et al. (1999), and Yagci (1999) also find similar evidence of divergence in India. Some of these authors have also found evidence against beta convergence in India. Rao et al. (1999) find that the growth of SDP per capita is positively related to initial levels for various sub-periods beginning in 1965 and ending in 1994–5. Yagci (1999) reports that higher-income states have grown faster since 1980 compared to lower-income states. Bajpai and Sachs (1996) also find evidence of a weak positive relationship between initial SDP and the economic growth rate in the time period 1971–93. However, Cashin and Sahay (1996) report evidence of weak beta convergence. But they also point out that the speed of convergence, 1.5 per cent per year, is slower than that of regional convergence in industrial economies (Australia, the US, Canada, and Japan), whose rate of convergence has been 2 per cent. In fact the speed of convergence is slower than between Organization for Economic Cooperation and Development (OECD) countries, which is a surprising result, as one would expect faster convergence within national borders.

Fiscal Structure and Regional Policies

There are several reasons for increasing regional inequality in India. The standard broad explanation could be that India is in an early stage of development and, is therefore, on the wrong side of the 'inverted

U' pattern of regional inequalities (Williamson 1965). However, this explanation is not very satisfying if one wants to understand in detail the dynamics of regional income distribution and the effects of government policies on such redistribution. The causes of regional disparity can be attributed to both economic forces and government interventions. As discussed earlier, economies of scale and scope, economies due to local knowledge spillovers, and thick factor markets cause both investment and skilled labour to converge in specific locations, leading to economic divergence (Fujita et al. 1999). On the other hand, government revenue and expenditure patterns, the intergovernmental transfer system, explicit industrial policies, regional development policies, and government-created barriers to inter-state trade also have an important effect on regional disparities.

In this chapter, we examine in detail India's fiscal structure and government policies that affect regional inequality. While we do not explicitly look at the economic forces shaping regional income patterns, we take into account the relationship between these forces and government policies. For example, where the central government spends its money on a certain sector, say defence, depends on the location of already existing defence industries. While regional balance may require spatial dispersal of government spending, economies of scale and scope may require the government to spend in areas with an already established industrial base, accentuating regional differences. Further, even if a government invests in a relatively backward region, the secondary benefits of that investment could flow to more advanced regions in the form of increased demand for intermediate goods and services.

There is substantial literature on India's fiscal structure, the regional development policies pursued by the central government, and state government revenue and expenditure patterns. Therefore, we present only a brief description of the Indian fiscal system, while focusing more closely on those aspects that have a bearing on regional inequality. In India, there are broadly four channels through which government finance and policy affect development in different states—explicit centre–state transfers, implicit inter-state transfers, central government policies, and state government policies. In this chapter, we discuss the first two channels. In the next sub-section, we show that explicit centre–state transfers designed to go to poorer states have created dependency and have not helped them catch up with richer regions. Next, we show that implicit transfers tend to flow to richer states, and as these transfers directly improve productive capacity, they have contributed to rising regional inequality.

Explicit Centre–State Transfers

Hypothetically, centre–state transfers have an impact on regional inequality through the magnitude of their share in state revenues, the measure of central discretion involved in making these grants, and the overall design of the transfer system. On the one hand, the central government can use these transfers as a redistributive mechanism to reduce regional disparities, while on the other hand these transfers can accentuate disparities by creating perverse incentives for state governments. This is an empirical question that we shall answer in the next section. In this sub-section, we present trends in explicit transfers by the centre to the states.

There are three explicit modes of transfers from the centre to the states in India—the constitutional mechanism of the Finance Commission (FC), transfers through the developmentally oriented Planning Commission (PC), and transfers from central government ministries. The FC decides on tax share and makes grants, the PC gives grants and loans for development plans. Various central ministries give grants (both fully funded and matching) to their counterparts in the states. Rao and Singh (1999, 2001) make a detailed analysis of these three mechanisms of intergovernmental transfers, and their constitutionality and legality. For our purposes, the important thing to note is that central government discretion is the least in FC transfers, high in PC transfers, and highest in the transfers from central ministries.

Table 8.16 presents the different types of centre–state transfers. The transfers are both in the form of grants (revenue transfers) and loans (capital transfers). The PC makes both capital and revenue transfers. Since 1969, plan transfers have been made on the basis of the 'Gadgil formula', which is approved (and modified) by the National Development Council (NDC) from time to time.[4] According to a modification in December 1991, 30 per cent of plan assistance is kept apart for special category states. These states, as mentioned earlier, are not included in our study. Our interest is in the remaining 70 per cent, which is distributed on the basis of population (60 per cent weight), per capita SDP (25 per cent weight), fiscal management (7.5 per cent weight), and special problems of states (7.5 per cent weight). Around 20 per cent of the funds with the 25 per cent weight on per capita SDP are allotted only to the states with less than average per capita SDP on the basis of an 'inverse formula', which is given by

$$\frac{P_i / Y_i}{\sum P_i / Y_i},$$

where Y_i and P_i represent the per capita SDP and the population respectively, of the ith state. The remaining 5 per cent of these funds are allocated to all the states according to the 'distance formula', which is given by

$$\frac{(Y_h - Y_i)P_i}{\sum (Y_h - Y_i)P_i}$$

where Y_h is the per capita SDP of the state with the highest per capita SDP. $Y_h - Y_i$ for the highest income state is calculated as the distance between the highest and the second highest per capita SDP. For the major states, which are of interest to us, plan assistance includes both loans and grants in the ratio of 70:30. Plan assistance is given both for state plan schemes, which are developed by state planning boards, and for implementing central plan schemes in the states (Rao and Singh 1999; Sato 1992).

TABLE 8.16
Characterization of All Transfers to States

	Capital transfers	Revenue transfers
Plan	PC	PC
Non-plan	Central government	FC, central government

FC transfers are entirely non-plan in the form of revenue sharing and grants. The FC assesses overall budgetary requirements of the centre and the states and determines the overall resources available for transfer during the period of recommendation (every five years). It then projects the states' own revenues and non-plan current expenditures. After this assessment, it first distributes assigned taxes on the basis of origin. These taxes include additional excise duties in lieu of sales tax, and grants in lieu of a repealed tax on railway passenger fares. Second, it distributes shareable taxes—personal income tax and union excise duties—between the centre and states and among the states. It finally makes up the deficit between projected expenditures and revenues after tax devolution with grants with the following formula.

$G_i = E_i - (R_{oi} + R_{ai} + R_{si})$

where G_i represents the grants receivable by the state i, if the right-hand side is positive. E_i represents projected non-plan current expenditures of state i, R_{oi} represents projected own revenues of state i, R_{oi} represents projected share of assigned revenues of state i, and R_{si} represents projected shared taxes of state i. This is generally called the 'gap-filling' approach (Rao and Singh 1999).

Apart from PC and FC transfers, states also get assistance from the centre in the form of central-sector and centrally sponsored schemes. These transfers are entirely discretionary and central ministries develop national programmes either by themselves or at the request of relevant state ministries. Central-sector schemes are funded entirely by central grants, and states merely execute these programmes. Centrally sponsored schemes are cost-sharing programmes, and central transfers take the form of both loans and grants. The amount and loan/grant components of central transfers vary from programme to programme. The rationale for these programmes is to finance activities that have inter-state spillovers or are in the nature of merit goods. Apart from these, states also get grants and loans in the case of natural disasters, ways and means advances (WMA) from the central government, loans to settle overdrafts at the Reserve Bank of India (RBI), special loans for reducing debts owed to the central government and small savings allotments (Rao and Singh 1999; Sato 1992).

Table 8.17 classifies the different transfers according to their levels of discretion. FC transfers involve the least discretion as they are decided by a neutral statutory body according to a preset formula. However, the discretionary element is not entirely absent as the President appoints the FC on the advice of the central cabinet, and its proposals have to be passed by Parliament, which means it needs the support of the ruling party or coalition. The grants and loans made on the recommendation of the PC for state plans are moderately discretionary as these are based on plans drawn up by the states in consultation with the PC. The central plan schemes involve a high level of central discretion as these are drawn up by the centre and implemented by the states. Finally, the other forms of central government assistance also involve a high level of central discretion as shown in the Table. This classification of discretion conforms to the classifications made in Sato (1992), Rao and Singh (2000), Biswas and Marjit (2000), Dasgupta et al. (2001), and Rao and Singh (2001).

TABLE 8.17
Categorization of All Transfers to States

	FC	PC	Central government
Low discretion	Shared taxes, non-plan grants		
Moderate discretion		Grants and loans for state plan schemes	
High discretion		Grants and loans for central plan schemes	Grants and loans for central sector and centrally sponsored schemes, small savings allotments, grants and loans in the case of natural disasters, WMAs from the central government, loans to settle overdrafts at the RBI, special loans for reducing debts owed to central government

Discretion is important as it is a measure of central government control over state policies. In terms of impacting regional inequality, one could hypothesize that high levels of central discretion can reduce regional disparity by directing transfers to poorer states. The alternative hypothesis would be that high levels of central discretion could create a dependency syndrome among state governments that would inhibit state initiatives for development. Further, high levels of central discretion could mean that transfers are influenced more by political than developmental motives, which could have detrimental effects on regional inequality. In fact, Rao and Singh (2000) and Dasgupta et al. (2001) find some evidence of this effect.

Overall Transfers

In the rest of this sub-section we first look at overall transfers—revenue and capital (grants and loans)—and we then discuss trends in each of these separately.[5] Table 8.18 presents trends in overall transfers from 1985 to 2001. The transfer statistics are presented both as shares in total state receipts (including capital and revenue receipts) and as component shares in overall transfers. We present these statistics based on the source of recommendation for these transfers, as well as by the degree of discretion involved in these transfers.

TABLE 8.18

Central Transfer Statistics—Revenue and Capital

	1985	1986	1987	1988	1989	1990	1991	1992	1993	1994	1995	1996	1997	1998	1999	2000	2001
Share of total transfers in total state receipts	47%	45%	45%	45%	43%	45%	42%	42%	43%	39%	39%	42%	41%	39%	39%	43%	43%
Central transfers by source as share of total state receipts—capital and revenue																	
FC transfers	17%	18%	18%	17%	19%	18%	17%	19%	18%	16%	18%	20%	18%	16%	15%	18%	18%
PC transfers	15%	15%	16%	15%	12%	13%	13%	13%	15%	15%	10%	13%	12%	11%	11%	11%	13%
Other non-plan central government transfers	15%	12%	11%	13%	12%	14%	12%	10%	10%	8%	10%	9%	11%	13%	14%	14%	13%
Central transfers by discretion as share of total receipts—capital and revenue																	
FC transfers (low)	17%	18%	18%	17%	19%	18%	17%	19%	18%	16%	18%	20%	18%	16%	15%	18%	18%
State plan schemes (moderate) (1)	14%	13%	14%	13%	11%	12%	12%	13%	14%	14%	9%	12%	11%	11%	11%	10%	12%
Central plan schemes and other central government transfers (high) (2)	17%	13%	13%	15%	13%	15%	12%	11%	11%	9%	11%	10%	12%	13%	14%	15%	14%
Total moderate and high discretionary transfers (1+2)	30%	27%	27%	28%	24%	27%	24%	24%	25%	23%	20%	22%	23%	24%	25%	25%	25%

Table 8.18 (contd...)

Table 8.18 (contd...)

	1985	1986	1987	1988	1989	1990	1991	1992	1993	1994	1995	1996	1997	1998	1999	2000	2001
Central transfers by source as share of total transfers—capital and revenue																	
FC transfers	36%	41%	40%	39%	44%	40%	42%	44%	42%	42%	47%	47%	44%	39%	38%	41%	41%
PC transfers	33%	33%	34%	33%	28%	28%	30%	32%	34%	38%	27%	31%	29%	29%	28%	26%	29%
Other non-plan central government transfers	31%	26%	25%	28%	28%	32%	28%	24%	24%	20%	26%	22%	27%	32%	34%	33%	30%
Central transfers by discretion as share of total transfers—capital and revenue																	
FC transfers (low)	36%	41%	40%	39%	44%	40%	42%	44%	42%	42%	47%	47%	44%	39%	38%	41%	41%
State plan schemes (moderate) (1)	29%	30%	31%	28%	26%	26%	29%	30%	32%	36%	25%	30%	28%	28%	27%	24%	27%
Central plan schemes and other central government transfers (high) (2)	35%	29%	29%	33%	30%	34%	29%	26%	26%	22%	28%	23%	28%	33%	35%	35%	32%
Total moderate and high discretionary transfers (1+2)	64%	59%	60%	61%	56%	60%	58%	56%	58%	58%	53%	53%	56%	61%	62%	59%	59%

Source: Authors' calculations based on data from the RBI and the World Bank.

Figure 8.4 shows that the share of overall central transfers in overall state receipts declined from 47 per cent in 1985 to 42 per cent in 1991 and has since remained relatively stable around 41 per cent. FC transfers as a share in overall state receipts have remained more or less stable around 18 per cent. PC transfer share has fluctuated around 13 per cent during the period 1985 to 2001. The share of other non-plan central government transfer has fluctuated around 12 per cent.

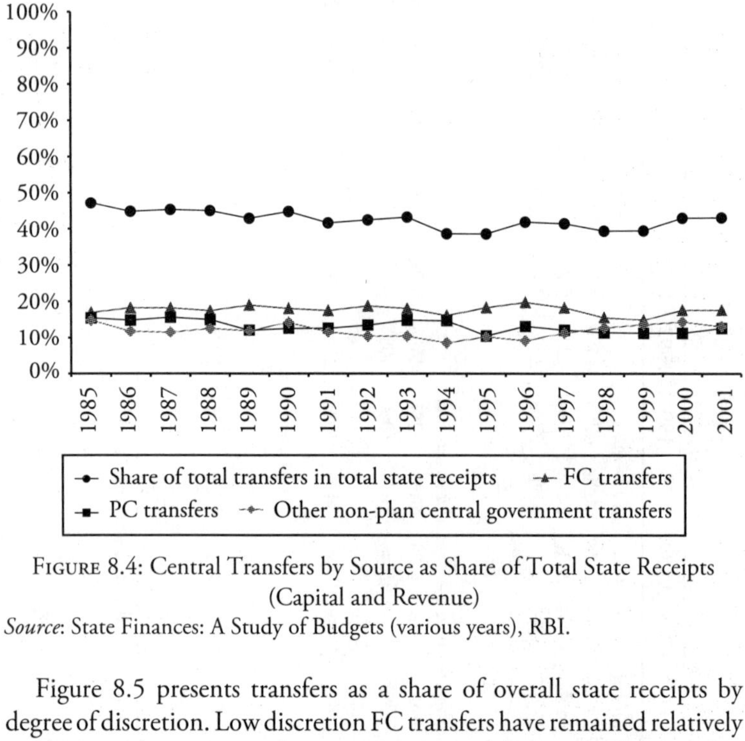

FIGURE 8.4: Central Transfers by Source as Share of Total State Receipts (Capital and Revenue)

Source: State Finances: A Study of Budgets (various years), RBI.

Figure 8.5 presents transfers as a share of overall state receipts by degree of discretion. Low discretion FC transfers have remained relatively stable around 18 per cent from 1985 to 2001. Moderately discretionary transfer share for state plan schemes has declined marginally from 14 per cent to 12 per cent. High discretion transfer share remained stable in the late 1980s around 14 per cent, declined to about 10 per cent in 1996 and then rose again to 14 per cent in 2001.

Figure 8.6 presents the different components of transfers by source of recommendation as a share of total transfers including capital and revenue transfers. FC transfer share increased from 36 per cent in 1985 to 47 per cent in 1996 and then declined to 41 per cent in 2001. PC transfer share declined in the late 1980s from 33 per cent in 1985 to 28

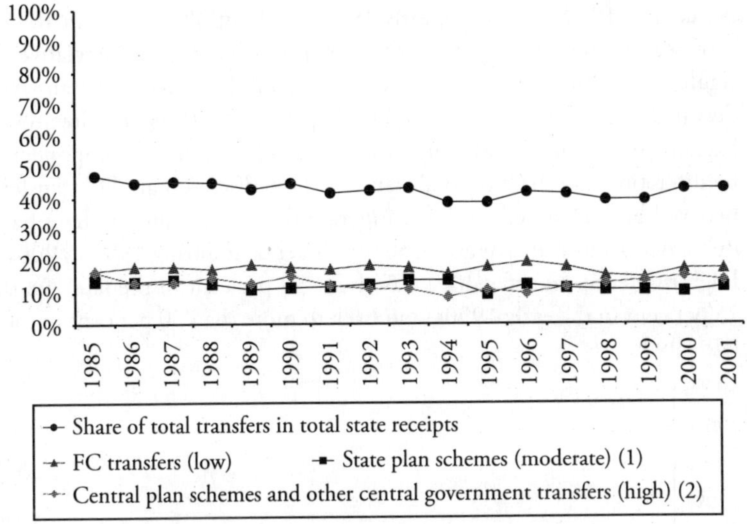

FIGURE 8.5: Central Transfers by Discretion as Share of Total State Receipts (Capital and Revenue)

Source: State Finances: A Study of Budgets (various years), RBI.

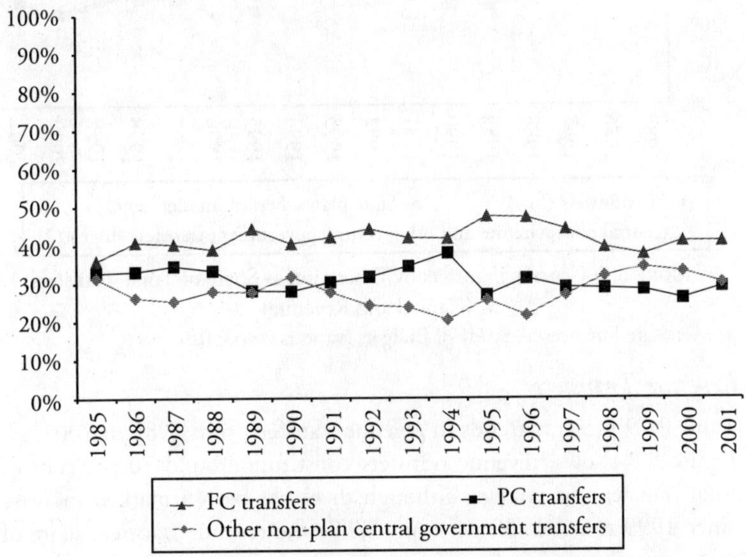

FIGURE 8.6: Central Transfers by Source as Share of Total Transfers (Capital and Revenue)

Source: State Finances: A Study of Budgets (various years), RBI.

per cent in 1989, rose in the early 1990s to about 38 per cent in 1994, dropped sharply to 27 per cent in 1995 and has remained relatively stable since. The share of other non-plan central government transfers declined from 31 per cent in 1985 to 20 per cent in 1994 and then rose back to 30 per cent in 2001. Figure 8.7 presents the transfer components by discretion as a share of total transfers. Low discretionary FC transfer behaved as mentioned earlier. Moderate discretion transfer share has fluctuated around an average of about 28 per cent during 1985 to 2001. High discretion transfer share was about 30 per cent in the late 1980s, 25 per cent in the early 1990s, and back to more than 30 per cent in the late 1990s.

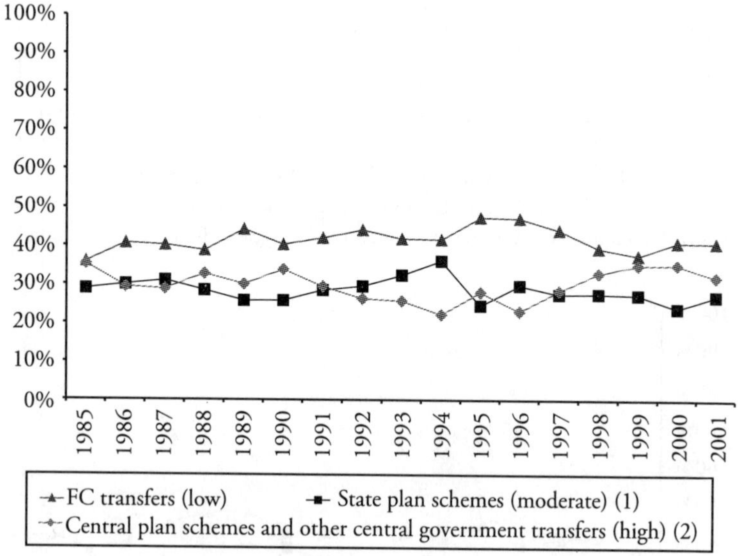

FIGURE 8.7: Central Transfers by Discretion as Share of Total Transfers (Capital and Revenue)

Source: State Finances: A Study of Budgets (various years), RBI.

Revenue Transfers

Table 8.19 presents trends in revenue transfers from 1985 to 2001. As Figure 8.8 shows, revenue transfers constitute around 70 per cent of total transfers on average, although there has been a marked increase since 1999 to about 80 per cent. While the revenue transfers share of total central transfers has increased, the revenue component of total state receipts has remained greater than 70 per cent except during 1998–2000. However, this trend masks trends in individual states that could be different.

TABLE 8.19

Central Transfer Statistics—Revenue

	1985	1986	1987	1988	1989	1990	1991	1992	1993	1994	1995	1996	1997	1998	1999	2000	2001
Share of revenue receipts in total state receipts	72%	74%	74%	75%	74%	73%	74%	75%	79%	74%	76%	78%	74%	67%	67%	69%	71%
Share of revenue transfers in total transfers	62%	67%	67%	67%	66%	66%	71%	75%	75%	70%	72%	71%	68%	61%	78%	80%	79%
Share of total revenue transfers in total state revenues	41%	40%	41%	40%	38%	40%	40%	42%	41%	37%	37%	38%	38%	36%	36%	40%	39%
Central transfers by source as share of total revenue																	
FC transfers	24%	25%	25%	23%	26%	25%	24%	25%	23%	22%	24%	25%	25%	23%	22%	26%	25%
PC transfers	11%	9%	10%	10%	7%	8%	9%	10%	11%	11%	7%	8%	8%	8%	8%	8%	8%
Other non-plan central government grants	6%	6%	7%	7%	5%	7%	7%	7%	7%	4%	5%	5%	5%	5%	5%	6%	6%
Central transfers by discretion as share of total revenue																	
FC transfers (low)	24%	25%	25%	23%	26%	25%	24%	25%	23%	22%	24%	25%	25%	23%	22%	26%	25%
Grants for state plan schemes (moderate) (1)	8%	8%	8%	7%	6%	7%	8%	9%	10%	10%	6%	8%	7%	8%	8%	6%	7%
Central plan schemes and other central	9%	8%	8%	10%	6%	8%	8%	9%	9%	5%	6%	5%	6%	5%	6%	8%	7%

Table 8.19 (*contd...*)

Table 8.19 (contd...)

	1985	1986	1987	1988	1989	1990	1991	1992	1993	1994	1995	1996	1997	1998	1999	2000	2001
government transfers (high) (2)																	
Total moderate and high discretionary transfers (1+2)	17%	16%	16%	17%	13%	16%	16%	17%	18%	15%	12%	13%	13%	13%	14%	14%	14%
Central transfers by source as share of total revenue transfers																	
FC transfers	58%	61%	60%	58%	67%	61%	59%	59%	56%	60%	66%	66%	65%	65%	62%	65%	64%
PC transfers	26%	23%	24%	24%	19%	21%	23%	23%	26%	29%	20%	22%	21%	23%	23%	19%	21%
Other non-plan central government grants	16%	16%	16%	18%	14%	18%	18%	18%	18%	12%	14%	12%	14%	13%	15%	16%	15%
Central transfers by discretion as share of total revenue transfers																	
FC transfers (low)	58%	61%	60%	58%	67%	61%	59%	59%	56%	60%	66%	66%	65%	65%	62%	65%	64%
Grants for state plan schemes (moderate) (1)	20%	19%	19%	17%	16%	18%	20%	21%	24%	26%	17%	20%	19%	21%	22%	16%	18%
Central plan schemes and other central government transfers (high) (2)	22%	20%	21%	25%	17%	21%	20%	20%	21%	14%	17%	13%	16%	14%	16%	19%	18%
Total moderate and high discretionary transfers (1+2)	42%	39%	40%	42%	33%	39%	41%	41%	44%	40%	34%	34%	35%	35%	38%	35%	36%

Source: Authors' calculations based on data from the RBI and the World Bank.

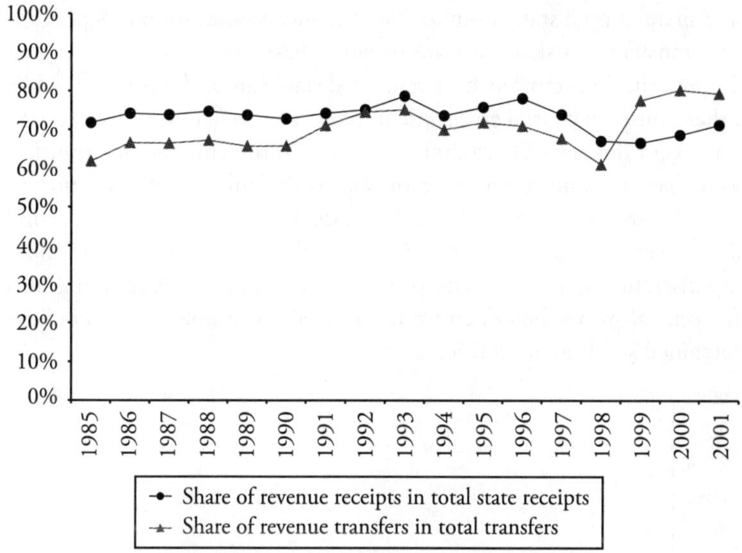

FIGURE 8.8: Revenue Receipts and Revenue Transfers
Source: State Finances: A Study of Budgets (various years), RBI.

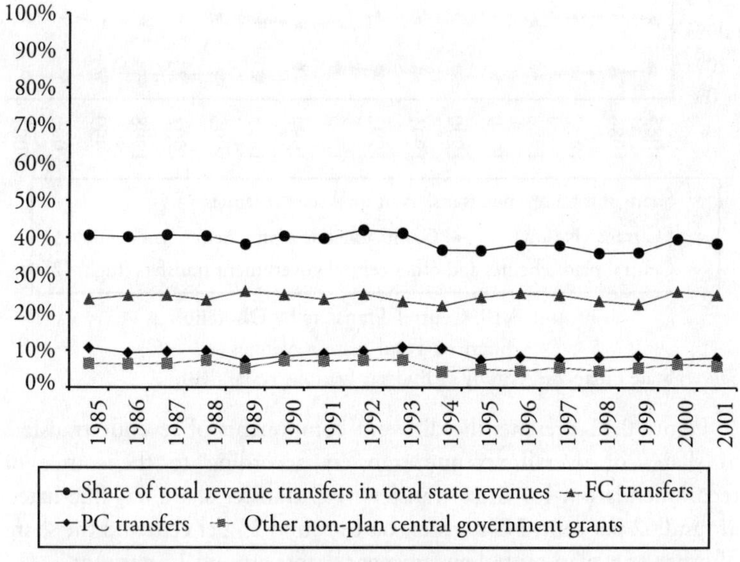

FIGURE 8.9: Central Transfers by Source as Share of Total State Revenues
Source: State Finances: A Study of Budgets (various years), RBI.

Figure 8.9 shows central revenue transfers by source of recommendation as a share of total state revenues. The share of total revenue transfers as a share of total state revenues has remained stable around 39 per cent. FC transfers as a share of state revenues have remained stable around 24 per cent, PC transfers have remained stable around 9 per cent, while other non-plan central government grants have remained stable around 6 per cent during 1985 to 2001. Figure 8.10 presents revenue transfers as a share of state revenues according to the amount of discretion involved. Low-discretion FC transfer share have remained stable around 24 per cent as already mentioned. Similarly, the shares of both moderate-discretion grants for state plan schemes and high-discretion grants for central plan schemes and other central government transfers have remained stable at around 8 per cent.

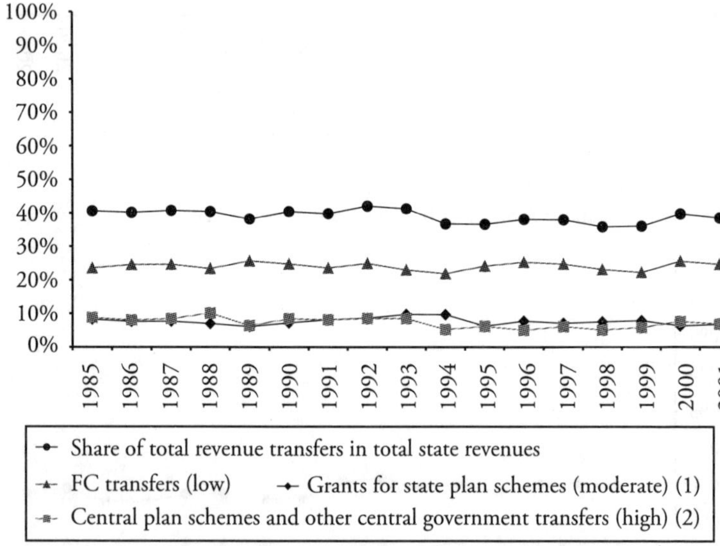

FIGURE 8.10: Central Transfers by Discretion as Share of Total State Revenues

Source: State Finances: A Study of Budgets (various years), RBI.

Figure 8.11 presents the different components of revenue transfers as shares of overall revenue transfers according to the source of recommendation for these transfers. FC transfer share has fluctuated around 62 per cent, PC transfer share around 23 per cent and the share of other non-plan central government grants around 15 per cent.

Figure 8.12 shows the different components of revenue transfers as a share of total revenue transfers according to the degree of central discretion. Again all the shares of the different components have remained relatively stable—low-discretion FC transfer share around

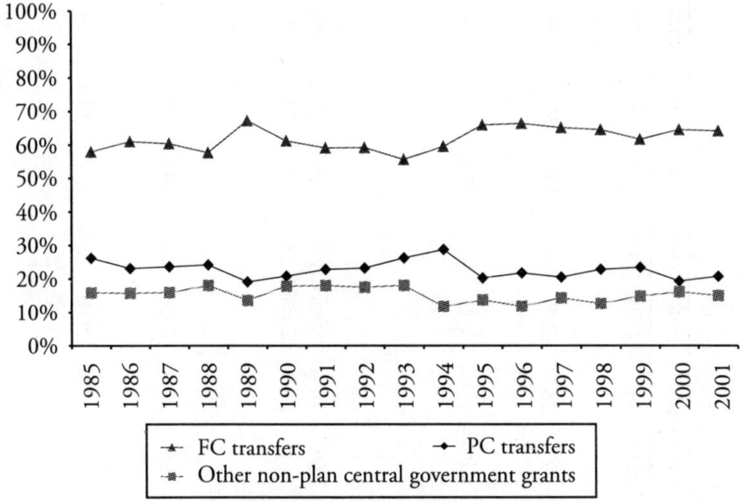

FIGURE 8.11: Central Transfers by Source as Share of Total Revenue Transfers

Source: State Finances: A Study of Budgets (various years), RBI.

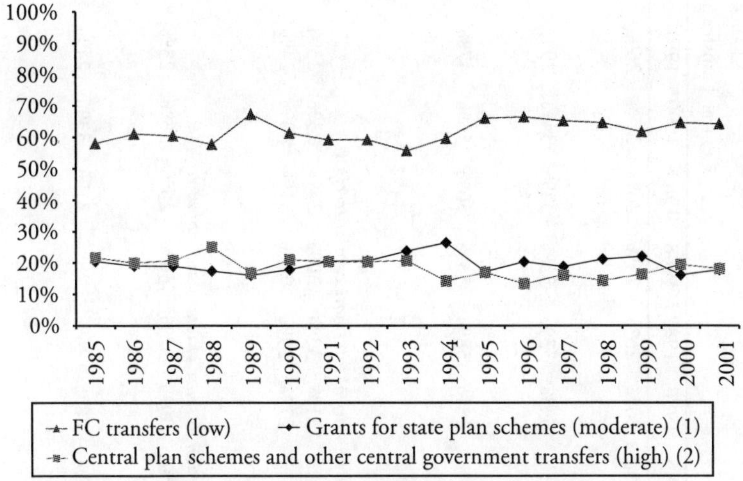

FIGURE 8.12: Central Transfers by Discretion as Share of Total Revenue Transfers

Source: State Finances: A Study of Budgets (various years), RBI.

62 per cent, grants for moderate-discretion state plan schemes around 20 per cent, and high-discretion share of central plan schemes and other central government transfers around 19 per cent.

Table 8.20

Central Transfer Statistics—Capital

	1985	1986	1987	1988	1989	1990	1991	1992	1993	1994	1995	1996	1997	1998	1999	2000	2001
Share of capital receipts in total state receipts	28%	26%	26%	25%	26%	27%	26%	25%	21%	26%	24%	22%	26%	33%	33%	31%	29%
Share of capital transfers in total transfers	38%	33%	33%	33%	34%	34%	29%	25%	25%	30%	28%	29%	32%	39%	39%	37%	36%
Share of total capital transfers in total state capital receipts	64%	58%	58%	58%	56%	56%	47%	44%	50%	44%	45%	55%	51%	47%	46%	50%	54%
Central transfers by source as share of total state capital receipts																	
PC transfers	28%	31%	32%	30%	25%	23%	23%	25%	30%	26%	20%	30%	24%	18%	17%	19%	24%
Other non-plan central government loans	36%	27%	25%	28%	31%	33%	24%	19%	21%	18%	25%	25%	27%	29%	30%	31%	31%
Central transfers by discretion as share of total state capital receipts																	
Loans for state plan schemes (moderate) (1)	27%	30%	32%	30%	25%	23%	23%	24%	30%	26%	20%	29%	24%	18%	17%	19%	24%
Central plan schemes and other central	37%	28%	26%	28%	31%	33%	24%	19%	21%	18%	25%	26%	28%	29%	30%	31%	31%

Table 8.20 (contd...)

Table 8.20 (*contd...*)

	1985	1986	1987	1988	1989	1990	1991	1992	1993	1994	1995	1996	1997	1998	1999	2000	2001
government transfers (high) (2)																	
Total moderate and high discretionary transfers (1+2)	64%	58%	58%	58%	56%	56%	47%	44%	50%	44%	45%	55%	51%	47%	46%	50%	54%
Central transfers by source as share of total capital transfers																	
PC transfers	43%	53%	56%	52%	45%	42%	49%	56%	59%	59%	44%	55%	47%	38%	36%	38%	44%
Other non-plan central government loans	57%	47%	44%	48%	55%	58%	51%	44%	41%	41%	56%	45%	53%	62%	64%	62%	56%
Central transfers by discretion as share of total capital transfers																	
Loans for state plan schemes (moderate) (1)	43%	52%	55%	51%	45%	41%	48%	56%	59%	59%	44%	53%	46%	38%	36%	37%	44%
Central plan schemes and other central government transfers (high) (2)	57%	48%	45%	49%	55%	59%	52%	44%	41%	41%	56%	47%	54%	62%	64%	63%	56%
Total moderate and high discretionary transfers (1+2)	100%	100%	100%	100%	100%	100%	100%	100%	100%	100%	100%	100%	100%	100%	100%	100%	100%

Source: Authors' calculations based on data from the RBI and the World Bank.

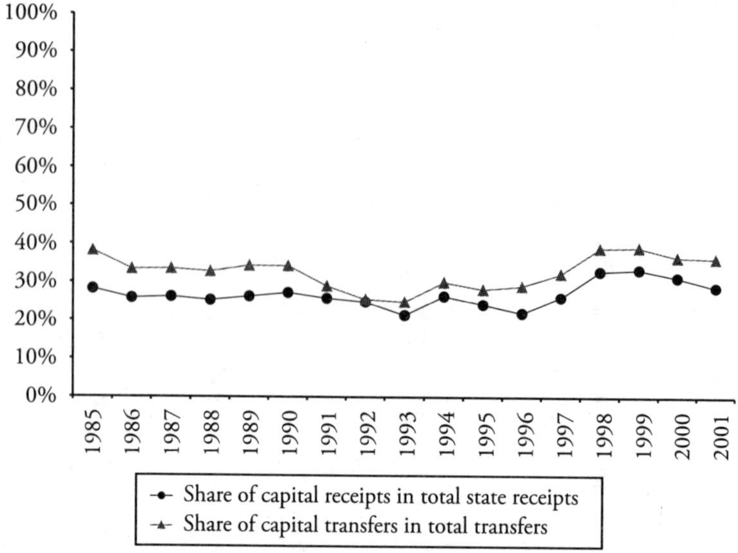

FIGURE 8.13: Central Receipts and Capital Transfers
Source: State Finances: A Study of Budgets (various years), RBI.

Capital Transfers

Table 8.20 presents the trends in capital transfers from 1985 to 2001. Figure 8.13 shows that capital transfers as a share of total transfers declined from 38 per cent in 1985 to 25 per cent in 1993 and then rose back to 36 per cent in 2001. Total capital receipts as a share of total state receipts have remained relatively stable around 27 per cent.

Figure 8.14 shows capital transfers by source of recommendation as a share of total state capital receipts. The share of total capital transfers in total state capital receipts declined steadily from 64 per cent in 1985 to 44 per cent in 1994, followed by a gradual increase to 54 per cent in 2001. PC transfer share fluctuated around an average of 25 per cent, while the share of other non-plan central government loans fluctuated around an average of 27 per cent. It is interesting to note that the PC transfer share has moved in a direction opposite to that of other non-plan central government loans. Figure 8.15 shows capital transfers by degree of discretion as a share of total state capital receipts. The share of moderately discretionary loans for state plan schemes fluctuated around 25 per cent, while the share of high-discretionary central plan schemes and other central government transfers fluctuated around 27 per cent. Again, both these shares moved in opposite directions.

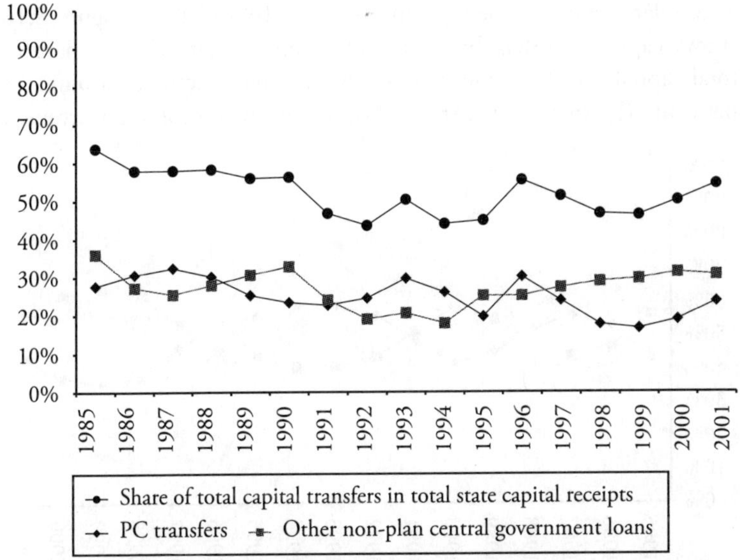

FIGURE 8.14: Central Transfers by Source as Share of Total State Capital Receipts

Source: State Finances: A Study of Budgets (various years), RBI.

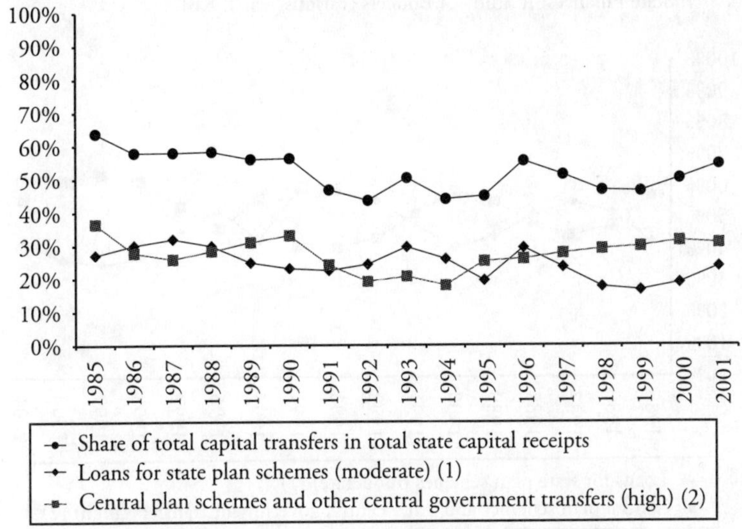

FIGURE 8.15: Central Transfers by Discretion as Share of Total State Capital Receipts

Source: State Finances: A Study of Budgets (various years), RBI.

Similar trends can be seen in Figures 8.16 and 8.17. Figure 8.16 shows capital transfers by source of recommendation as a share of total capital transfers. The share of PC transfers fluctuated around 48 per cent. The trend in the share of other non-plan central government

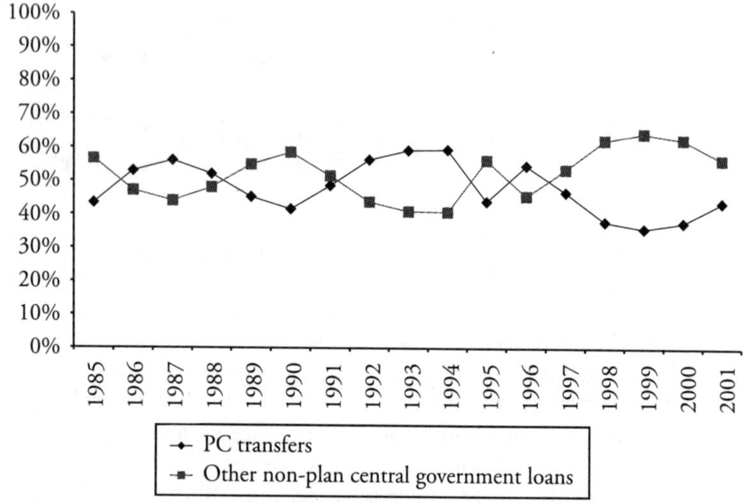

FIGURE 8.16: Central Transfers by Source as Share of Total Capital Transfers
Source: State Finances: A Study of Budgets (various years), RBI.

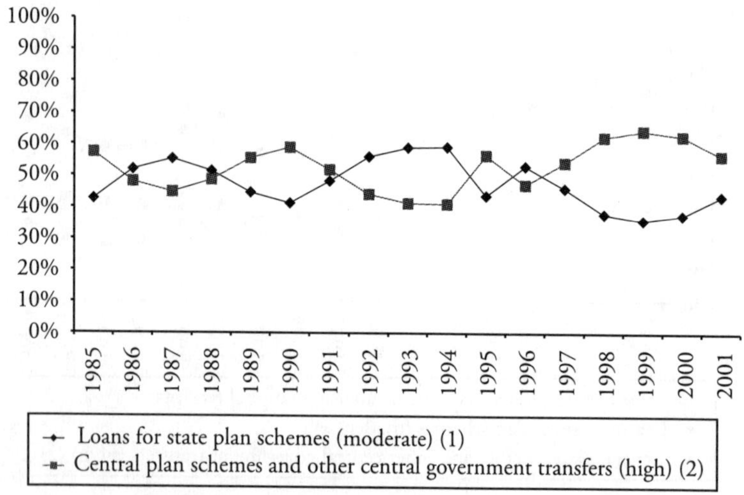

FIGURE 8.17: Central Transfers by Discretion as Share of Total Capital Transfers
Source: State Finances: A Study of Budgets (various years), RBI.

loans, which fluctuated around an average of 52 per cent, is the mirror image of the trend in the share of PC transfers. Figure 8.17 presents capital transfers by the degree of discretion as a share of total capital transfers. The share of moderately discretionary loans for state plan schemes fluctuated around 47 per cent till 1998, while the share of high-discretion central plan schemes and other central government transfers fluctuated around 53 per cent.

Inter-state Differences in Explicit Centre–State Transfers and Impact on Regional Inequality

The analysis so far has looked at the aggregate picture and masked the differences between states. Now we turn to the question of what effect these transfers have had on regional inequality.

Table 8.21 captures the differences in the magnitude of central transfers as a share of state revenues. It shows own revenue shares for the fourteen states under study from 1985 to 2001. It clearly shows that richer states have higher own revenue shares, while poorer ones are more dependent on central transfers.

Figure 8.18 shows this more clearly. In this graph, we have calculated the dependency quotient of each state as the average share of central transfers for the period 1997–2001 divided by average own revenue share for the same period in total state revenues. We took the average to smooth out any random effects in any particular year. It clearly shows that low-income states are more dependent on central transfers than higher-income states. This is clearly to be expected, given the gap-filling approach for central transfers and the higher weight given to poorer states. However, the key point here is that these higher transfers to poorer states have not had the effect of making them catch up with the richer states in terms of per capita gross state domestic product (GSDP), as we discussed in the previous section. Figure 8.2 captures this when it shows the richer states pulling away from the poorer ones.

In fact the poorer states have been dependent on central transfers for many years. Figure 8.19 shows this where it compares the dependency quotient for the years 1992–6 with 1997–2001. The dependence ranking of the states does not change. In fact, the quotient has been stable in most cases and has actually increased significantly in the case of poorer states such as Bihar and Orissa. This clearly shows that explicit central transfers have not led to a reduction in regional disparities, on the contrary, they might be having the opposite effect by creating a culture of dependency in the poorer states.

TABLE 8.21

States' Own Revenue Share

(in ascending order according to 2001 per capita GSDP)

	1985	1986	1987	1988	1989	1990	1991	1992	1993	1994	1995	1996	1997	1998	1999	2000	2001
Bihar	45	45	48	48	49	44	38	39	40	41	39	41	32	41	43	33	26
Orissa	44	40	41	41	42	40	38	39	40	44	45	43	42	45	41	40	30
Uttar Pradesh	47	49	49	49	49	47	47	45	48	51	52	48	47	54	53	45	48
Madhya Pradesh	60	58	59	59	61	57	59	59	58	59	61	61	58	61	63	52	53
Rajasthan	58	53	52	53	58	56	55	56	56	57	65	59	59	62	62	57	59
West Bengal	56	55	56	58	62	57	58	55	54	59	60	57	55	55	56	50	53
Andhra Pradesh	66	64	67	69	69	64	64	63	63	66	58	58	64	69	68	67	65
Kerala	64	65	70	66	69	64	67	65	68	68	72	72	71	72	72	74	77
Karnataka	71	71	72	72	73	73	74	72	72	74	76	74	72	75	72	71	70
Tamil Nadu	68	70	67	67	68	69	72	68	68	72	76	74	72	76	75	76	75
Haryana	79	76	80	80	84	83	82	80	84	91	87	87	85	85	83	83	85
Gujarat	74	84	71	75	83	83	86	78	76	80	81	79	79	81	80	74	72
Punjab	74	78	80	78	82	78	86	75	78	87	85	84	85	83	84	80	83
Maharashtra	80	79	79	79	79	79	79	79	78	82	83	80	85	82	84	84	86

Source: Authors' calculations based on data from the RBI and the World Bank.

Implicit Inter-regional Transfers

Apart from the explicit inter-governmental transfers discussed above, according to Rao and Singh (1999), there are three other channels

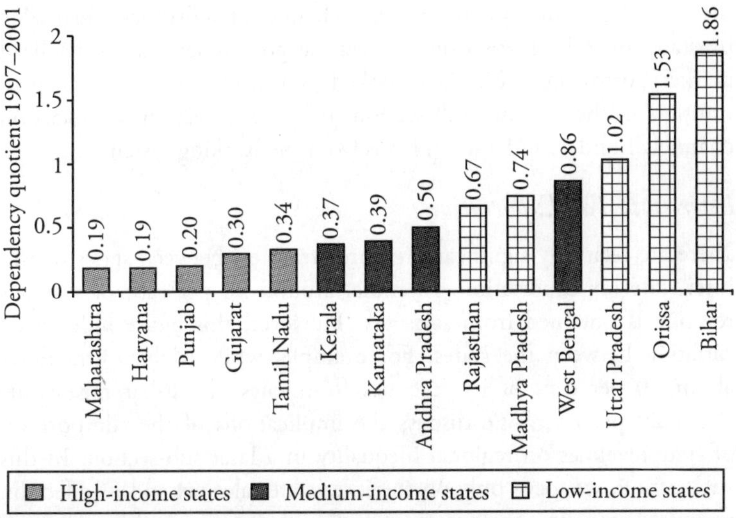

FIGURE 8.18: States in Increasing Order of Dependence on Central Transfers
Source: State Finances: A Study of Budgets (various years), RBI.

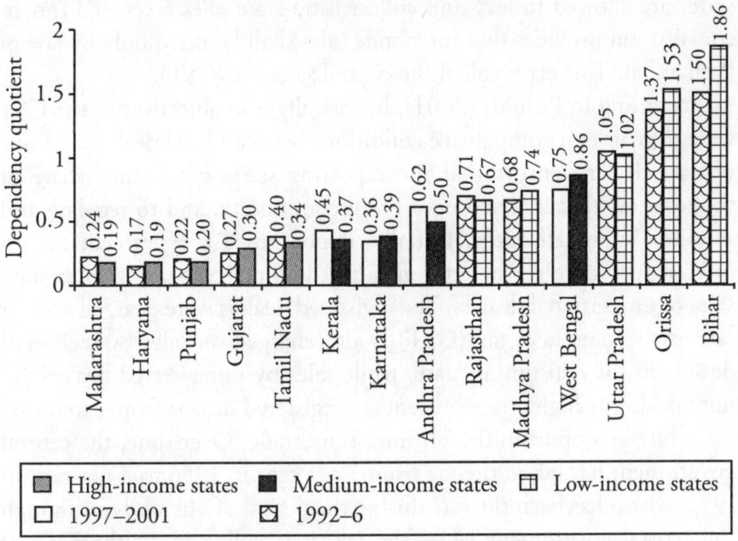

FIGURE 8.19: Trend in State Dependence on Central Transfers, 1992–6 vs 1997–2007
Source: State Finances: A Study of Budgets (various years), RBI.

of inter-state resource transfers—(1) inter-state tax exportation; (2) subsidized lending by banking and financial institutions to the private sector (including lending by All-India Financial Institutions [AIFIs][6]); (3) subsidized borrowing by states from the central government and the central banking system. The last channel of subsidized borrowing by states includes loans from the central government and subsidized market borrowings. We have looked at central government capital transfers in the previous sub-section. In this sub-section, we focus on channels 1 and 2, and also on loans from the banking system.

Inter-state Tax Exportation

There are relatively significant resource transfers between states due to inter-state tax exportation. In India, around 30 per cent of a state's revenue is obtained from sales tax. However, this figure hides wide variation between the states. For example, while Maharashtra raises about 40 per cent of its revenues from sales tax, Bihar raises only about 20 per cent. We discuss the implications of the composition of state revenues on regional inequality in a later sub-section. In this sub-section, we focus only on the inter-state sales tax and its effect on regional inequality. Sales taxes in India are composed of broadly two parts—taxes on intra-state sales and taxes on inter-state sales.[7] While states are allowed to levy and collect intra-state sales taxes, the Indian constitution provides that inter-state sales shall be taxed only by law of Parliament. This tax is called the central sales tax (CST).

According to Purohit (2001), historically, the objectives of the CST were to maintain competitive conditions between local dealers and out-of-state dealers, ensure that the exporting states get a small share of the total tax that is levied on a given commodity, and to regulate and monitor inter-state trade. Initially, it prescribed a 1 per cent tax on inter-state sales to registered dealers and a 10 per cent tax on inter-state sales to unregistered dealers. The registered dealers were charged a lower rate as the state sales tax (GST) is also charged on sales by registered dealers in the consuming state, while sales by unregistered dealers are not taxed. The higher rate prevents unregistered dealers from exploiting tax arbitrage opportunities on inter-state trade. Over time, the central government has raised the tax from 1 per cent in 1956 to 4 per cent in 1975, which has been the rate during the period of our study. Although the central government levies the tax, it is collected on the basis of origin by the state where the goods sold came from. In fact, the CST is administered by local sales tax authorities in each state. The state sales tax law is also applicable in several respects, the CST Act makes provisions for very few procedures and rules. With regard to provisions like return, assessment, and appeals, the provisions of the sales tax law of the state apply. Therefore, the amount of CST collected depends to some extent on local provisions and local tax effort. However, as the rate, the base, and any exemptions are decided by the central government, the CST is like any other form of unconditional central transfer. In effect, it is akin to the shareable taxes that the FC assigns, except that it is assigned entirely to the state where it is collected.

The CST has several harmful economic implications, some of which have a direct bearing on regional inequality. One, it hampers the creation of an internal common market within the country. If we assume that free trade between states would lead to income convergence, then the CST is a barrier to such convergence. The CST forms about 4–5 per cent of all states' revenues and 0.45–0.55 per cent of all states' GDP on average each year. On the other hand, even if we assume that free trade may cause divergence, the CST does not help reduce inequality. In fact, as we shall show, the CST by its very nature, leads to resource flow from the poorer to the richer states. The CST discriminates against consuming states to the benefit of the producing states. To the extent that richer states produce more, there is a net resource flow from the poorer to the richer states. The states dispatching the raw materials first levy CST on inputs, the states manufacturing goods that are exported to other states again levy CST. As Rao and Singh (1998: 21) point out, in a developing economy with only limited internal and external competition, the tax is fully shifted forward, so input taxes cascade onto the final consumer. Thus a net consuming less-developed state bears most of the burden of the CST, while an industrialized state with the most value-added collects most of the revenue. The effect is worsened due to tax cascading as inputs and each stage of processing (if by a different firm) are taxed, either by the GST if the inputs or intermediate goods are obtained locally or by the CST if they were obtained from another state. The CST has other economically negative effects by making imports from other countries more competitive, and exports to other countries that use inputs from other states less competitive. In terms of regional inequality, the import effect is in favour of the net importing states, while states that export to other states and abroad are hurt by the import effect and the export effect, respectively.

Table 8.22 shows that richer states tend to have higher collections of CST. The Table is arranged according to descending order of per capita

TABLE 8.22
Central Sales Tax Statistics

		1994	1995	1996	1997	1998	1999
High-income states							
Maharashtra	Per capita CST (Current Rs)	115.4	134.4	142.6	144.3	148.8	182.5
	CST as % of state revenues	6.4%	7.0%	6.5%	6.3%	6.1%	6.6%
Gujarat	Per capita CST (Current Rs)	116.6	122.8	130.1	145.5	158.5	199.3
	CST as % of state revenues	6.6%	6.5%	6.2%	6.1%	5.9%	6.9%
Punjab	Per capita CST (Current Rs)	105.2	90.7	112.0	120.7	111.9	n.a.
	CST as % of state revenues	4.3%	3.9%	4.5%	4.4%	4.5%	n.a.
Haryana	Per capita CST (Current Rs)	166.1	245.2	212.2	257.4	249.3	311.4
	CST as % of state revenues	5.1%	9.0%	6.6%	8.3%	8.8%	10.6%
Tamil Nadu	Per capita CST (Current Rs)	95.3	118.7	111.6	171.3	117.1	134.8
	CST as % of state revenues	6.0%	6.6%	5.6%	7.6%	5.0%	5.1%
Middle-income states							
Karnataka	Per capita CST (Current Rs)	105.1	49.1	28.0	42.2	87.6	106.3
	CST as % of state revenues	7.3%	2.8%	1.4%	2.0%	4.0%	4.3%
Kerala	Per capita CST (Current Rs)	53.0	54.2	54.3	51.8	85.8	89.5
	CST as % of state revenues	3.5%	3.1%	2.8%	2.3%	3.8%	3.6%
Andhra Pradesh	Per capita CST (Current Rs)	68.5	72.6	75.0	84.9	60.4	74.8
	CST as % of state revenues	5.5%	5.3%	4.9%	4.5%	3.1%	3.3%
West Bengal	Per capita CST (Current Rs)	55.1	57.6	57.4	43.5	36.6	34.4
	CST as % of state revenues	5.8%	5.8%	5.2%	3.7%	3.0%	2.6%

Table 8.22 (contd...)

Table 8.22 (contd...)

		1994	1995	1996	1997	1998	1999
Low-income states							
Rajasthan	Per capita CST (Current Rs)	14.2	16.6	19.5	22.5	25.7	27.2
	CST as % of state revenues	1.1%	1.1%	1.3%	1.4%	1.6%	1.5%
Madhya Pradesh	Per capita CST (Current Rs)	38.9	46.5	48.4	56.6	58.2	59.8
	CST as % of state revenues	3.7%	4.0%	3.6%	3.8%	4.0%	3.6%
Uttar Pradesh	Per capita CST (Current Rs)	0.0	9.6	9.0	14.7	11.1	25.2
	CST as % of state revenues	0.0%	1.0%	0.9%	1.3%	1.0%	2.0%
Orissa	Per capita CST (Current Rs)	0.1	0.0	0.0	0.0	0.0	12.8
	CST as % of state revenues	0.0%	0.0%	0.0%	0.0%	0.0%	0.8%
Bihar	Per capita CST (Current Rs)	28.1	0.0	34.8	37.0	34.4	42.5
	CST as % of state revenues	3.8%	0.0%	4.1%	4.1%	3.6%	3.4%
All India	CST as % of state revenues	4.0%	3.6%	3.6%	3.7%	3.5%	4.5%
Correlation between per capita SDP and per capita CST		*0.9*	*0.8*	*0.8*	*0.8*	*0.8*	*0.8*

Source: Authors' calculations based on data from the RBI and the World Bank.

income. During the period 1994–9 for which data were available, richer states tended to have higher collections of CST per capita. They also tended to have higher collections of CST as a percentage of state revenues. As the richer states also have higher overall revenues, the total CST collections are more than proportionately higher than in poorer states.

Figure 8.20 shows a scatter plot of per capita CST with per capita SDP for the year 1997. As other years show a similar relationship, we have not reproduced charts for each year. As the Figure shows there is a broad positive relationship between per capita SDP and per capita CST. The relationship is confirmed in the last row in Table 8.22, which shows that the Pearson correlation coefficient between per capita SDP and per capita CST in each of the years is around 0.8. We also computed the Pearson correlation coefficients between per capita CST and per capita manufacturing SDP, and per capita CST and per capita industry SDP (includes manufacturing, mining, construction, and electricity, gas and water supply). These had similar magnitudes (around 0.8) to the correlation coefficient between per capita CST and per capita SDP.

In Table 8.23, we compute the net per capita inflow of CST into each state. This computation was done as follows. If X_i is the CST collected by the state i, then

$$X_i = \sum_{\substack{j=1 \\ j \neq i}}^{N} x_{ij}; \qquad \text{(Equation 1)}$$

where x_{ij} is the CST collected by state i from sales to state j, and N is the total number of states. In our case, N = 15,[8] the fourteen major states

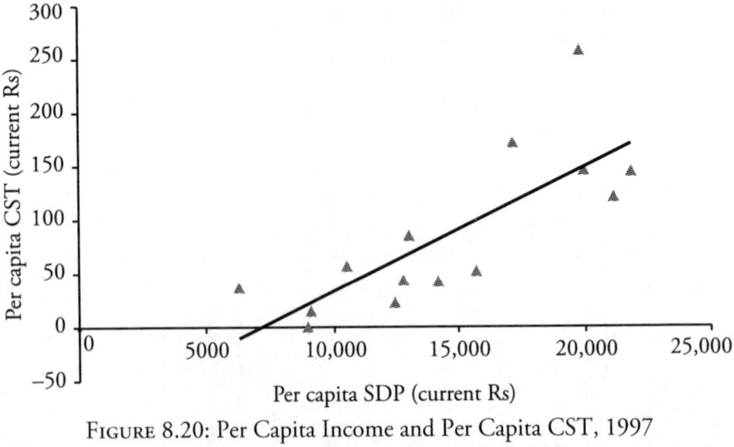

FIGURE 8.20: Per Capita Income and Per Capita CST, 1997

Source: State Finances: A Study of Budgets (various years), RBI.

under consideration and the 'rest of India', which is considered as one entity for this purpose. x_{ij} was calculated as follows:

$$x_{ij} = X_i * \frac{Y_j}{\sum_{j=1}^{N} Y_j};$$

$$j \neq i \qquad \text{(Equation 2)}$$

where Y_j is the SDP of state j. This is of course based on the assumption that the CST collected by state i from exports to state j is directly proportional to the SDP of state j as a share of all states' GDP. This is a reasonable assumption as we would expect richer states to import more. We are also making another assumption that exports from one state to another do not depend on the physical distance between them, or on the nature of their economies. For example, iron exporters would export the metal only to states with steel factories, and not to others. However, we can assume such differences to be somewhat random and that they somewhat balance out at aggregate level. In addition, we assume that the effective rate of tax on a state's exports is the same for all states. This means that the effect of exemptions, tax rate differences on selected goods, and tax rate differences according to the classification of buyers is similar for the different states.[9] Finally, we do not take into account the effects of inter-state income redistribution by the central government, which would raise consumption in the poorer states. Therefore, we must be careful of these assumptions while interpreting the data, and we would suggest that looking the direction of flow of resources is more meaningful than the magnitude of flow. We discuss the implications of these assumptions at the end of this sub-section. Having said this, we estimate the outflow of CST from state j as follows:

$$Z_j = \sum_{i}^{N} x_{ij};$$

$$i \neq j \qquad \text{(Equation 3)}$$

where Z_j is the sum of the CST paid by state j to each of the other states. Finally, we calculate the net inflow of CST in state i as shown below, X_i being the total CST collected and Z_i being the total CST paid by consumers in state i.[10]

$$I_i = X_i - Z_i \qquad \text{(Equation 4)}$$

In Table 8.23, we present the net inflow per capita $i_i = I_i/P_i$, both in current rupees and constant 1993–4 rupees for each of the years 1994–9. is the population of state i. We see that all the high-income states have

TABLE 8.23
Net Per Capita Inflow of CST

		1994	1995	1996	1997	1998	1999
High-income states							
Maharashtra	Current rupees	45.5	66.4	70.2	60.4	74.7	89.6
	Constant 1993–4 rupees	40.7	54.5	54.5	44.4	52.1	59.3
Gujarat	Current rupees	42.4	52.5	50.3	57.9	77.5	109.0
	Constant 1993–4 rupees	38.8	44.9	41.2	45.3	58.2	78.1
Punjab	Current rupees	19.1	8.0	23.2	21.2	18.9	n.a.
	Constant 1993–4 rupees	17.4	6.7	18.2	15.7	12.9	n.a.
Haryana	Current rupees	88.0	173.3	129.8	167.4	164.7	209.5
	Constant 1993–4 rupees	79.4	141.0	98.5	119.1	108.7	134.5
Tamil Nadu	Current rupees	35.2	62.1	49.2	100.8	45.8	47.3
	Constant 1993–4 rupees	33.1	53.2	38.7	74.1	31.1	31.2
Middle-income states							
Karnataka	Current rupees	53.5	–5.1	–33.1	–25.2	23.6	27.8
	Constant 1993–4 rupees	48.4	–4.2	–25.3	–18.5	16.4	18.6
Kerala	Current rupees	–5.5	–6.2	–11.4	–23.4	15.8	–0.3
	Constant 1993–4 rupees	–4.9	–4.8	–7.9	–15.1	9.3	–0.1
Andhra Pradesh	Current rupees	17.6	23.2	21.8	27.1	2.0	5.6
	Constant 1993–4 rupees	15.6	18.8	16.7	19.2	1.4	3.6
West Bengal	Current rupees	9.9	12.3	9.6	–16.2	–22.3	–41.0
	Constant 1993–4 rupees	9.1	10.2	7.7	–11.7	–14.6	–25.1

Table 8.23 (contd...)

Table 8.23 (contd...)

		1994	1995	1996	1997	1998	1999
Low-income states							
Rajasthan	Current rupees	–35.0	–30.4	–34.0	–37.8	–30.8	–36.8
	Constant 1993–4 rupees	–32.7	–25.7	–26.2	–29.2	–21.5	–24.3
Madhya Pradesh	Current rupees	–5.5	5.1	3.8	8.0	13.5	3.7
	Constant 1993–4 rupees	–5.1	4.5	3.1	6.1	9.8	n.a
Uttar Pradesh	Current rupees	–38.9	–26.3	–31.4	–28.6	–30.4	–23.2
	Constant 1993–4 rupees	–35.3	–21.9	–24.2	–20.6	–20.3	–14.9
Orissa	Current rupees	–37.2	–38.6	–35.6	–44.4	–40.4	–36.1
	Constant 1993–4 rupees	–32.6	–29.1	–26.2	–30.4	–25.8	–21.8
Bihar	Current rupees	1.6	–23.9	9.2	7.6	7.8	10.8
	Constant 1993–4 rupees	1.5	–21.3	7.5	5.8	5.8	7.6

Source: Authors' calculations based on data from the RBI and the World Bank.

net positive inflows in all the years. The magnitudes of these inflows are also relatively high compared to the other states with positive inflows. Haryana has the highest inflows, followed by Maharashtra, Guajarat, and Tamil Nadu. Haryana's high CST inflows could perhaps be explained by the setting up of industries in Gurgaon and Faridabad close to its border with Delhi, the national capital. Except for Punjab, the other high income states with high per capita net inflows of CST are also more industrialized, as can be seen by above-average manufacturing shares in SDP. On average, manufacturing share of SDP in these states was around 25 per cent, while the all-India average was around 16 per cent.

Among the middle-income states, Karnataka has had net outflows in the years 1995–7, followed by net inflows in 1998 and 1999. Kerala has had net outflows for all the years, except 1998. Andhra Pradesh has had net inflows, while West Bengal has moved from net inflows during 1994–6 to net outflows during 1997–9. Almost all the low-income states, except Madhya Pradesh and Bihar have had net outflows. Although Bihar and Madhya Pradesh have had net inflows, the magnitudes are small, and much of the CST inflows can be explained by the exports of natural resources. While mining and quarrying forms about 2.2 per cent of all-India GDP during this period, in Bihar mining and quarrying formed about 6.3 per cent of SDP and in Madhya Pradesh this share was 4.5 per cent. Both states had about a 12 per cent share each of overall mining and quarrying output in the country. The other three low-income states—Rajasthan, Orissa, and Uttar Pradesh—have all seen significant net outflows.

Figure 8.21 shows the net per capita CST inflows in 1998. The states are arranged in order of increasing per capita SDP. This 1998 figure, which is also reasonably representative of the other years, shows that higher-income states have higher per capita CST inflows, except Punjab, which has a relatively low manufacturing SDP share of about 15 per cent for a rich state.

Rao and Singh (1999) present their estimates of inter-state tax exportation for 1993–4. They find the same directional effect of resource transfer from the poorer to the richer regions as we do; however, their estimates of per capita inflows are smaller than ours. Their calculation is based on the difference between sales tax shares and corresponding consumption shares (household + government). They find that higher-income states have higher sales tax shares than consumptions shares, which is a measure of the tax exportation from these states. However, as they acknowledge, at least part of the difference could be due to better tax effort in more advanced states. Rao and Singh (1998) perhaps adopted this method as they did not have the breakdown of sales tax into intra-state and inter-state sales taxes. Our analysis is based on only the inter-state CST; therefore, we avoid the effects of differences in tax rates and tax efforts on intra-state sales. The tax effort issue remains for the CST, but even if we assume that higher CST collections in higher-income states are due to better tax effort, the effect of resource transfer between rich and poor states remains.

To look at whether higher-income states collect more CST due to better tax effort, we studied the correlation between the share of overall sales taxes (or intra-state sales taxes) in state revenues and the share of CST in overall state revenues for each of the states for the time period 1994–9. If tax effort determined the shares of sales tax collections, we would expect a strong positive correlation between the shares. However, we find no relationship in most of the states. Further, some states with high shares of CST have low shares of overall sales taxes in state revenues. For example, Haryana collected above-average CST as a share in state revenues (around 8 per cent compared to the all-India figure of around 4 per cent), but it collected below-average shares of intra-state sales taxes (around 18 per cent compared to the all-India of around 23 per cent). Again, Bihar and Madhya Pradesh collected close

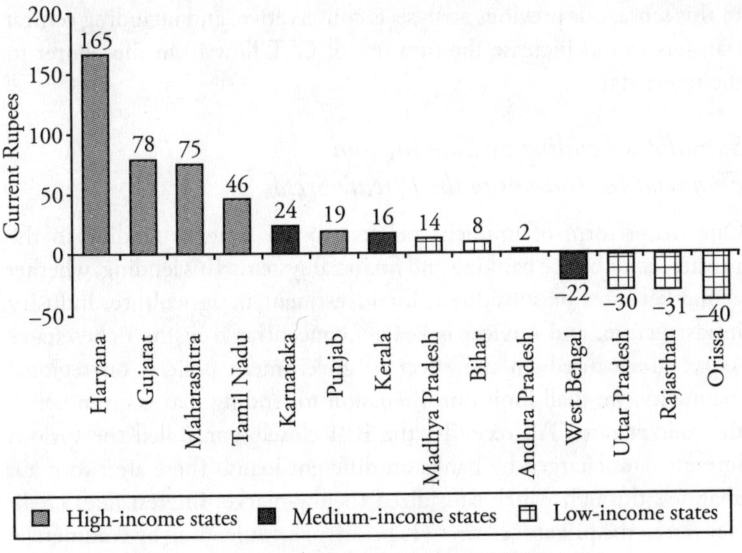

FIGURE 8.21: Net Per Capita Flow of CST, 1998

Source: State Finances: A Study of Budgets (various years), RBI.

to the all-India average of CST as a share of state revenues, but their overall or intra-state sales tax collections were significantly below the national average. On the other hand CST shares in Kerala were below the national average, while the intra-state sales tax shares were above the national average. The differences in intra-state sales tax collections could be due to differences in tax rates, tax bases, and tax effort. The CST tax rates are the same throughout the country. Therefore, the differences in CST collections would be due to tax base and tax effort. As we have shown, tax effort is perhaps only part of the explanation. So resource transfers to rich states through tax exportation are mostly due to their more advanced production base.

Finally, we briefly discuss the implications of some of our assumptions. One assumption was that centre–state transfers did not impact the CST flows. However, if we relax this assumption, we see that consumption would rise in poorer states compared to richer ones. This would only reinforce our results, increasing the magnitude of the CST flow from the poorer to the richer states. For example, in a state like Bihar, which receives more than 60 per cent of its revenues as transfers from the central government, consumption of households and the government is raised more than proportionately as compared to other states. This significant increase in consumption could actually change it from a state with a small net inflow to one with net outflow. In this sense, our previous analysis is conservative, and including central transfers would increase the measure of CST flow from the poorer to the richer states.

Subsidized Lending by Banking and Financial Institutions to the Private Sector

One major form of implicit transfers to the states is lending to the private sector by the banking and financial system. This lending, whether at market rates or subsidized, for investment in agriculture, industry, infrastructure, and services is heavily concentrated in the richer states. As we are focused on the effect of government policies on regional inequality, we shall limit our discussion to lending that is given below the market rate. Till recently, the RBI closely controlled the various interest rates charged by banks on different loans. There are two main channels through which subsidized (below-market interest rate) credit is given to the private sector—(1) priority sector lending by commercial banks (public, private, and foreign) and (2) financial assistance from all financial institutions (AFIs).

The objectives of priority-sector lending, which began with bank nationalization in 1969, were to extend and expand credit on a priority basis to sectors of crucial importance in terms of income and employments and to those sectors that had limited access to institutional credit. The RBI sets targets of lending to the priority sector and to some of the components of this sector such as agriculture, small-scale industries (SSI), exports, and credit to weaker sections of society.[11] Currently, if a domestic bank does not achieve the RBI target for the priority sector, it has to contribute the shortfall to the Rural Infrastructure Development Fund (RIDF). The interest rates and periods on these deposits are decided by the central government every year. For a foreign bank, they have to deposit the shortfall amount with the Small Industries Development Bank of India (SIDBI) for one year at the below-market interest rate of 8 per cent. The rate of interest for loans under the priority sector cannot exceed the prime lending rate (PLR) of the bank for small amounts below Rs 200,000. For amounts above this, the banks are free to determine the interest rate.

Initially, the sectors identified for prioritized lending were agriculture, small industry, and self-employment. According to Shajahan (1998) priority-sector lending was relatively successful in meeting its goals, and credit extended to priority sectors increased from 14.6 per cent of total net bank credit in 1969 to 40.9 per cent in 1991. Shajahan (1999), however, finds that priority-sector lending by public-sector banks declined from 40.09 per cent of total net bank credit in 1991 to 37.8 per cent in 1996, after which it rose to 43.5 per cent in 1999. But this increase in 1999 is at least partly due to a broader definition of the priority sector.[12] In 2000, the priority sector consisted of agriculture, small-scale industry, setting up of industrial estates, small road and water transport operators, retail trade, small business, professionals and self-employed, education and consumption loans, housing, software, venture capital, and exports.

Table 8.24 presents lending by all commercial banks under priority sector by state in descending order of per capita income. The numbers presented are the priority-sector advances or amounts outstanding for each state for the years 1996 to 2000. The Table shows that high-income states obtained the largest shares of priority-sector credit. Richest Maharashtra had 16.73 per cent of the overall credit in 1996 compared to just 3.43 per cent in poorest Bihar, although Maharashtra has only 90 per cent of Bihar's population. The gap widened to 20.62 per cent and 2.54 per cent respectively in 2000. On a per capita basis,

Table 8.24

Scheduled Commercial Banks' Advances under Priority Sectors by State

	1996			1997			1998		
	Amount outstanding (Rs million)	Per cent share of all-India	Amount outstanding per capita (Rs)	Amount outstanding (Rs million)	Per cent share of all-India	Amount outstanding per capita (Rs)	Amount outstanding (Rs million)	Per cent share of all-India	Amount outstanding per capita (Rs)
High-income states									
Maharashtra	135,218.9	16.73%	1574	160,231.9	17.08%	1835	191,250.8	17.56%	2159
Gujarat	46,130.2	5.71%	1021	50,472	5.38%	1100	60,184.4	5.53%	1292
Punjab	42,698.7	5.28%	1923	48,100	5.13%	2128	56,699.6	5.21%	2476
Haryana	23,389.1	2.89%	1271	25,413.4	2.71%	1352	29,873.8	2.74%	1564
Tamil Nadu	99,065.5	12.26%	1676	114,455	12.20%	1914	126,532.8	11.62%	2095
Middle-income states									
Karnataka	58,885.1	7.28%	1202	72,289.2	7.71%	1452	84,699.9	7.78%	1677
Kerala	38,181.3	4.72%	1240	48,912.5	5.21%	1568	51,229.7	4.70%	1626
Andhra Pradesh	67,867.2	8.40%	947	78,152.7	8.33%	1076	95,968.5	8.81%	1307
West Bengal	44,642.4	5.52%	603	53,560.2	5.71%	711	59,471.5	5.46%	778
Low-income states									
Rajasthan	26,674.1	3.30%	542	31,491.7	3.36%	626	40,942.4	3.76%	798
Madhya Pradesh	37,643.9	4.66%	512	42,655.2	4.55%	569	50,268.4	4.62%	658
Uttar Pradesh	71,098.4	8.80%	458	77,499.4	8.26%	489	86,545.9	7.95%	536
Orissa	15,338	1.90%	448	19,114	2.04%	551	21,009.2	1.93%	600
Bihar	27,725.6	3.43%	300	29,958.8	3.19%	319	31,102.5	2.86%	325
All-India	*808,312.4*	*100%*	*872*	*938,070.6*	*100%*	*994*	*1,089,052.5*	*100%*	*1136*
Correlation with per capita SDP			*086*			*0.86*			*0.88*

Table 8.24 (contd...)

Table 8.24 (contd...)

	1999			2000		
	Amount outstanding (Rs million)	Per cent share of all-India	Amount outstanding per capita (Rs)	Amount outstanding (Rs million)	Per cent share of all-India	Amount outstanding per capita (Rs)
High-income states						
Maharashtra	23,731.3	18.79%	2646	321,270	20.62%	3542
Gujarat	69,376.1	5.49%	1467	79,170	5.08%	1649
Punjab	68,120.2	5.39%	2936	81,050	5.20%	3464
Haryana	36,779.6	2.91%	1896	43,340	2.78%	2200
Tamil Nadu	140,260.9	11.10%	2299	165,410	10.62%	2685
Middle-income states						
Karnataka	101,291.7	8.02%	1978	109,180	7.01%	2108
Kerala	57,870.3	4.58%	1814	69,510	4.46%	2165
Andhra Pradesh	104,098.7	8.24%	1401	125,600	8.06%	1672
West Bengal	65,799	5.21%	849	76,070	4.88%	968
Low-income states						
Rajasthan	48,654.6	3.85%	932	54,290	3.49%	1020
Madhya Pradesh	57,524.3	4.55%	739	70,060	4.50%	885
Uttar Pradesh	96,199.3	7.62%	583	138,870	8.91%	824
Orissa	21,233.4	1.68%	600	24,120	1.55%	676
Bihar	36,181.5	2.86%	371	39,560	2.54%	399
All-India	*1,263,090.1*	*100%*	*1296*	*1,557,790*	*100%*	*1573*
Correlation with per capita SDP			*0.92*			*n.a.*

Source: Authors' calculations from RBI Banking Statistics.

Maharashtra obtained more than five times as much credit as Bihar. The last row of the Table shows that the Pearson correlation coefficient between per capita SDP and per capita outstanding advances to priority sectors was close to 0.9 during 1996 to 1999.

The fourteen states under consideration obtained about 90 per cent of all-India credit. Of the remaining 10 per cent, one city-state, Delhi, with a population slightly more than one-eighth that of Bihar, obtained 6 per cent, almost twice the credit obtained by Bihar. We mention this even though Delhi does not form part of our study to show that most of the priority-sector credit flows to areas of industrial concentration. One can also see it from the Table, which shows that relatively industrialized states such as Maharashtra, Tamil Nadu, and Karnataka get the lion's share of the credit. In addition, we believe that most of this credit goes to particular cities in these states such as Mumbai, Bangalore, and Chennai. Figure 8.22 presents per capita priority sector advances for 2000, which is representative of other years. The figure confirms the conclusions that we draw from the Table.

Table 8.24 and Figure 8.22, which show the distribution of aggregate priority-sector advances hide the details of their composition. These details are important from the view of economic development in these states. Table 8.25 presents the percentage of credit that the different states get in each of the priority sectors in 1998, which is representative of the other years. The percentage figures are the ratio of the credit that a state obtains in a sector to the total all-India credit in that sector. The

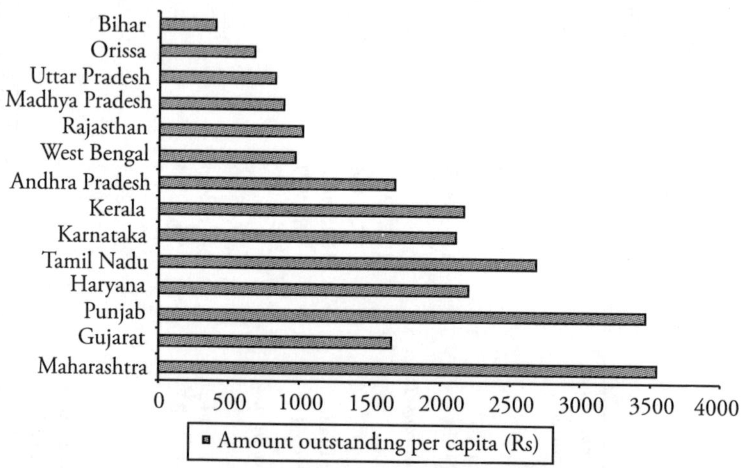

FIGURE 8.22: Per Capita Priority-sector Advances, 2000

Source: RBI.

TABLE 8.25

Composition of Priority Lending by Sectors, 1998

	Agriculture			Small-scale industries	Other priority sectors	Exports	All priority sectors
	Direct	Indirect	Total				
High-income states							
Maharashtra	9.41%	19.26%	11.16%	20.83%	14.75%	53.36%	17.56%
Gujarat	4.90%	8.21%	5.49%	6.84%	3.84%	1.60%	5.53%
Punjab	6.73%	4.32%	6.30%	5.87%	2.96%	1.57%	5.21%
Haryana	3.70%	1.62%	3.33%	3.01%	1.75%	0.60%	2.74%
Tamil Nadu	13.32%	10.42%	12.81%	13.20%	7.48%	8.40%	11.62%
Delhi	0.94%	7.44%	2.09%	8.60%	4.49%	16.69%	5.91%
Middle-income states							
Karnataka	9.64%	9.02%	9.53%	6.11%	8.92%	3.31%	7.78%
Kerala	5.02%	3.51%	4.76%	3.67%	7.76%	0.64%	4.70%
Andhra Pradesh	13.09%	10.03%	12.55%	5.82%	8.30%	2.09%	8.81%
West Bengal	4.34%	6.79%	4.77%	5.64%	5.66%	8.83%	5.46%
Low-income states							
Rajasthan	4.52%	4.41%	4.50%	3.47%	4.04%	0.12%	3.76%
Madhya Pradesh	6.62%	5.18%	6.36%	3.25%	5.61%	0.56%	4.62%
Uttar Pradesh	9.51%	4.02%	8.54%	7.46%	9.64%	1.40%	7.95%
Orissa	2.06%	1.12%	1.90%	1.15%	3.41%	0.08%	1.93%
Bihar	3.37%	1.34%	3.01%	2.00%	5.11%	–	2.86%
Total (as per cent of total priority-sector advances)	27.04%	5.82%	32.85%	42.03%	20.08%	4.57%	99.52%

Source: Authors' calculations from RBI Banking Statistics.

last row gives all-India credit in each sector as a percentage of all priority sectors' credit.

Overall priority-sector credit consisted of about 40 per cent of all bank credit in 1998. The agriculture sector cumulatively comprised 32.85 per cent of all priority-sector lending, the small scale industries sector 42.03 per cent, other priority sectors 20.08 per cent, and exports 4.57 per cent. Agriculture had two components—'direct' and 'indirect'. Direct advances are credit to farmers for agricultural purposes, while indirect advances are loans for activities allied to agriculture such as distribution of inputs such as fertilizers and seeds, loans to electricity boards for connections and improvements, and loans under other government schemes.[13] Other priority sectors include small road and water transport operators, retail trade, small businesses, professionals and self-employed, consumption and education loans, and housing.

Table 8.25 shows that relatively rich industrialized states such as Maharashtra, Gujarat, Delhi, and Haryana have above-average (compared to the overall last column) shares of credit under the small-scale industries sector. Maharashtra also gets over 50 per cent of the credit for the exports sector. Delhi also has a big share of export-sector credit, followed by West Bengal and Tamil Nadu, which are coastal states. Most of the other states have above-average credit in agriculture. The middle- and low-income states also have above-average credit shares for other priority sectors in contrast to the high-income states. This could be due to the larger share of the informal sector in these states. These numbers are not surprising. They just show that to some extent, investment follows development, even investment by regulation or subsidy. Government has not succeeded in regional equalization of investment, and it is not clear if that would be desirable as priority lending is probably flowing to areas with higher returns. Less-developed areas may not have the capacity to absorb higher investments, and individuals and small companies in poorer states may be less qualified to take and use loans productively.

In addition to lending by commercial banks to priority sectors, there is a plethora of financial institutions that provide various financial products and services to the industrial sector. National-level institutions are known as the All-India Financial Institutions (AIFIs). They comprise six all-India development banks (AIDBs), two specialized financial institutions (SFIs), and three investment institutions. At state level, there are eighteen State Financial Corporations (SFCs) and twenty-eight State Industrial Development Corporations (SIDCs). The all-

India institutions, AIFIs, along with the state-level institutions together are called all financial institutions (AFIs).[14] Four of the development banks provide financial assistance to medium and large industries. These are the Industrial Development Bank of India (IDBI), Industrial Finance Corporation of India (IFCI), Industrial Credit and Investment Corporation of India (ICICI), and Industrial Investment Bank of India (IIBI). Of the other two AIDBs, the Industrial Development Finance Company (IDFC) caters to the infrastructure sector, while the Small Industries Development Bank of India (SIDBI) services the small-scale sector. One of the SFIs focuses on exports and imports and the other on agriculture and other economic activities in rural areas. The investment institutions deal with insurance cover, mobilize savings of small investors, invest in the corporate sector. The SFCs cater to small and medium enterprises, while the SIDCs cater to medium- and large-scale enterprises in their respective states.[15]

The assistance provided by both AIFIs and the all-inclusive AFIs is highly skewed in favour of the richer states. Table 8.26 shows the amounts of assistance sanctioned and disbursed by AIFIs to the different states for the years 1996–2000, and the aggregate sanctions and disbursements till the end of March 2001. As usual, the richer and more industrialized states get the biggest chunk of assistance, while the poor states get but a pittance. The five richest states with less than a quarter of the country's population get around 50 per cent of the financial assistance. The five poorest states with around 45 per cent of the country's population get around 15 per cent of the financial assistance provided by these institutions.

Table 8.27 presents the per capita financial assistance sanctioned and disbursed to the states for the years 1996–2000 and the cumulative per capita assistance sanctioned and disbursed till the end of March 2001. Figure 8.23 shows the cumulative per capita financial assistance disbursed till the end of March 2001 for the different states in increasing order of per capita SDP. Both the table and the figure show that the richer a state, the higher the financial assistance it obtained. Further, the more industrialized states get higher levels of financial assistance from the AIFIs. The last two rows of Table 8.27 show this. While there is a high positive Pearson correlation of around 0.7 per capita assistance with per capita SDP, the Pearson correlation with per capita manufacturing SDP is even higher at about 0.9.

Table 8.28 presents similar results, but for the assistance provided by the AFIs. The AFIs include state-level financial institutions. These

Table 8.26

State-wise Assistance Sanctioned and Disbursed by AIFIs

(Rs million)

	1996				1997				1998			
	S	% share	D	% share	S	% share	D	% share	S	% share	D	% share
High-income states												
Maharashtra	85,163.5	18.78%	85,737.5	21.72%	147,117.9	20.93%	119,434.5	23.32%	240,336.6	31.09%	152,356.4	27.99%
Gujarat	74,782.1	16.49%	61,965.8	15.70%	121,924.4	17.34%	103,493.4	20.20%	84,099.6	10.88%	73,015.1	13.41%
Punjab	8383.4	1.85%	6680.5	1.69%	11,357.9	1.62%	10,869.5	2.12%	18,918.8	2.45%	12,076.6	2.22%
Haryana	13,169	2.90%	10,502.5	2.66%	16,980	2.42%	11,947.2	2.33%	17,576.3	2.27%	13,047.6	2.40%
Tamil Nadu	39,497	8.71%	33,680.5	8.53%	63,295.3	9.00%	30,152.2	5.89%	81,371.6	10.53%	40,808.1	7.50%
Middle-income states												
Karnataka	38,323.4	8.45%	25,875.6	6.56%	36,516.4	5.19%	34,208	6.68%	46,996.6	6.08%	35,161.8	6.46%
Kerala	6324	1.39%	6855.8	1.74%	10,863.1	1.55%	6213.2	1.21%	10,580.7	1.37%	6792.6	1.25%
Andhra Pradesh	26,597	5.86%	25,048.5	6.35%	46,555.1	6.62%	38,422.9	7.50%	46,290.8	5.99%	28,178.4	5.18%
West Bengal	20,571.5	4.54%	12,499	3.17%	32,117.3	4.57%	23,331.6	4.55%	34,705.6	4.49%	29,564.6	5.43%
Low-income states												
Rajasthan	22,734.3	5.01%	15,166.8	3.84%	25,703.1	3.66%	12,730.6	2.49%	15,285.8	1.98%	14,937.7	2.74%
Madhya Pradesh	13,955.7	3.08%	17,159.9	4.35%	59,363.5	8.44%	17,014.5	3.32%	27,395.2	3.54%	20,988.5	3.86%
Uttar Pradesh	26,475.5	5.84%	31,098.1	7.88%	26,203.2	3.73%	25,421.7	4.96%	38,981.9	5.04%	22,228.7	4.08%
Orissa	7237.9	1.60%	4169.8	1.06%	12,628.2	1.80%	5832.6	1.14%	12,269.5	1.59%	10,937.5	2.01%
Bihar	4676.4	1.03%	2621.1	0.66%	11,122.5	1.58%	7824.8	1.53%	11,374.9	1.47%	7057.6	1.30%
Total	453,572		394,700		702,947		512,242		773,035		544,329	

Table 8.26 (contd...)

Table 8.26 (contd...)

	1999				2000				Cumulative up to end March 2001			
	S	% share	D	% share	S	% share	D	% share	S	% share	D	% share
High-income states												
Maharashtra	224,602.1	23.19%	159,099.4	24.84%	310,944.2	27.42%	190,992	27.27%	1,632,455.9	23.83%	1,119,165.6	23.77%
Gujarat	131,910.5	13.62%	84,319.9	13.16%	140,018.6	12.35%	47,040.5	6.72%	970,128.4	14.16%	616,657.2	13.09%
Punjab	20,147.6	2.08%	13,318.3	2.08%	29,706.3	2.62%	18,647.7	2.66%	150,523.1	2.20%	107,885.7	2.29%
Haryana	18,930.1	1.95%	14,299.9	2.23%	49,108.9	4.33%	16,616.5	2.37%	179,458.1	2.62%	111,438.2	2.37%
Tamil Nadu	89,947.5	9.29%	44,162.2	6.89%	68,241.5	6.02%	45,535.2	6.50%	583,045.8	8.51%	364,945.8	7.75%
Middle-income states												
Karnataka	55,043	5.68%	40,650.8	6.35%	60,832.8	5.36%	49,604	7.08%	416,740	6.08%	297,250.6	6.31%
Kerala	8236.1	0.85%	8660	1.35%	9451.9	0.83%	9339.6	1.33%	87,916.4	1.28%	71,002.4	1.51%
Andhra Pradesh	91,624.3	9.46%	39,188.6	6.12%	56,125.5	4.95%	36,080.3	5.15%	455,572.4	6.65%	296,385.1	6.29%
West Bengal	38,821.8	4.01%	33,071	5.16%	49,707.1	4.38%	37,330	5.33%	289,681.6	4.23%	211,621.8	4.49%
Low-income states												
Rajasthan	17,278.2	1.78%	14,417.1	2.25%	24,062.1	2.12%	15,667.2	2.24%	209,689.2	3.06%	157,410.9	3.34%
Madhya Pradesh	22,908.8	2.37%	14,500.6	2.26%	25,892.5	2.28%	16,841.1	2.40%	278,045	4.06%	180,493.7	3.83%
Uttar Pradesh	35,986.3	3.72%	25,694.5	4.01%	45,518.5	4.01%	26,310.8	3.76%	373,322.2	5.45%	273,827.2	5.81%
Orissa	28,300.3	2.92%	10,350.2	1.62%	14,697	1.30%	10,143.6	1.45%	118,896.7	1.74%	74,374	1.58%
Bihar	10,436.4	1.08%	9903.4	1.55%	2658.1	0.23%	3075.9	0.44%	75,744.3	1.11%	59,930.3	1.27%
Total	968,606		640,555		1,133,899		700,438		6,849,769		4,709,132	

Source: Authors' Calculations based on statistics from the IDBI Report on Development Banking in India.

TABLE 8.27

State-wise Per Capita Assistance Sanctioned and Disbursed by AIFIs

(Rs)

	1996		1997		1998		1999		2000		Cumulative up to end March 2001	
	S	D	S	D	S	D	S	D	S	D	S	D
High-income states												
Maharashtra	954.9	961.3	1616.3	1312.1	2587.2	1640.1	2369.1	1678.2	3213.6	1974	16,872.5	11,567.3
Gujarat	1602.9	1328.2	2560.9	2173.8	1730.9	1502.8	2660.5	1700.6	2767.3	929.7	19,173.6	12,187.6
Punjab	371	295.6	493.6	472.4	807.5	515.5	844.6	558.3	1223	767.7	6197.1	4441.7
Haryana	689.6	549.9	867.4	610.3	875.9	650.2	920.4	695.3	2329.3	788.1	8512	5285.7
Tamil Nadu	663.5	565.8	1052	501.2	1338.2	671.1	1463.6	718.6	1098.7	733.1	9387.2	5875.7
Middle-income states												
Karnataka	774.5	522.9	726.3	680.4	920	688.3	1060.5	783.2	1153.6	940.6	7902.7	5636.8
Kerala	205.9	223.2	350.5	200.5	338.4	217.2	261	274.5	296.9	293.3	2761.3	2230.1
Andhra Pradesh	369.9	348.4	639.2	527.5	627.4	381.9	1225.7	524.3	741.2	476.4	6015.9	3913.8
West Bengal	273.8	166.4	420.6	305.5	447.1	380.8	491.9	419.1	619.6	465.3	3611	2638
Low-income states												
Rajasthan	444.8	296.7	490.5	242.9	284.5	278	313.7	261.7	426.1	277.4	3713.1	2787.4
Madhya Pradesh	186.5	229.4	777.5	222.8	351.5	269.3	288	182.3	321.2	208.9	3351.2	2152.1
Uttar Pradesh	171.1	201	166.4	161.4	243.2	138.6	220.6	157.5	263.7	152.4	2108.2	1563.9
Orissa	211.3	121.7	363.8	168	348.9	311	794.2	290.4	407	280.9	3292.9	2059.8
Bihar	55.5	31.1	132.5	93.2	136.1	84.5	125.4	119	26.3	30.5	678.6	533.2
All-India	*487.9*	*424.6*	*744.2*	*542.3*	*805.5*	*567.2*	*993.2*	*656.8*	*1105*	*682.4*	*6673.5*	*4587.9*
Correlation with per capita SDP	**0.71**	**0.74**	**0.65**	**0.66**	**0.75**	**0.73**	**0.63**	**0.70**	**n.a.**	**n.a.**	**n.a.**	**n.a.**
Correlation with per capita manufacturing SDP	**0.92**	**0.95**	**0.91**	**0.90**	**0.86**	**0.90**	**0.88**	**0.93**	**n.a.**	**n.a.**	**n.a.**	**n.a.**

Source: *Report on Currency and Finance*, RBI.

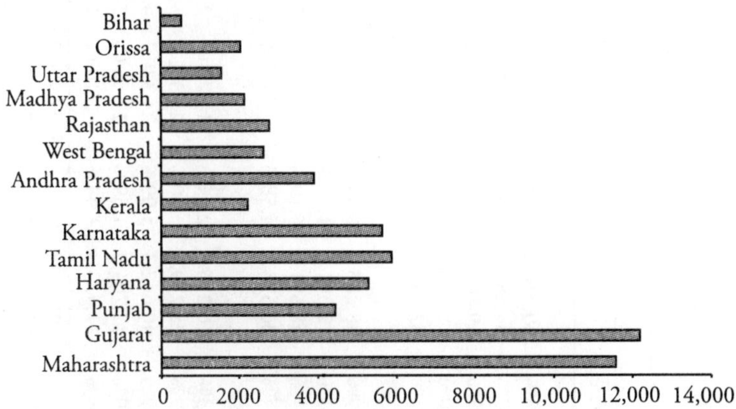

FIGURE 8.23: Per Capita Assistance Disbursed by AIFIs (Cumulative in Rs up to March 2001)

Source: RBI.

are far less important than the national-level institutions. The AIFIs, the national institutions, provide about 95 per cent of the total assistance provided by AFIs. Therefore, the picture for the state-wise distribution of assistance would not be very dissimilar if we include the state-level institutions. However, the results are presented in the Table. As expected, the richer and more industrialized states get most of the assistance. Table 8.29 and Figure 8.24 (with states in increasing order of per capita SDP) show that states with higher per capita SDP get higher per capita financial assistance from all AFIs. Further, the last two rows of Table 8.29 show that the Pearson correlation between per capita manufacturing SDP and per capita assistance is higher (0.9) than the Pearson correlation between per capita SDP and per capita assistance (0.7). This provides further backing to our previously stated claim that investment flows to regions with existing industrial bases, perhaps because they provide better returns due to economies of scale and agglomeration. Apart from economies of scale, relatively developed regions may have entrepreneurs with more experience and skill in taking advantage of government assistance. These regions also have more and bigger existing corporations that may be better able to avail and utilize financial assistance.

In this sub-section, we have shown that financial assistance from banks and financial institutions flowed primarily to more developed areas. This is probably due to better opportunities for investment in these areas. This is also an example of the trade-off that the government

Table 8.28

State-wise Assistance Sanctioned and Disbursed by AFIs

(Rs million)

	1996				1997				1998			
	S	% share	D	% share	S	% share	D	% share	S	% share	D	% share
High-income states												
Maharashtra	87,903.4	17.96%	90,433.5	21.32%	151,616	20.79%	122,447.2	22.93%	249,310.5	31.25%	162,308.6	28.52%
Gujarat	77,060.3	15.74%	64,358.6	15.17%	123,853.1	16.98%	105,044.4	19.67%	84,581.6	10.60%	73,654.9	12.94%
Punjab	9343.8	1.91%	7645.1	1.80%	13,567.3	1.86%	12,458.3	2.33%	19,862.7	2.49%	12,954.6	2.28%
Haryana	14,460.8	2.95%	11,581.4	2.73%	18,315.3	2.51%	12,814	2.40%	18,398.3	2.31%	13,571.4	2.38%
Tamil Nadu	42,701.5	8.72%	36,178.2	8.53%	64,619.6	8.86%	31,123.4	5.83%	82,247.3	10.31%	41,364.9	7.27%
Middle-income states												
Karnataka	48,372.7	9.88%	32,096.7	7.57%	40,620.6	5.57%	38,912.1	7.29%	48,283.4	6.05%	37,840.3	6.65%
Kerala	8319.3	1.70%	8665.2	2.04%	12,572.2	1.72%	7552	1.41%	12,391.7	1.55%	8298.1	1.46%
Andhra Pradesh	27,389.2	5.59%	25,973.5	6.12%	47,805.1	6.56%	39,365	7.37%	48,651.9	6.10%	29,275.2	5.14%
West Bengal	21,263.6	434%	13,123.7	3.09%	33,190.6	4.55%	24,222.5	4.54%	36,573.1	4.58%	31,986	5.62%
Low-income states												
Rajasthan	24,113.9	9.93%	15,965.2	3.76%	26,579.4	3.64%	13,521	2.53%	16,276.3	2.04%	15,760.4	2.77%
Madhya Pradesh	14,887.1	3.04%	17,837.9	4.21%	60,253.5	8.26%	17,592.5	3.29%	28,729.1	3.60%	21,366.9	3.75%
Uttar Pradesh	34,053.7	6.96%	36,220	8.54%	30,086	4.13%	28,770.2	5.39%	40,642.3	5.09%	24,320.1	4.27%
Orissa	8147.9	1.66%	5027.6	1.19%	12,989.7	1.78%	6387.4	1.20%	12,704.9	1.59%	11,564.9	2.03%
Bihar	4942.6	1.01%	2762.4	0.65%	11,297.3	1.55%	7930.1	1.48%	11,423.3	1.43%	7109.1	1.25%
Total	489,538		424,110		729,203		534,061		797,734		569,032	

Table 8.28 (contd...)

Table 8.28 (contd...)

	1999				2000				Cumulative up to end March 2001			
	S	% share	D	% share	S	% share	D	% share	S	% share	D	% share
High-income states												
Maharashtra	231,857.8	23.44%	168,612.8	25.52%	322,096.3	27.67%	200,222.1	27.69%	1,702,842.9	23.91%	1,182,706	23.85%
Gujarat	134,943.7	13.64%	87,504	13.25%	142,331.5	12.23%	48,431.7	6.70%	1,004,627.3	14.11%	643,946.1	12.98%
Punjab	20,525.8	2.08%	13,578.6	2.06%	29,289	2.52%	18,755.1	2.59%	163,329.8	2.29%	119,754	2.41%
Haryana	19,594.1	1.98%	14,918.8	2.26%	50,500.9	4.34%	17,351.3	2.40%	190,382.7	2.67%	121,283.6	2.45%
Tamil Nadu	90,706.9	9.17%	44,330.5	6.71%	70,192.6	6.03%	46,909	6.49%	605,400.6	8.50%	380,271.5	7.67%
Middle-income states												
Karnataka	56,048.1	5.67%	41,419.5	6.27%	61,739.1	5.30%	49,997.4	6.91%	451,528.4	6.34%	330,016.5	6.65%
Kerala	9601.7	0.97%	9698.1	1.47%	11,979.3	1.03%	11,175.1	1.55%	103,297	1.45%	84,186.6	1.70%
Andhra Pradesh	93,414	9.44%	40,669.8	6.16%	58,072.1	4.99%	37,814.3	5.23%	465,805.7	6.54%	309,228.1	6.24%
West Bengal	39,340.9	3.98%	33,591.1	5.09%	52,023.7	4.47%	39,521.5	5.47%	303,424.6	4.26%	224,383	4.52%
Low-income states												
Rajasthan	18,576.3	1.88%	14,935.6	2.26%	25,335.4	2.18%	16,963.2	2.35%	215,657.7	3.03%	167,360.6	3.37%
Madhya Pradesh	23,703	2.40%	15,181.5	2.30%	26,679.5	2.29%	17,378.3	2.40%	279,544.4	3.93%	183,329.5	3.70%
Uttar Pradesh	36,114	3.65%	26,265.4	3.98%	46,541.3	4.00%	26,770	3.70%	393,207.6	5.52%	296,199.2	5.97%
Orissa	28,924.1	2.92%	10,823.7	1.64%	14,972.3	1.29%	10,513.9	1.45%	123,982.4	1.74%	81,246.7	1.64%
Bihar	10,448.4	1.06%	9935.5	1.50%	2665.4	0.23%	3109.8	0.43%	79,011.6	1.11%	61,957.9	1.25%
Total	989,121		660,580		1,164,026		723,076		7,120,758		4,959,257	

Source: Authors' calculations based on statistics from the IDBI Report on Development Banking in India.

Table 8.29
State-wise Per Capita Assistance Sanctioned and Disbursed by AFIs

(Rs)

	1996		1997		1998		1999		2000		Cumulative up to end March 2001	
	S	D	S	D	S	D	S	D	S	D	S	D
High-income states												
Maharashtra	985.6	1014	1665.7	1345.2	2683.8	1747.3	2445.7	1778.6	3329.1	2069.4	17,600	12,224.1
Gujarat	1651.7	1379.5	2601.4	2206.3	1740.9	1516	2721.7	1764.9	2813	957.2	19,855.5	12,727
Punjab	413.5	338.3	589.6	541.4	847.8	552.9	860.4	569.2	1205.8	772.2	6724.4	4930.3
Haryana	757.5	606.4	935.6	654.6	916.9	676.4	952.7	725.3	2395.3	823	9030.2	5752.7
Tamil Nadu	717.3	607.7	1074	517.3	1352.6	680.3	1476	721.3	1130.1	755.2	9747.1	6122.5
Middle-income states												
Karnataka	977.6	648.6	808	774	945.2	740.8	1079.9	978	1170.8	948.1	8562.4	6258.1
Kerala	270.9	282.1	405.7	243.7	396.3	265.4	304.3	307.4	376.3	351	3244.4	2644.2
Andhra Pradesh	381	361.3	656.3	540.5	659.4	396.8	1249.7	544.1	766.9	499.3	6151.1	4083.4
West Bengal	283	174.7	434.6	317.2	471.1	412	498.5	425.7	648.5	492.7	3782.4	2797.1
Low-income states												
Rajasthan	471.8	312.4	507.2	258	303	293.4	337.2	271.2	448.6	300.4	3818.8	2963.5
Madhya Pradesh	198.5	237.8	788.7	230.3	369.3	274.6	299.3	191.7	331.0	215.6	3468.3	2274.6
Uttar Pradesh	215.0	228.7	186.3	178.1	246.5	147.5	214.2	155.8	269.6	155.1	2278.1	1716.1
Orissa	237.8	146.8	374.2	184	361.2	328.8	811.7	303.7	407.9	286.4	3377.6	2213.4
Bihar	52.58	29.39	118.05	82.86	117.28	72.99	105.33	100.16	26.39	30.79	782.3	613.4
All-India	*526.6*	*456.2*	*772*	*565.4*	*831.2*	*592.9*	*1014*	*677.4*	*1133*	*704.1*	*6933.4*	*4828.8*
Correlation with per capita SDP	**0.71**	**0.75**	**0.68**	**0.68**	**0.76**	**0.74**	**0.64**	**0.70**	**n.a.**	**n.a.**	**n.a.**	**n.a.**
Correlation with per capita manufacturing SDP	**0.90**	**0.95**	**0.92**	**0.90**	**0.85**	**0.89**	**0.88**	**0.92**	**n.a.**	**n.a.**	**n.a.**	**n.a.**

Source: Authors' calculations based on statistics from the IDBI Report on Development Banking in India.

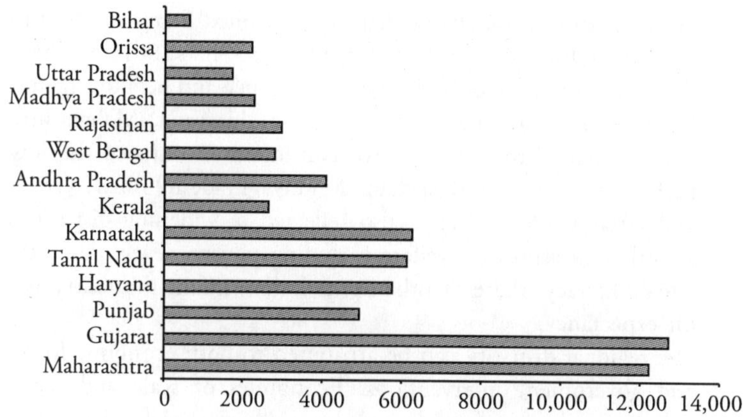

FIGURE 8.24: Per Capita Assistance Disbursed by AFIs (Cumulative in Rs up to March 2001)

Source: RBI.

faces between economic growth for the whole country versus reducing regional inequality.

Policy Implications

In this chapter, we have shown that regional inequality, especially as measured by the SDP per capita has increased in India in the last twenty years. We have also discussed different policies affecting regional development and have shown that these have not been successful in reducing inter-state disparities. Specifically, we have focused on two types of policy-driven mechanisms—(1) explicit centre–state transfers that while redistributing income from rich to poor states have created dependency in the poor states, and (2) implicit inter-regional transfers that have concentrated productive investments towards the richer states. In the rest of this section we summarize our findings and then suggest future research areas that will shed more light on the relationship between regional development policies and regional inequality.

Summary of Findings

In this chapter we studied the relationship between regional development policies and regional inequality in fourteen major states in India, which contain close to 93 per cent of the country's population and 85 per cent of the country's GDP. Our main findings are as follows:

1. India has seen constant and unambiguous rise in regional disparity from 1980 to 1999, the period of our study. Its level of inequality

has risen from about twice that of the United States in 1990 to more than three times in 1997 (Shankar and Shah 2001). We have shown the presence of both sigma divergence and beta divergence. High-performing states such as Punjab, Haryana, Maharashtra, Gujarat, and Tamil Nadu have continued to outpace the low-performing states of Rajasthan, Madhya Pradesh, Bihar, Orissa, and Uttar Pradesh. This is also reflected in widening disparities on other measures of welfare including poverty levels, sex ratio, female literacy, share of urban population, infant mortality, and life expectancy.

2. The regional disparity can be attributed to both economic forces and government interventions. Economies of scale and scope, economies due to local knowledge spillovers, and thick factor markets cause both investments and skilled labour to converge in specific locations, leading to economic divergence. On the other hand, government revenue and expenditure patterns, the inter-governmental transfer system, explicit industrial policies, regional development policies, and government-created barriers to inter-state trade also have an important effect on regional disparities. In this chapter, we looked in detail at India's fiscal structure and some of its policies that affect regional inequality. In India, there are broadly four channels through which government finance and policy affects development in different states—explicit centre–state transfers, implicit inter-state transfers, central government policies, and state government policies. This chapter focused on the effect of the first two and examined their impact on regional disparities in India.
3. There are three explicit modes of transfers from centre to states—the constitutional mechanism of the FC, transfers through the developmentally oriented PC, and transfers from central government ministries. Central government discretion is least in FC transfers, high in PC transfers, and highest in the transfers from central ministries. Discretion is important as it is a measure of central government control over state policies. In terms of impact on regional inequality, one could hypothesize that high levels of central discretion can reduce regional disparity by directing transfers to poorer states. The alternative hypothesis would be that high levels of central discretion could create a dependency syndrome among state governments that would inhibit state initiatives for development. Further, high levels of central discretion could mean that transfers

are influenced more by political than developmental motives, which could have detrimental effects on regional inequality. In this chapter, we find some evidence to support the latter hypothesis that discretionary explicit transfers have contributed to increasing regional disparities in India.

4. Low-discretion FC transfers have remained relatively stable around 18 per cent from 1985 to 2001. The moderately discretionary transfer share for state plan schemes has declined marginally from 14 per cent to 12 per cent. The high-discretion transfer share remained stable in the late 1980s at around 14 per cent, declined to about 10 per cent in 1996, and then rose again to 14 per cent in 2001. Revenue transfers constitute around 70 per cent of total transfers on average, although there has been a marked increase since 1999 to about 80 per cent. While the revenue transfers share of total central transfers has increased, the revenue component of total state receipts has remained greater than 70 per cent except during 1998–2000. Capital transfers as a share of total transfers declined from 38 per cent in 1985 to 25 per cent in 1993 and then rose back to 36 per cent in 2001. Total capital receipts as a share of total state receipts has remained relatively stable around 27 per cent.
5. Richer states have higher own revenue shares, while poorer ones are more dependent on central transfers for their revenues. We calculated the dependency quotient of each state as the average share of central transfers for the period 1997–2001 divided by average own revenue share for the same period in total state revenues and showed that low-income states are more dependent on central transfers than higher-income states. This is clearly to be expected, given the gap-filling approach for central transfers and the higher weight given to poorer states. However, the key point we highlight is that these higher transfers to poorer states have not had the effect of making them catch up with the richer states in terms of per capita GSDP, rather richer states are pulling away from the poorer states. In fact, the poorer states have been dependent on central transfers for some time. We compared the dependency quotient for the years 1992–6 with 1997–2001 and found that the dependence ranking of the states does not change. In fact, the quotient has been stable in most cases and has actually increased significantly in the case of poorer states such as Bihar and Orissa. This clearly shows that explicit central transfers have not led to a reduction in regional

disparities; on the contrary, they may be having the opposite effect by creating a culture of dependency in the poorer states.

6. Apart from the explicit intergovernmental transfers, there are three other channels of inter-state resource transfers—(i) inter-state tax exportation; (ii) subsidized lending by banking and financial institutions to the agricultural and industrial sectors (including lending by the AIFI); (iii) subsidized borrowing by states from the central government and the central banking system. We looked in detail at channels 1 and 2, and also at loans from the banking system.
7. There are relatively significant resource transfers between states due to inter-state tax exportation. Sales taxes in India are composed of broadly two parts—taxes on intra-state sales and taxes on inter-state sales. While states are allowed to levy and collect intra-state sales taxes, the Indian constitution provides that inter-state sales shall be taxed only by law of Parliament. This tax is called the central sales tax (CST). The CST has several harmful economic implications, some of which have a direct bearing on regional inequality. One, it hampers the creation of an internal common market within the country. If we assume that free trade between states would lead to income convergence, then the CST is a barrier to such convergence. The CST forms about 4–5 per cent of all states' revenues and 0.45–0.55 per cent of all states' GDP on average each year. On the other hand, even if we assume that free trade may cause divergence, the CST does not help reduce inequality. In fact, as we show, the CST by its very nature, leads to resource flow from the poorer to richer states. The CST discriminates against consuming states to the benefit of the producing states. To the extent that richer states produce more, there is a net resource flow from the poorer to the richer states. The states dispatching the raw materials first levy CST on inputs, the states manufacturing goods that are exported to other states again levy CST. As Rao and Singh (1998: 21) point out, in a developing economy with only limited internal and external competition, the tax is fully shifted forward, so input taxes cascade onto the final consumer. Thus a net consuming less-developed state bears most of the burden of the CST, while an industrialized state with the most value added collects most of the revenue. We looked at net per capita CST inflows in 1998, which is also reasonably representative of the other years, and found that higher-income states have higher per capita CST inflows. To look

at whether higher-income states collect more CST due to better tax effort, we also looked at the correlation between the share of overall sales taxes (or intra-state sales taxes) in state revenues and the share of the CST in overall state revenues for each of the states for the time period 1994–9 and found no relationship in most of the states. The differences in intra-state sales tax collections could be due to differences in tax rates, tax bases, and tax effort. The CST tax rates are the same throughout the country. Therefore, the differences in CST collections would be due to tax base and tax effort. As we have shown, tax effort is perhaps only part of the explanation. So the resource transfer to rich states through tax exportation is mostly due to their more advanced production base. We also discuss the implications of some of our assumptions on which our calculations were based. One assumption was that centre–state transfers did not impact the CST flows. However, if we relax this assumption, we see that consumption would rise disproportionately in poorer states with higher transfer shares compared to richer ones with lower transfer shares. This would only reinforce our results, increasing the magnitude of the CST flow from the poorer to the richer states. In this sense, our analysis is conservative, and including central transfers would increase the measure of CST flow from the poorer to the richer states.

8. Another major form of implicit transfers to the states is lending to different agricultural and industrial sectors by the banking and financial system. This lending, whether at market rates or subsidized, for investment in agriculture, industry, infrastructure, and services is heavily concentrated in the richer states. There are two main channels through which subsidized (below-market interest rate) credit has been given—(i) priority-sector lending by commercial banks (public, private, and foreign) and (ii) financial assistance from AFIs. We looked at per capita priority-sector advances for 2000, which is representative of other years, and showed that most of the subsidized credit goes to the richer states. In addition to lending by commercial banks to priority sectors, there are a plethora of financial institutions at both the centre and state levels that provide various financial products and services to the industrial sector. The assistance provided by these institutions is highly skewed in favour of the richer states. We showed that the more industrialized states get higher levels of financial assistance from the AIFIs. We found a high positive Pearson correlation of around 0.7 of per capita

assistance with per capita SDP, and the Pearson correlation with per capita manufacturing SDP was even higher at about 0.9.

The main conclusions are that regional inequality between Indian states has increased since 1980. Explicit government transfers have not been successful in reducing regional inequality. Rather, they may be contributing to increased inequality by creating dependency in poorer states. Implicit transfers such as subsidized lending have gone disproportionately to the richer states. This could primarily be due to better opportunities for investment in these areas. In this sense, implicit transfers (including CST) shift resources to more productive states, while explicit transfers transfer some income to the poorer states that use these transfers to buy goods and services produced in the richer states, providing additional fillip to their development. Therefore, government policies have not reduced regional disparity as they have not been aimed at helping or forcing poorer states to catch up in productivity terms.

Suggested Future Research

We suggest two broad directions for future research. First, we think that the approach developed in this chapter could be applied to other large developing countries such as China, Brazil, and Indonesia. This research could explore the resource flows in these countries from the centre to the regions and resource flows between the regions due to government policies and examine the impact of these policies on regional disparities. Specifically, these studies can be targeted to addressing the question of whether paternalistic strong central governments or decentralized, relatively independent regional governments are better at regional development.

Second, we would recommend broadening the study to look at the impact of direct central government expenditures on regional disparities. We believe that central government expenditures can be classified into two types. One, they could increase direct consumption in each state through spending, job creation, income grants, etc. Second, they could invest in policies that raise the productive capacity of individual states. These could include investments in education, health, and infrastructure. It would be interesting to examine which of these expenditures predominate in the richer states and which ones in the poorer states. This examination would then shed much-needed light on how central government expenditures actually impact regional disparities—and help shape future policies to reduce these disparities.

Notes

1. A more detailed discussion of these studies can be found in Shankar and Shah (2001).
2. The states included are Andhra Pradesh, Bihar, Gujarat, Haryana, Karnataka, Kerala, Madhya Pradesh, Maharashtra, Orissa, Punjab, Rajasthan, Tamil Nadu, Uttar Pradesh, and West Bengal.
3. These poverty statistics have been taken from the South Asia office at the World Bank.
4. The NDC consists of all central cabinet ministers, state chief ministers, and the members of the PC. It is chaired by the Prime Minister.
5. In this sub-section, we present statistics that include data for all the states and union territories as a whole. In later sections, where we look in detail at the relationship between fiscal structure and government policies, we analyse data only on the fourteen major states, that comprise almost 93 per cent of the country's population and 85 per cent of the country's GDP.
6. AIFIs refer to all-India development banks, specialized financial institutions, and investment institutions. The national-level development banks are Industrial Development Bank of India, Industrial Finance Corporation of India, Industrial Credit and Investment Corporation of India, Small Industries Development Bank of India, Industrial Reconstruction Bank of India and Shipping Credit and Investment Company of India. The specialized financial institutions are Technology Development & Information Company of India Limited, Risk Capital & Technology Finance Corporation Limited and Tourism Finance Corporation of India. The investment institutions are Unit Trust of India, General Insurance Corporation of India and Life Insurance Corporation of India.
7. There are other more minor components of the sales tax such as taxes on motor spirits and lubricants, sales tax surcharge and turnover tax. However, these are not pertinent to the current discussion, as we focus only on inter-state sales.
8. For 1999, N = 14, as there was a data problem for Punjab. We also excluded Punjab from the 'rest of India' for this computation for the same reason. Excluding Punjab we are assuming that there are no exports to or imports from Punjab, which would certainly bias our estimates for 1999. However, as Punjab has been a net exporting state for the previous years, there is no reason to assume any different for 1999. Given that, the net inflow figure for other states would be biased upward. This would mean that our estimates of tax exportation for 1999 are conservative, and that if Punjab were included, the measured negative effects on the poorer states would be more pronounced.

9. For a detailed description of the CST—definitions, bases, rates, exemptions and concessions, see http://dateyvs.com/indexis.htm. Purohit (2001) also presents a brief description of the CST and its economic drawbacks.
10. Here we are also assuming that the CST is passed on completely to the consumer, which in the case of a developing country like India with limited competition, is a reasonable assumption. We have discussed this earlier in this sub-section.
11. These targets are different for domestic and foreign banks and can be found on the RBI website http://www.rbi.org.in.
12. For a detailed discussion on priority-sector lending and its evolution over time, see Shajahan (1998, 1999) and Khundrakpam (2000). The RBI also has detailed data on the components of priority-sector lending from 1995 onwards on its website http://www.rbi.org.in. Data prior to 1995 can also be obtained from various issues of RBI reports on banking.
13. Details of direct and indirect agriculture advances can be found on the RBI website.
14. For a detailed description of these institutions, see IDBI (2000–1).
15. For a detailed discussion of these institutions, see IDBI (2000–1).

References

Akita, Takahiro and Rizal Affandi Lukman (1995). 'Interregional Inequalities in Indonesia: A Sectoral Decomposition Analysis for 1975–92', *Bulletin of Indonesian Economic Studies*, 31(2): 61–81.

Asra, Abuzar (1989). 'Inequality Trends in Indonesia', *Bulletin of Indonesian Economic Studies*, 25(2): 100–10.

Atkinson, Anthony B. and François Bourguignon (eds). (2000). *Handbook of Income Distribution*, Vol. 1. Amsterdam, Netherlands: Elsevier Science B.V.

Bajpai, Nirupam and Jeffrey D. Sachs (1996). 'Trends in Inter-State Inequalities of Income in India', Development Discussion Paper No. 528, Harvard Institute for International Development, Cambridge.

Barro, R.J. and Xavier Sala-i-Martin (1995). *Economic Growth*. New York: McGraw-Hill.

________ (1992). 'Convergence', *Journal of Political Economy*, 100, pp. 223–51.

________ (1991). 'Convergence across States and Regions', *Brookings Papers on Economic Activity*, 2, pp. 107–58.

Biswas, R. and S. Marjit (2000). 'Political Lobbying and Discretionary Finance in India: An Aspect of Regional Political Influence in a Representative Democracy', processed, Centre for Studies in Social Science, Calcutta.

Boldrin, Michelle (2001). 'Inequality and Convergence: Reconsidering European Regional Policies', *Economic Policy*, 16(32): 205–53.

Canova, Fabio and Albert Marcet (1995). 'The Poor Stay Poor: Non-convergence across Countries and Regions', CEPR Discussion Paper, No. 1265, London, Centre for Economic Policy Research.

Cashin, Paul and Ratna Sahay (1996). 'Regional Economic Growth and Convergence in India', *Finance & Development*, 33, March, pp. 49–52.

Chen, Jian and Belton M. Fleisher (1996). 'Regional Income Inequality and Economic Growth in China', *Journal of Comparative Economics*, 22, pp. 141–64.

Das, Sandwip Kumar and Alokesh Barua (1996). 'Regional Inequalities, Economic Growth and Liberalisation: A Study of the Indian Economy', *The Journal of Development Studies*, UK, 32, Feb., pp. 364–90.

Dasgupta, Sugato, Amrita Dhillon, and Bhaskar Dutta (2001). 'Electoral Goals and Centre–State Transfers in India', processed, Indian Statistical Institute, New Delhi.

Decressin, Jörg (1999) 'Regional Income Redistribution and Risk Sharing: How Does Italy Compare in Europe?', IMF Working Paper WP/99/123, International Monetary Fund, Washington D. C., September.

Dev, S. Mahendra (2000). 'Economic Reforms, Poverty, Income Distribution and Employment', *Economic and Political Weekly*, 35(10): 823–35.

Easterly, William (2001a). 'The Lost Decades: Developing Countries' Stagnation in Spite of Policy Reform 1980–98', *Journal of Economic Growth*, 6(2): 135–57.

________ (2001b). *The Elusive Quest for Growth—Economists' Adventures and Misadventures in the Tropics*. Cambridge, Massachusetts: MIT Press.

Easterly, William and Ross Levine (2001). 'It's Not Factor Accumulation: Stylized Facts and Growth Models', The World Bank, Washington D.C.

Fujita, Masahisa, Paul Krugman, Anthony J. Venables (1999). *The Spatial Economy: Cities, Regions and International Trade*. Cambridge, MA: MIT Press.

Garcia, Jorge Garcia and Lana Soelistianingsih (1998). 'Why Do Differences in Provincial Incomes Persist in Indonesia?', *Bulletin of Indonesian Economic Studies*, 34(1): 95–120.

Giugale, Marcelo M., Vinh Nguyen, Fernando Rojas, and Steven B. Webb (2000). 'Overview', in Marcelo M. Giugale and Steven B. Webb (eds), *Achievements and Challenges of Fiscal Decentralization—Lessons from Mexico*. The World Bank, Washington D.C.

IDBI (2000–1). *Report on Development Banking in India.* Industrial Development Bank of India, http://www.idbi.com/devbnk02.html.

Jian, Tianlun, Jeffrey Sachs, and Andrew M. Warner (1996). 'Trends in Regional Inequality in China', Working Paper 5412, National Bureau of Economic Research.

Jha, Raghbendra (2000). 'Growth, Inequality and Poverty in India—Spatial and Temporal Characteristics', *Economic and Political Weekly*, 35(11): 921–8.

Kakwani, Nanak C. (1990). *Large Sample Distribution of Several Inequality Measures—With Application to Côte d'Ivore.* Washington D.C.: The World Bank.

________ (1980). *Inequality and Poverty—Methods of Estimation and Policy Applications.* Washington D.C.: The World Bank and Oxford University Press.

Kanbur, Ravi and Xiaobo Zhang (2005). 'Fifty Years of Regional Inequality in China: A Journey through Central Planning, Reform, and Openness', *Review of Development Economics*, 9(1): 87–106.

Khundrakpam, J.K. (2000). 'Priority Sector Bank Lending—Some Important Issues', *Economic and Political Weekly*, 1 April, pp. 1209–11.

Krugman, P. (1991). 'Increasing Returns and Economic Geography', *Journal of Political Economy*, 99(3): 483–99.

Kurian, N.J. (2000). 'Widening Regional Disparities in India', *Economic and Political Weekly*, 35(7): 538–50.

Kuznets, Simon (1955). 'Economic Growth and Income Inequality', *American Economic Review*, 45: 1–28.

Lyons, Thomas P. (1991). 'Interprovincial Disparities in China: Output and Consumption, 1952–87', *Economic Development and Cultural Change*, 39, April, pp. 471–506.

Markusen, Ann (1994). 'The Interaction between Regional and Industrial Policies: Evidence from Four Countries (Korea, Brazil, Japan and the United States)', Annual Bank Conference on Development Economics, 28–9 April, Washington D.C.

Nagaraj, R., A. Varoudakis, and M.A. Veganzones (2000). 'Long Run Growth Trends and Convergence across Indian States', *Journal of International Development*, 12(1): 45–70.

Pritchett, Lant (1997). 'Where Has All the Education Gone?' World Bank Policy Research Working Paper No. 1581, The World Bank, Washington D.C.

Purohit, Mahesh C. (2001). 'National and Sub-National VATs—A Road Map for India', *Economic and Political Weekly*, 36(9): 757–72.

Raiser, Martin (1998). 'Subsidizing Inequality: Economic Reforms, Fiscal

Transfers and Convergence across Chinese Provinces', *The Journal of Development Studies*, 34(3): 1–26.

Rao, M. Govinda, R.T. Shand, and K.P. Kalirajan (1999). 'Convergence of Income across Indian States', *Economic and Political Weekly*, 34, 27 March.

Rao, M. Govinda and Nirvikar Singh (2001). 'Federalism in India: Political Economy and Reform', Working Paper Series, University of California, Santa Cruz, http://econ.ucsc.edu/faculty/workpapers.html.

________ (2000). 'The Political Economy of Centre-State Fiscal Transfers in India', paper presented at Columbia University—World Bank Conference on Institutional Elements of Tax Design and Reform, 18–19 February, forthcoming in John McLaren (ed.).

________ (1999). 'An Analysis of Explicit and Implicit Intergovernmental Transfers in India', Working Paper Series, University of California, Santa Cruz, http://econ.ucsc.edu/faculty/workpapers.html.

Romer, P. (1990). 'Endogenous Technical Change', *Journal of Political Economy*, 98, pp. S71–S102.

Sacks, Michael Paul (1999). 'Regional Inequality and Branch Employment in Russia Between 1990 and 1995', *Post-Communist Economies*, 11(2): 149–59.

Sato, Hiroshi (1992). 'The Political Economy of Central Budgetary Transfers to States in India, 1972–84', *The Developing Economies*, 30(4).

Shah, Anwar and Raja Shankar (Forthcoming). *Regional Development Policies: Helping Regions or Building Transfer Dependencies?* Washington, D.C.: World Bank.

Shah, Anwar (2000). Federalism and Regional Equity: Building Partnerships or Transfer Dependencies, paper presented at the International Conference on Federalism organized by the Forum of Federations, Brasilia, Brazil, May.

________ (1994). '*The Reform of Intergovernmental Fiscal Relations in Developing and Emerging Market Economies*', Policy and Research Series No. 23, World Bank; Washington, D.C.

Shajahan, K.M. (1999). 'Priority Sector Bank Lending—How Useful?' *Economic and Political Weekly*, 18 December, pp. 3572–4.

________ (1998). 'Priority Sector Bank Lending—Some Important Issues', *Economic and Political Weekly*, 33, 17–23/24–30 October, pp. 2749–56.

Shankar, Raja and Anwar Shah (2001). 'Bridging the Economic Divide within Nations—A Scorecard on the Performance of Regional Development Policies in Reducing Regional Income Disparities', Policy Research Working Paper 2717, The World Bank, Washington, D.C.

Solow, Robert (1956). 'A Contribution to the Theory of Economic Growth', *Quarterly Journal of Economics*, 70, pp. 65–94.

Theil, Henri (1967). *Economics and Information Theory*. Amsterdam: North-Holland Publishing Company.

Tsui, Kai-yuen (1996). 'Economic Reform and Interprovincial Inequalities in China', *Journal of Development Economics*, 50, August, pp. 353–68.

Williamson, Jeffrey G. (1965). 'Regional Inequality and Process of National Development: A Description of the Patterns', *Economic Development and Cultural Change*, Part II, July, 13(4): 2–84.

World Bank (1997). 'India—1997 Economic Update: Sustaining Rapid Growth', Report No. 16506-IN, 30 May.

Yagci, F. (1999). 'Narrowing Inter-state Disparities Agenda for Fiscal and Sector Reforms', The World Bank, Washington D.C.

Yao, Shujie and Jirui Liu (1998). 'Economic Reforms and Regional Segmentation in Rural China', *Regional Studies*, November, 32(8):

Contributors

PINAKI CHAKRABORTY, Senior Fellow, National Institute of Public Finance and Policy, New Delhi.

P.R. JENA, Fellow, National Institute of Public Finance and Policy, New Delhi.

SOMIK V. LALL, Senior Economist, Spatial and Local Development Unit, Sustainable Development Network, World Bank.

SUBRATA MANDAL, Senior Economist, National Institute of Public Finance and Policy, New Delhi.

PARTHA MUKHOPADHYAY, Professor, Centre for Policy Research, New Delhi.

M. GOVINDA RAO, Director, National Institute of Public Finance and Policy, New Delhi.

R. KAVITA RAO, Senior Fellow, National Institute of Public Finance and Policy, New Delhi.

ANWAR SHAH, Lead Economist and Programme Leader, Public Sector Governance, World Bank Institute, Washington, D.C.

RAJA SHANKAR, Head of Economic, Financial and Business Consulting, Happold Consulting, London.

D.K. SRIVASTAVA, Director, Madras School of Economics, Chennai.